W9-AVE-706

Russia's First Modern Jews

REAPPRAISALS IN JEWISH SOCIAL
AND INTELLECTUAL HISTORY

General Editor: Robert M. Seltzer

Martin Buber's Social and Religious Thought:
Alienation and the Quest for Meaning
LAURENCE J. SILBERSTEIN

The American Judaism of Mordecai M. Kaplan
EDITED BY EMANUEL S. GOLDSMITH, MEL SCULT,
AND ROBERT M. SELTZER

On Socialists and "the Jewish Question" after Marx
JACK JACOBS

Easter in Kishinev: Anatomy of a Pogrom
EDWARD H. JUDGE

Jewish Responses to Modernity:
New Voices from America and Eastern Europe
ELI LEDERHENDLER

Rabbi Abraham Isaac Kook and Jewish Spirituality
EDITED BY LAWRENCE J. KAPLAN AND DAVID SHATZ

Russia's First Modern Jews:
The Jews of Shklov
DAVID E. FISHMAN

DAVID E. FISHMAN

RUSSIA'S FIRST MODERN JEWS

The Jews of Shklov

NEW YORK UNIVERSITY PRESS
NEW YORK & LONDON

NEW YORK UNIVERSITY PRESS
New York and London

Library of Congress Cataloging-in-Publication Data
Fishman, David E., 1957–
Russia's first modern Jews : the Jews of Shklov / David E.
Fishman.
p. cm. — (Reappraisals in Jewish social and intellectual
history)
Includes bibliographical references and index.
ISBN 0-8147-2614-3
1. Jews—Belarus—Shkloŭ—Intellectual life. 2. Shkloŭ (Belarus) —
Intellectual life. 3. Haskalah—Belarus—Shkloŭ—History—18th
century. I. Title. II. Series.
DS135.B38F57 1995
947'.656—dc20   94-29482
CIP

New York University Press books are printed on acid-free paper,
and their binding materials are chosen for strength and durability.

Manufactured in the United States of America
10   9   8   7   6   5   4   3   2   1

מײַנע טאַטע-מאַמע
מיט דאַנקשאַפֿט און ליבשאַפֿט

Contents

List of Illustrations

Acknowledgments

I began my research on the topic of this book under the exacting guidance of Isadore Twersky of Harvard University, who supervised the dissertation on which it is based. I am grateful to him and to my other teachers at Harvard, Yosef Yershalmi and Bernard Septimus, for their guidance and for the model they set of the highest standards of scholarship. The advice and friendship of Allan Nadler, Lois Dubin, and Aron Rodrigue, who read earlier drafts of this work, were especially valuable to me. Others who assisted with suggestions and advice include Israel Bartal, Immanuel Etkes, Eli Lederhendler, David Roskies, Robert Seltzer, Peter Shaw, Shaul Stampfer, and the late Shmuel Ettinger.

I am grateful to the libraries, archives, and individuals that helped provide materials for this study: Widener Library, Harvard; Dina Abramowicz and Marek Web of the YIVO Institute for Jewish Research; Jerry Schwarzbard of the Library of the Jewish Theological Seminary of America; Mordechai Nadav of the Jewish National and University Library, Jerusalem; the Slavonic and Jewish Divisions of the New York Public Library; Buttler Library, Columbia University; the New York and Cincinnati libraries of Hebrew Union College—Jewish Institute of Religion; the Leo Baeck Institute, New York; Viktor Kelner of the St. Petersburg Public Library; and Dmitry Feldman of the Russian State Archive of Ancient Acts.

I owe a tremendous debt to the academic institutions with which I have been affiliated. I remember fondly the years I spent at Brandeis University; Marvin Fox, former Director of the Lown School of Near Eastern and Judaic Studies, provided me with invaluable encouragement and guidance. The YIVO Institute for Jewish

Research, where I have been a Research Associate and member of the faculty of the Max Weinreich Center for Advanced Jewish Studies, has been a source of much stimulation and inspiration for me. Most of all I am indebted to the Jewish Theological Seminary of America which has been my intellectual home for the past six years. Chancellor Ismar Schorsch and my colleagues in the Department of Jewish History have provided me with a uniquely supportive environment for teaching and studying Jewish history.

It is a pleasure for me to acknowledge the financial assistance of the Memorial Foundation for Jewish Culture; the National Foundation for Jewish Culture; the Strook Faculty Fellowship of the Jewish Theological Seminary of America; and the Max Weinreich Center for Advanced Jewish Studies in supporting this study.

I am grateful for permission to use (in revised form) material from my article "A Polish Rabbi Meets the Berlin Haskalah: The Case of R. Barukh Schick," *Association for Jewish Studies Review* 12, no. 1 (Spring 1987): 95–121.

On a more personal level, I wish to recall the memory of two of my mentors, now deceased, Yudl Mark and Chaim Grade. Both were Lithuanian Jewish intellectuals who strived—not totally unlike the subjects of this study—to combine tradition and modernity, Jewishness and worldliness. My brother Avi helped me write this book by opening up his home, and offering me something precious: a quiet place to work. My wife, Marion, and our children Arele, Nesanel, and Tsivye-Rokhl, have been a constant reminder to me that joy can (and should) be derived from life in the present. My parents, to whom I dedicate this book, first taught me to study and cherish the riches of the Jewish past in Eastern Europe.

A Note on Transliteration

In transliterating Hebrew and Russian, I have followed the Library of Congress rules, except that I have eliminated most diacritical marks. For Hebrew words, I have not used diacritical marks to distinguish between the letters *het* and *hei*, and have rendered the letter *tsadi* as *ts*. In transliterating Yiddish, I have followed the system devised by the YIVO Institute for Jewish Research.

Place names are usually offered in their Russian form, unless there is a familiar English variation. Personal names are presented in a variety of forms, based upon the cultural context in which the individual was most active.

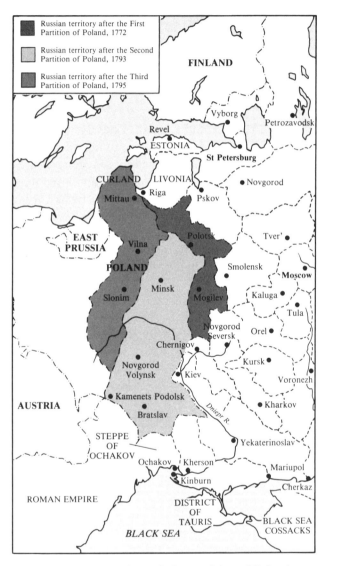

FINLAND

Vyborg

Petrozavodsk

Revel

ESTONIA

St Petersburg

CURLAND LIVONIA

Mittau

Riga

Pskov

Novgorod

EAST
PRUSSIA

Vilna

Polotsk

Tver'

POLAND

Smolensk

Moscow

Slonim

Minsk

Mogilev

Kaluga

Tula

Novgorod
Seversk

Orel

Chernigov

Novgorod
Volynsk

Kiev

Kursk

Voronezh

Kamenets Podolsk

AUSTRIA

Bratslav

Dniepr R.

Kharkov

STEPPE
OF
OCHAKOV

Yekaterinoslav

Ochakov

Kherson

Mariupol

Kinburn

Cherkaz

ROMAN EMPIRE

DISTRICT
OF
TAURIS

BLACK SEA
COSSACKS

BLACK SEA

The Russian Empire and the partition of Poland.

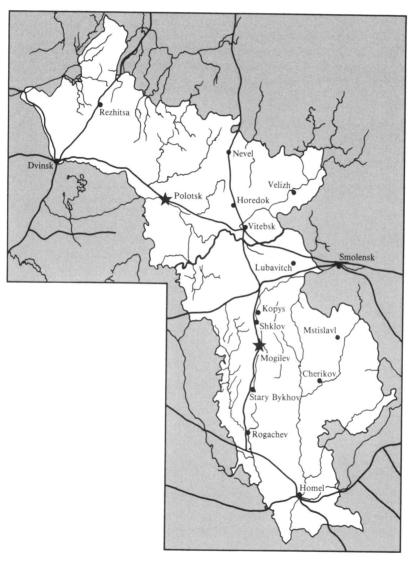

The Mogilev and Polotsk provinces. *(Evreiskaia entsiklopediia)*

Introduction: The Jews
in the "Land of Russia"

Long before there were Jewish communities in the land of the Tsars,
Jews inhabited a region which they called *medinat rusiya*, "the
land of Russia." Situated along the banks of the Dniepr and Dvina
rivers, "the land of Russia" occupied the far eastern corner of the
Polish-Lithuanian Commonwealth, and corresponded to the Mohylew, Mtsislavl, and Witebsk districts of the Lithuanian Grand-
Duchy.

In this region of what is today eastern Belarus, most of the
Christian inhabitants were followers of the Orthodox church, and
spoke a Slavic dialect much closer to Russian than to either Polish
or Ukrainian. Commerce with Smolensk and Moscow was the main-
stay of the economy, and Russian merchants were a major presence
at fairs and marketplaces. Cultural ties with Muscovy were also
strong. In the mid-seventeenth century, Tsar Aleksei Mikhailovitch
invited artists and craftsmen from the Mohylew district to orna-
ment the Kremlin. The Jewish geographical appelation was very
much on the mark. This was Russia, in essence if not in fact, even
before it was annexed by the Tsarist Empire in 1772.[1]

Jews first settled here in the second half of the sixteenth century.
They established communities in the district capitals of Mogilev
(Polish: Mohylew), Vitebsk (Polish: Witebsk), Mtsislavl, and elsewhere, and struggled to secure royal charters confirming their rights
of residence and trade. By 1631, the communities had become suffi-
ciently large and established for them to be represented as a separate district on the *va'ad ha-medinah*, the governing council for
Jewish communities in Lithuania.[2]

Although the Jews of "the land of Russia" were spared the devastation wrought by the Chmielnicki uprising of 1648, catastrophe struck them six years later, in the Russian invasion of Poland, which was accompanied by the killing, looting, and forced conversion of Jews. The communities scattered to escape the Russian onslaught; many of those who did not flee were taken captive by the Muscovites. The most famous incident was in Mogilev, where the townsmen agreed to surrender to the Russians peacefully, if the Jews were expelled and their property divided among the remaining inhabitants. Tsar Aleksei Mikhailovitch acceded to this condition, which was incorporated into Mogilev's treaty of surrender. After a delay of several months, the Jews were rounded up by Russian troops, and escorted to the outskirts of town. But instead of being expelled, they were ruthlessly massacred.[3]

Jewish life reestablished itself in the region after the 1667 peace of Andrusova. New communities emerged, the most prominent of which was in Shklov (Polish: Szklow), chartered in 1668. Under the ownership of the Sieniawski and, later, the Czartoryski family of Polish magnates, Shklov became one of the most powerful commercial centers in Byelorussia, and, in the words of a diplomat who visited the town in 1699, Jews were "the richest and most influential class of people in the city." In 1727, more than a third of the shops in the town's marketplace were owned by Jews, and in 1760—more than half.[4] The town's Jewish population grew at an impressive pace, and the 1766 census recorded 1,367 Jews in Shklov, a number roughly equal to that of such older centers as Slutsk, Pinsk, and Minsk.[5]

The communities in the "land of Russia" were organized in a regional council, the *va'ad medinat rusiya*, whose primary task was the apportionment and collection of taxes among its constituent members. As the region grew in wealth during the course of the eighteenth century, *medinat rusiya* contributed an increasing proportion of the Jewish head tax for Lithuania. In 1717, it paid 9,800 zlotys, or 16.3 percent of the total; in 1762—16,440 zlotys, or 27.4 percent of the total. The *va'ad* also served as the highest legislative and judicial body for the Jews of the region. It regulated economic activity, including the purchase and orderly transfer of leases (*ar-*

enda), and decided disputes between kahals, or between individuals and kahals.[6]

One striking feature of organized Jewish life in "the land of Russia" was its centralization, and the enormous power wielded by the va'ad's highest official, the provincial rabbi. The rav ha-medinah, as he was called, directed the va'ad's fiscal affairs between one meeting and the next, and enjoyed extensive freedom in determining the apportionment of taxes and the use of funds. Local communal rabbis were subject to his authority; in fact, their salaries were paid out of his budget. On several occasions, communities lodged complaints with Lithuanian magnates and tribunals concerning alleged abuses of power by the provincial rabbi, and, in 1746, Shklov and Kopys briefly seceded from the va'ad medinat rusiya in protest at the rabbi's unfair tax-apportionment practices.[7]

Prior to its annexation by Russia, "the land of Russia" was anything but a center of rabbinic culture. There were no Hebrew printing presses within its boundaries, no world-renowned rabbis or prestigious yeshivas. The closest citadel of Talmudic learning was in Minsk, to the west, where R. Arye Leyb Ginzburg (called the Sha'agat arye [Roar of the Lion], after his volumes of novellae) and R. Yehiel Halperin (author of Seder ha-dorot [The Order of Generations]) headed yeshivas. Promising Talmudic students were sent to study with Ginzburg, Halperin, or R. Avraham Katzenellenbogen in Brest-Litovsk.[8]

Most of the region's communal rabbis were involved primarily in judicial and administrative affairs, and did not distinguish themselves as authors on halakhah, Kabbalah, and homiletics. Shklov was something of an exception in this regard, with several of its rabbis being men of scholarly accomplishment. These included R. Israel Yaffe, whose work on the Zohar and the Shulhan arukh, Or yisrael (Light of Israel; Frankfurt, 1702), received the approbation of the rabbinic court of the Council of Lithuania; R. Elijah Pines, author of Tana de-ve eliyahu (Teachings from the House of Elijah; Zolkiew, 1753), who was famed for his knowledge of whole tractates of the Talmud by heart; and R. Jacob b. Judah Schick, whose high standing in rabbinic circles was consolidated by his marriage to the sister of the Sha'agat arye.[9] But even these men and their works belonged, at best, to the second tier of rabbinic scholarship in Eastern Europe.

In 1772, "the land of Russia" and its neighboring districts were severed from the Polish-Lithuanian Commonwealth and annexed by Tsarist Russia in the first partition of Poland. The region, with approximately 65,000 Jews,[10] was cut off from the heartland of Jewish life in Eastern Europe and was forced to become an independent, self-sustaining center. It needed to create its own religious leadership and institutions, now that it was separated from the traditional seats of learning, piety, and authority. This task was compounded by the nascent conflict between Hasidim and Mitnagdim which would rack "the land of Russia" and Jewish Eastern Europe at large, and which opened a whole slew of questions on the nature of Jewish piety and the criteria for Jewish religious leadership.

The Jews of eastern Byelorussia also needed to establish an effective political leadership of their own, which would protect Jewish interests vis-à-vis their new rulers. Relationships needed to be forged with the Tsarist authorities, who had previously bannned and banished Jews from Russia's territory. The region's Jews now had to fend for themselves in the high-stakes struggle for economic and political survival.

In short, the Jews of the "land of Russia" were thrust into the task of intensive community building during the years following their annexation by the Tsarist Empire, and remained preoccupied with this task at least until 1793–95, when the communities of western Byelorussia and Lithuania came under Russian rule in the second and third partitions of Poland. The effort to forge a strong identity for this previously underdeveloped hinterland resulted in a remarkably intense cultural ferment. The three great currents in East European Jewish life—Hasidism, Mitnagdic rabbinism, and Haskalah—all converged on the virgin soil of "the land of Russia," where they clashed and competed. Disciples of R. Shneur Zalman of Liady, the Vilna Gaon, and Moses Mendelssohn championed rival views of Judaism and the universe, at a distance of a few kilometers—and sometimes a few hundred meters.

One indicator of the intellectual ferment which engulfed the region is the sudden flourishing of Hebrew printing. Hebrew books were published in Shklov beginning in 1783, and the town was, in fact, the very first center of Hebrew printing in Byelorussia and Lithuania. Between 1783 and 1799, when the famed Romm press was established in Vilna, ninety-seven Hebrew titles were published in Shklov, thirty-seven of which were original works. Forty-two additional titles were issued between 1800 and the outbreak of the French-Russian war of 1812. No other center of Hebrew printing in Eastern Europe equaled these figures during that span of time.[11]

The period between Shklov's annexation by Russia and its brief conquest by Napoleon (1772–1812) was the town's golden era, when it was the metropolis of Russian Jewry. Mitnagdim referred to it as "the Yavne of Byelorussia," due to its circle of disciples of the Vilna Gaon, and its renowned yeshiva. Habad Hasidism boasted that "the Hasidim of Shklov were the loftiest of all, and were tied to our Rebbe with endless bonds of love." And Maskilim pointed to the town as "a city full of wisemen and scribes, whose inhabitants are the wealthiest and most honored men in the land." The city's Great Synagogue, built in 1790, was described as "a glorious building, without equal among the synagogues of Lithuania and Poland; it is said that it was like the Temple of Herod." And folk memory recalls that Shklov was then compared to the Land of Israel—a land flowing with milk and honey.[12]

The emergence of a Haskalah circle in Shklov is particularly intriguing. Most historians have been of the opinion that the Russian Haskalah did not begin in earnest until the publication of Isaac Ber Levinsohn's monumental manifesto *Teudah be-yisrael* (Testimony in Israel), in 1828, and Levinsohn has been referred to by many as "the Russian Mendelssohn." Earlier voices calling for the reform of Jewish education and culture along European lines, and the transformation of the Jews' social and legal position in relation to their neighbors, have been lumped together under the rubric of "forerunners of the Haskalah."[13] The assumption underlying this characterization is that Jewish reformists and enlighteners before Levinsohn were isolated and idiosyncratic individuals, whose ideas were inchoate and whose impact on Jewish society was negligible. According to this conventional view, Russian Jewry remained entrenched in religious piety during the late eighteenth century and

at the turn of the nineteenth—a piety which flourished in rival
Hasidic-mystical and Mitnagdic-rabbinic variations—and faced the
challenges of Enlightenment and modernity only later.

The appearance of Haskalah and acculturation in Shklov and its
environs flies in the face of this view. In the course of a generation,
the town's Jewish community witnessed an explosion of interest in
science, languages, and European culture, a flurry of programs to
reform Jewish life, and the transformation of the lifestyle of many
of its members. These new trends spread among merchants whose
business dealings drew them into the orbit of the Russian Imperial
court in St. Petersburg, intellectuals who were swayed by the ideas
emanating from the Mendelssohnian circle in Berlin, and even
among rabbis with ties to the Vilna Gaon and the Lithuanian rabbinic establishment. The lines of dissemination were by no means
narrow or uniform.

These developments have been noted in passing by Jewish historians, but have not received the close consideration that they merit,
by virtue of their incongruity with the conventional view of Russian Jewish history.[14] The appearance of Haskalah and acculturation in Shklov suggest a much more variegated Jewish cultural
landscape in the late eighteenth century, and an earlier intrusion
of modernity than has been appreciated. It is on this intriguing
corner of the Jewish past that we now focus our attention.

CHAPTER I

The Great Divide:
Hasidim and Mitnagdim

Prehistory: Before the Partition

When the Jews of eastern Byelorussia came under the control of the Tsarist Empire, in August of 1772, they were in the throws of a tense and volatile internal religious conflict. The "land of Russia" was the birthplace of the struggle between Hasidim and Mitnagdim; a conflict which spread from Shklov to Vilna, and from Vilna to the rest of Jewish Eastern Europe. The division between the two camps became the defining cultural feature of Jewish life in Russia for several decades to come.[1]

In the years immediately prior to the partition, the "land of Russia" was a center of radical, eccentric, and aggressive Hasidim, whose activities provoked a fierce backlash among rabbis and communal leaders. Their behavior and its historical consequences were described by R. Shneur Zalman of Liady (1745–1813), the founder of Lubavitch-Habad Hasidism, in a letter to his colleague R. Avraham Kalisker (1741–1810), the leading Hasidic figure in eastern Byelorussia in the pre-partition years. Writing in the context of an angry feud which developed between them, R. Shneur Zalman reminded R. Avraham of his youthful sins. He recalled an emergency meeting of Hasidic leaders in the summer of 1772, after the first flurry of bans against their movement, and noted:

My eyes saw and my ears heard how [the Magid, R. Dov-Ber of Mezeritch] spoke sternly to you concerning your poor leadership of our people in the land of Russia. . . . Their daily speech was full of wildness and bufoonery, scoffing at the scholars and scorning them, throwing off the yoke [of the

7

Torah], and engaging in great levity. They also constantly performed somersaults (which are called *kulyen zikh*) in the marketplaces and streets, and the name of God was desecrated in the eyes of the gentiles. And other sorts of mockery and derision in the streets of Kalisk. And in the winter of 5532 [1771–72], after the disputation in Shklov, at which you could not find a response regarding this and similar behavior, the scholars of Shklov wrote to the late Vilna Gaon and persuaded him to rule that we should be "cast down," God forbid, as is the law regarding heretics and those who disgrace scholars.[2]

R. Shneur Zalman's picture of Hasidim run amok in eastern Byelorussia was elaborated upon in oral traditions within Lubavitch Hasidism. They speak of the *haside talk* or *tolk* who established an eccentric, violent order or regime—the meaning of the word *tolk* in Yiddish—which included not only somersaults in the streets and the mocking of Talmudists, but acts of wanton vandalism and violence. The goal of their antisocial behavior was "to turn the world upside down."[3] An anti-Hasidic polemicist from the end of the eighteenth century reports in a similar vein that the communal rabbis of Shklov and Lubavitch (the latter being at the time a non-Hasidic town in the Mogilev district) were harassed by the Hasidim during those years, and there is evidence that R. Jacob b. Judah Schick of Shklov was forced to flee his community because of Hasidic harassment.[4]

As R. Shneur Zalman's above-cited letter indicates, the community of Shklov responded to this antisocial outburst by convening a public disputation with R. Avraham Kalisker in the winter of 1771–72. Hasidism was put on trial and its representative was subjected to interrogation, along the lines of the Christian-Jewish disputations in the Middle Ages.[5] R. Avraham's inability to respond convincingly to some of the charges is attested to not only by R. Shneur Zalman, but also by a contemporaneous Mitnagdic source, which adds that the Shklov community proceeded to "pronounce them [the Hasidim] total heretics."[6]

This was a fateful, epoque-making decision. The halakhic ruling that Hasidim were heretics officially sanctioned their persecution from the perspective of Jewish religious law (see Maimonides, *Mishne Torah*, hilkhot mamrim, chapters 3 and 4). The ruling was communicated to the Vilna Gaon, R. Elijah b. Shlomo Zalman (1720–96), who endorsed it fully.

When the writings from Shklov reached us here in Vilna, the Gaon said "the law is according to the community of Shklov. This is a family of heretics; they are to be cast down [into a pit] and not elevated [from it]." ('Avodah Zarah 26b)[7]

The Shklov ruling spurred the Vilna Gaon to mobilize the Vilna community against Hasidism; the great Vilna *herem* against them was issued in May 1772, and letters were dispatched to communities throughout Eastern Europe calling for the suppression of the "sect."[8]

The Jews of eastern Byelorussia had thus gone through a full first round of Hasidic-Mitnagdic warfare, with provocations and acts of violence, a public confrontation, and formal excommunication of the Hasidim, in the months immediately prior to the annexation of their region by Russia. The clash in "the land of Russia" drew the Vilna Gaon into the fray, and sparked the nationwide campaign to suppress the Hasidic movement.

The Kahal in Russia, 1772–1794

The new Russian rulers of eastern Byelorussia were not directly interested in the religious disputes which engaged their recently acquired Jewish subjects. Their immediate concerns following the partition were of a more general nature: to establish control over the region, integrate it into the Russian administrative and legal system, and ensure that the inhabitants accepted Russian rule and its laws. Maintaining order and securing the steady flow of taxes to the Imperial treasury were of vital importance.[9]

Due to these considerations, the Russian authorities decided shortly after the partition to invest the corporate Jewish communities, the kahals, with broad administrative powers. General-Governor Z. G. Chernyshev, the official in charge of the annexed territories, ordered all Jews to register with the kahals, and empowered the latter to act as the state's agent in collecting the Russian head tax among Jews. Chernyshev left the apportionment of the tax burden to the discretion of the kahal elders, and also entrusted them with "making among [the Jews] the appropriate order." This broad mandate for regulating the affairs of the Jewish community included, after 1776, the authority to control travel and mobility through the issuance of official passports.[10] Chernyshev confirmed the jurisdiction of Jewish courts over both religious and civil affairs, and ordered the establishment of district and provincial kahals (*uyezdnie, gubernskie kagali*), which were to serve as appellate courts and as the highest authorities in internal Jewish disputes.[11]

Taken together, these actions by the Russian authorities constituted the rehabilitation of Jewish communal self-government on the local and regional levels, as it had been practiced in the Polish-Lithuanian Commonwealth before 1764, when the regional and national kahal councils were abolished by royal decree. The system of autonomous kahals was under intense attack from many quarters in Poland in the 1770s, and the councils (*va'adim*) had been completely dismantled there. But these very structures were embraced and resuscitated by the authorities in Tsarist Russia, for the sake of political stability and the steady flow of taxes in their newly annexed territories.[12]

The Jews took full advantage of this opportunity to revive their tradition of regional autonomy. In the newly created Mogilev province, the *va'ad medinat rusiya* was reestablished, and recognized by the Russian authorities as the Mogilev *gubernskii kagal*. The *va'ad*, which consisted in this period of representatives from five communities (Shklov, Mogilev, Mtsislavl, Stary Bykhov, and Chaus), reasserted its authority in supervising the affairs of the kahals under its jurisdiction. When intense conflicts arose in the Jewish community of Petrovitz in 1777, the *va'ad* appointed a rabbinic court to write new bylaws for its kahal. From their contents, we learn that the *va'ad medinat rusiya* was the recipient of the taxes collected by the kahals of the Mogilev province, and that its *bet din* was the appellate court for internal Jewish disputes. The *va'ad*'s rabbinic court also intervened to resolve a territorial dispute between Old Mtsislavl and New Mtsislavl (Slobeda) between 1777 and 1781.[13]

The control of the reconstituted *va'ad medinat rusiya* over internal Jewish affairs was so strong, that a complaint was submitted to the Russian Senate in 1783 "by Jews who were dissatisfied with the decisions of the *gubernskii kagal*, asking where one can submit an appeal [of its decisions], so that a situation not arise in which innocently accused people are forced, at times, to suffer."[14]

The kahal's broad powers were subsequently curtailed in the

mid-1780s, when the Jews' legal status was reformed, and they were formally integrated into the urban classes (*kupechestvo* and *meshchanstvo*). The Tsarist authorities withdrew their official sanction for Jewish courts to adjudicate civil cases, and affluent Jews who joined the ranks of the merchant guilds began to pay certain taxes directly to the Imperial treasury. But even after these reforms, the official powers retained by the kahal in Russia were impressive, especially when compared to the situation in Poland and Austria at the time. The Jewish "charter" of 1786 explicitly authorized the *gubernskii kagal* to adjudicate all cases related to Jewish religious and ritual matters, and sanctioned the collection of both Imperial and internal (that is, communal) taxes by the local kahals. The charter left the system of officially recognized organs of Jewish self-government, on both the local and regional levels, essentially intact.[15] The *va'ad medinat rusiya* and its rabbinic court continued to function into the 1790s.[16]

The Suppression of Hasidism in the Mogilev Province

This situation had far-reaching consequences for the course of the Hasidic-Mitnagdic conflict in Russia in the late eighteenth century. In the Mogilev province, the *va'ad medinat rusiya* led a coordinated campaign against Hasidism among the communities under its jurisdiction, and successfully suppressed the movement there for more than twenty years. Such regional coordination and enforcement were impossible in Poland, where the *va'adim* had been abolished, and the battle against Hasidism had to be waged on a community-by-community basis, with uncertain and varying results.

The driving ideological force behind the anti-Hasidic movement in the Mogilev province was provided by the "Sages of Shklov," a circle of disciples and devotees of the Vilna Gaon led by R. Benjamin b. Shlomo Zalman Rivlin (1728–1812).[17] This group of Talmudists convened a public disputation with leaders of the Hasidic "sect" in 1775, at which the public uproar against the Hasidim was so great, that their representatives, R. Shneur Zalman of Liady and R. Avraham Kalisker, were manhandled and physically mistreated.[18] And in 1787, the *va'ad medinat rusiya* held a special session in Shklov, at which it issued a set of anti-Hasidic

ordinances, signed by R. Benjamin Rivlin, R. Issachar Ber b. Judah
Leyb (the communal rabbi of Shklov and Rivlin's brother-in-law),
as well as other local *dayyanim*, scholars, and notables. Hasidic
traditions refer to additional bans and meetings, and one Hasidic
author notes that "when the great Mitnagdic rabbis used to gather
in order to ban our rabbis and those who followed them, the city of
Shklov was their metropolis. Most of the meetings and actions took
place there."[19]

The accusations lodged against the movement by the "Sages of
Shklov" were typical of Mitnagdim in general: sectarian separatism;
disdain for Torah study and Talmudic scholars; a dissolute and
licentious lifestyle characterized by endless celebrations; the alter-
ation of the traditional liturgy and praying "with great madness";
the violation of halakhic regulations regarding prayer and *shehita*;
false claims to perform miracles; and the dissemination of heretical
religious doctrines.[20]

The novelty of their campaign lay not in the realm of ideology
and polemics, but rather in the sphere of politics and organization.
In the Mogilev province, the anti-Hasidic movement was conducted
under the auspices of the *va'ad medinat rusiya*, with close inter-
communal coordination and unified action on the regional level.
When a Hasidic *shohet* from Vohlyn crossed into the Mogilev province's southern district and was detected by the community of Krichev, it immediately reported the matter to heads of the *vaa'd* in
Mogilev, who arranged for the unfortunate trespasser, Ayzik Zas-
laver, to be apprehended and interrogated. This "breach" was
deemed adequate cause for convening the special meeting of the
va'ad in 1787, to which communal elders and leaders from across
the province were summoned.[21]

The high level of regional discipline among the *Va'ad*'s constituent communities is reflected in a letter from the rabbi of Mtsislavl
apologizing for his inability to attend the gathering. The rabbi
assured the *va'ad* of his total support for the Mitnagdic cause, and
urged it to adopt the most severe measures against the Hasidim. He
reported to them that "I and the members of my community swear
by heaven and earth . . . that there are no members of this evil sect
in our city, thank God. Not even one."[22]

The ordinances passed at the meeting were formulated as a series of directives from the *va'ad medinat rusiya* to the communities under its jurisdiction. They read as follows:

It is obligatory for every single community to issue ordinances, and to enforce them with all possible means of coercion, in order to ensure that the restrictions listed below are observed. These should be recorded in the minute book of every single community and city, as an eternal precaution and reminder. . . .

The following are the restrictions which we adopted at this meeting:

1. To decree a public fast on the 25th of Teveth.
2. To employ all means to destroy the altars of these heretics, and prevent them from gathering.
3. To ensure that no one study their books, and to conduct searches for this purpose.
4. To enforce the validity of the ordinances passed in Brody and Vilna prohibiting travel to the leaders of the sect.
5. Meat slaughtered by their *shohtim* is forbidden and treif, and all meat coming from outside city limits will be considered treif, unless it has a writ of *kashrut* from a well-known person, who does not belong to their sect.
6. It is forbidden to provide lodging to anyone of their sect.
7. No community may accept one of them as a cantor, rabbi, or preacher, and particular attention should be paid to the *melamdim* (teachers), to ensure that none of them teach boys without an appropriate certificate from the rabbis.
8. To announce in all the communities that anyone who knows anything about them, whether favorable or negative, should report it to the rabbinic court.[23]

These anti-Hasidic directives were squarely within the parameters of the *va'ad's* officially granted authority to supervise Jewish religious matters, and "make order" among the communities. According to historian P. Marek, the minutes of an earlier meeting of the *va'ad medinat rusiya* noted explicitly that Russian law gave them the right to punish the sectarians (i.e., the Hasidim).[24] It is safe to assume that the *va'ad* would have used its power of tax apportionment to punish a recalcitrant community which refused to implement its anti-Hasidic measures. Hence the eagerness of the rabbi of Mtsislavl to reassure the *va'ad* that, despite his inability to attend, he was firmly on their side.

A number of letters by R. Shneur Zalman of Liady bear testimony to the effectiveness of the anti-Hasidic measures taken in the Mogilev province. They offer a portrait of a persecuted, endangered movement, driven underground by its adversaries, and fearful for the physical safety of its adherents. Writing to a group of Hasidim in or around 1780, R. Shneur Zalman conceded that it was simply too dangerous to convene separate Hasidic *minyanim*, and asked that they be discontinued throughout "the entire land."

"It is a time of trouble for Jacob, but out of it he shall be saved" [Jer. 30:7]. It is therefore my advice unto the entire land to fulfill the verses "hide yourself for a little moment, until the fury has passed" [Is. 26:20], "it is a time to do unto the Lord, and abrogate the Torah" [Psalms 119:126]. Take heed for the sake of your souls, and do not confront those who have risen up against you by praying in a separate *minyan*. I put my trust in the Lord, that he will not forsake us, and that He will soon return the crown to its ancient glory.[25]

This is an extraordinary document in the history of Hasidism. Nowhere else in Eastern Europe was a Hasidic leader forced to call upon his followers in an entire province to cease and desist from organized Hasidic prayer. The Hasidic prayer group was the movement's primary institution, in the technical sociological sense of the term. It was the focal point of Hasidic religious life, where the quest for *dvekut*, communion with God, was pursued on an individual and collective basis.[26] Without it, Hasidism was a dead letter.

In 1787, following the issuance of the anti-Hasidic ordinances by the *va'ad medinat rusiya*, R. Shneur Zalman addressed an impassioned appeal to its leaders, pleading for mercy and justice. He invoked the language of the book of Esther, thereby comparing the *va'ad*'s actions to the evil decrees of Haman. "The letters were sent by couriers to all the districts (*uyezdn*), containing terrible decrees and injunctions. . . . For we are sold, I and my people. And we shall be redeemed not by silver, but by mercy and the supplications which we put before you."[27]

Most revelatory is R. Shneur Zalman's description of the suffering inflicted upon Hasidim as a result of the *va'ad*'s ordinances:

The masses have acted to harm us, treating us like children of wickedness and total heretics, [believing] that whoever kills us first merits reward, and brings merit on the community. Were it not for fear of the authorities, men would swallow each other alive and consider it an act of goodness. And in secret, things that must not be done have been done, and permission has been granted to go after people's lives and livelihoods to the extent possible. . . . Add to this the humiliation and bloodshed. For our blood has been shed like water, and we have been put to shame before the Gentiles and humiliated among our brethren the children of Israel.

Earth, oh earth, do not cover our blood, be not the place for our cries.[28]

R. Shneur Zalman's complaint of anti-Hasidic terror and bloodshed in the Mogilev province should not be dismissed as hyperbole. Local traditions have been preserved concerning the ruthlessness with which the Shklov kahal dealt with rebels and informers. "If the waters of the Dnieper could speak, they would tell a great deal about the informers who were drowned to death according to the decision of the kahal of the Shklov region."[29] The Hasidim, who were deemed to be a heretical sect, were no doubt treated just as severely. The practice of depriving Hasidim of their livelihoods, probably through unfair competitive practices which caused them to lose their *arendas* (leases), is attested to in other sources. Letters by Byelorussian Hasidim to their masters in the Land of Israel complained bitterly that they were suffering from economic harassment.[30]

Taken together, these sources substantiate the view preserved in Lubavitch oral tradition, that anti-Hasidic persecution was considerably greater in Russian-controlled territory (i.e., in the Mogilev province) than in Poland and the Ukraine.[31] The unique powers of the *va'ad medinat rusiya* made effective persecution possible; the strong Mitnagdic leadership of the "Sages of Shklov" made it a reality.

The Dominance of Hasidism in the Polotsk Province

The Hasidim faced no such difficulties in the Polotsk province to the north of Mogilev. The boundaries of the province, which was established by the Russian authorities in 1772, corresponded to the area of greatest Hasidic strength. R. Avraham Kalisker, R. Menahem Mendl of Vitebsk, and R. Shneur Zalman of Liady all hailed from this territory. Shortly after the region's annexation by Russia, R. Menahem Mendl returned there from Minsk (where he had resided for a number of years) and settled in the town of Horodok. Under his leadership, Hasidism gained tremendous popularity in the province, as numerous inhabitants flocked to his court in Horodok and were affected by his teachings.[32]

In 1777, R. Menahem Mendl and R. Avraham Kalisker emigrated with a sizable group of Hasidim to the Land of Israel. They continued, however, to serve as the spiritual leaders of Byelorussian Hasidism after their departure, employing frequent correspondence and personal emissaries to communicate with their followers. As it became apparent that this model of long-distance leadership was unsatisfactory, R. Menahem Mendl and R. Avraham gradually shifted the burden of responsibility to R. Shneur Zalman of Liady, who was appointed leader in 1786. From that point on, his residence in the town of Liozna became the movement's focal point.[33]

Hasidism predominated in the Polotsk province. Not a single *herem* against the movement is known to have been issued within its borders. Indeed, the local kahals appear to have been under Hasidic control. When the first Hasidic emissary from the Holy Land sought to raise funds for his struggling brethren in Palestine, he addressed a request for aid to the heads of the Vitebsk kahal, rather than to the *gabaim* of the local Hasidic conventicle. The communal body had been co-opted by the movement, and so there was no need to circumvent it or utilize an alternative institutional structure.[34]

R. Menahem Mendl, writing from Palestine, gave voice to the Hasidic confidence that the province was theirs:

The land has been subdued before us, for all the inhabitants of the land have melted away before us. And those who rose up against us, God brought their counsel to nought.[35]

R. Shneur Zalman proposed in his above-mentioned 1787 letter to the Mogilev *va'ad medinat rusiya* that the leaders of the Hasidic and Mitnagdic camps meet before an impartial tribunal "either in our province (*ba-guberniya shelanu*) or in your province, or in a place in between the two provinces."[36] Clearly he also considered the Polotsk region to be Hasidic territory.

This is not to say that there were no non-Hasidic congregations and rabbis in the province. There were; and they were magnanimously tolerated by the Hasidic majority. But the Mitnagdim were outnumbered and overpowered. The writings of R. Phinehas b. Judah of Polotsk, a preacher and theologian who lived in Polotsk between 1767 and 1785, testify to this fact. R. Phinehas's works are full of anguish and dismay that the Satanic forces of Hasidism are

1. The great synagogue of Shklov, built in 1790. (YIVO Archives)

2. R. Shneur Zalman b. Barukh. (YIVO Archives)

3. The Vilna Gaon, R. Elijah b. Shlomo Zalman. (YIVO Archives)

4. Semion Gavrilovich Zorich.
(Stolitsa i usad' ba)

5. Students of the Shklov Nobility
Academy in uniform. *(Stolitsa i
usad' ba)*

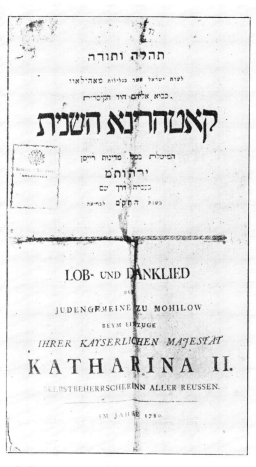

6. Poem presented by the Jews of the Mogilev province to Empress Catherine II. (*Historische shriftn fun YIVO*)

הַלּוּז וְעַרְמוֹן הָרִמּוֹן הַשָּׁקֵד

וְתָמָר וְשָׁנוּ וְשִׁנְאוּ וְשִׁנַּסְנוּ

וְנָאוּ וְעָלוּ אַלְגּוּמִים אַלְמֻגִּים אֶזְרָח

תִּדְהָר אֹרֶן אֵלָה אַלּוֹן בְּרוֹשׁ

בְּרוֹתִים תְּאַשּׁוּר נֹפֶר הֲדַס כֹּפֶר

לִבְנֶה נַהֲלֹלִים קָנֶה עַרְעָר עֲרָבִים

צַפְצָפָה רֹתֶם תִּרְזָה וְעָרְפוּ

בִּיתְרוֹן שָׂרוֹחַ וְשָׁאָר עֲלֵיהֶם

עֲפָאֵיהֶם טַרְפֵּיהֶם וְנוֹסְפוּ וְנִסְפּוּ חֲטֻרְיּוֹתֵיהֶם

סַקְלוֹתֵיהֶם מַטֻּוֹתֵיהֶם שָׁבְטֵיהֶם שַׂרְבִיטֵירֶם עֻוּטֵיהֶם

7. Naftali Hirtz Schulman's edition of
Zekher rav (Shklov, 1804).

№ 945.

Государь мой Нота Хаимовичъ!

Получаю поднесеннаго мною въ прошломъ 1800 году мнѣнія, о живущихъ въ бѣлоцкой губерніи Евреяхъ, Государь Императоръ высочайше учредить изволилъ комитетъ, относительно устройства ихъ на общую государственную, ихъ самыхъ пользу. — Члены комитета, каковыхъ и я высочайше удостоенъ, испросили всеподданнѣйшимъ докладомъ у Его Императорскаго величества позволеніе избрать себѣ сверхъ предположенныхъ изъ губерній депутатовъ, подобному тому же изъ про свѣщеннѣйшихъ и извѣстныхъ въ честности Евреевъ. Я будучи нѣсколько уже лѣтъ извѣстенъ башимъ къ общему благу и послѣднихъ дня народа, которые удостоены —

8. Draft of letter inviting Nota Notkin to serve as adviser to the State Committee on the Jews. (I. Gessen, *Istoriia evreiskogo naroda v rossii*)

ВОПЛЬ

ДЩЕРИ ІУДЕЙСКОЙ.

Сочиненіе

ЛЕЙБЫ НЕВАХОВИЧА.

Сᴕ Указнаго дозволенія.

Санктпетербургъ,
печатано въ привилегированной Врейткопфовой Типографіи,
1803го года.

9. Nevakhovich's *Lament of the Daughter of Judah* (Russian: St. Petersburg, 1803;

קול שועת בת יהודה

והוא מליצה ישרה עבור עם יהודה,
להסיר ממנו תלונות העמים ·

חובר בלשון רוסיא

מאת הרבני טוהר"ר

יהודא ליב במו' נח ז"ל
מלעטיטשוב

ונדפס בעיר מלוכה·

פעטרס בארג

ברשיון מקום הממשלה

לשם

האדון יועץ חרשים

בעניניס שבתוך המדינה
נראף וויקטאר פאוולאוויטש
קאטשוב יי'

וכעת נעתק ע"י המחבר עצמו ללשון עברי

ונדפס

בשקלאוו

שנת תקסד לפק

9. (Cont.) Hebrew: Shklov, 1804)

10. Abraham Perets
*(Dekabrist grigorii ab-
ramovich perets)*

11. Grigorii (Hirsh) Per-
ets, ca. 1820. *(Dekabrist
grigorii abramovich
perets)*

defeating rabbinic Judaism, and contain bitter complaints that the younger generation has abandoned Talmudic study for other religious pursuits.[37] Fearing that Hasidism might spread to his own family, R. Phinehas took the extraordinary step of requiring his son to take an oath that he "would not join the sect of the Hasidim, . . . not pray in their minyanim . . . , and never visit their rabbis."[38]

In the Polotsk province, the structure of Jewish regional governance differed from that of the Mogilev province. Instead of forming a council of kahals along the lines of the va'ad medinat rusiya, the highest regional authority was a provincial rabbinic court, which consisted of R. Israel of Polotsk, R. Issachar Ber of Lubavitch, and R. Shneur Zalman of Liady. Historian Immanuel Etkes has pointed out that these three figures acted as the collective second-tier Hasidic leadership of Byelorussia during the early 1780s, when R. Menahem Mendl and R. Avraham Kalisker guided the movement from their residence in the Land of Israel.[39] But closer examination of the trio's pronouncements and epistles indicates that they acted as an officially constituted high rabbinic court. They issued decrees and herems on civil affairs, such as a ban on using funds raised for the inhabitants of the Holy Land to support local paupers, whose formulaic language suggests that the authors were not an ad hoc Hasidic leadership, but rather the functioning provincial bet din of a region under Hasidic control.[40]

In 1786, the bet din structure gave way to a centralized system headed by a provincial rabbi, and R. Shneur Zalman of Liady was appointed to this position of leadership by his senior colleagues in Palestine. The language used by R. Avraham Kalisker in referring to his appointment was that of traditional rabbinic ordination: "We have anointed him to be the rabbi [moreh tsedek] in your land, so that the congregation of God not be like sheep without a shepherd."[41]

As provincial rabbi, R. Shneur Zalman imposed fees and collections upon the inhabitants of the region, which he enforced by threat of excommunication. Wielding the same power of herem as his Mitnagdic counterparts in the Mogilev province, he decreed:

Whoever will not give the amount assessed of him, in cash or at least in security, should be distanced from us through all forms of ostracization.

. . . He has no portion nor inheritance with us in all matters of holiness, and should not even be counted in a *minyan*. He should be banished until he repents.[42]

In his capacity as provincial rabbi, R. Shneur Zalman was also the region's ultimate halakhic authority. The rabbinic courts of the Vitebsk and Polotsk kahals submitted inquiries to him on matters of religious divorces, to which he replied with responsa.[43]

Scholars have characterized R. Shneur Zalman's style of leadership as less charismatic and more conventionally rabbinic than other Hasidic masters.[44] This was not only a matter of personal style or outlook, but a reflection of his institutional roles. From 1786 on, R. Shneur Zalman was not only spiritual master to his Hasidim, but also the official regional authority in the Polotsk province for fiscal and halakhic affairs. R. Shneur Zalman was both *tsadik* and *rav*— and he was referred to by the latter title in many sources.

The battle between Hasidim and Mitnagdim was thus drawn along sharp geographic lines. In the Mogilev province, Hasidism was suppressed by the regional *va'ad*, while in the Polotosk province it reigned supreme and was in control of the kahals and provincial rabbinate. This was the state of affairs which prevailed until the mid-1790s.

The Shift in Russian Policy and Its Consequences

With the second and third partitions of Poland, in 1793 and 1795, Russia acquired seven hundred thousand new Jewish subjects, more than it had ever wanted or imagined, and the Tsarist authorities began to revise their policies toward the Jews. Restrictions on Jewish residence, the establishment of the Pale of Settlement, and the introduction of double taxation of Jewish merchants and townsmen were the most famous features of the new policy of suspicion and hostility.[45]

The kahal and the regional bodies of Jewish self-government also came under closer governmental scrutiny. Catherine the Great became intent upon bringing the Jewish population under the undivided jurisdiction of the civil authorities, and sought to severely diminish the realm of Jewish autonomy. Although the full attainment of this goal eluded her—as it did her successors—her actions did yield limited success, which, in turn, changed the balance of power between Hasidim and Mitnagdim in Russia.

An Imperial *ukaz* (decree) issued on May 3, 1795, in the aftermath of the third Polish partition, decreed that the Jews were to be treated as an urban class, subordinate to the city magistrates, and stipulated that the *gubernskie kagali* were "not authorized to deal with any matters other than religious rites and rituals."[46] The decree was interpreted by provincial officials as categorically rescinding the civil, judicial, and police powers of the Jewish regional bodies. The latter were stripped of the authority to serve as the final arbiters of all internal Jewish disputes and to issue binding decrees, enforceable by power of the *herem*.

The *ukaz* was a turning point in the history of the Hasidic-Mitnagdic conflict in Russia, and its impact is alluded to in the literature of both camps. R. Avigdor of Pinsk, a fanatical Mitnaged who denounced the Hasidic movement to Tsar Paul I in 1800, attributed the movement's resurgence to the weakened status of Jewish autonomous bodies. Hasidism, he complained, could no longer be banned by Jewish communal leaders via judicial or administrative fiat.

From time immemorial it has been our custom that only our scholars could decide matters of justice. . . . And when the Empress, may she rest in peace, assumed the throne, she decreed that Jewish disputes should be decided by the Jews' scholars.

But certain rich men who did not approve of this, cunningly brought about that the decisions of Jewish courts in such disputes should remain ineffectual. . . .

The truth of the matter is that if now, as in the past, the Jews' affairs were subject to the judgment of their own scholars, the latter would have—based on the order of the authorities and in accordance with the supreme laws of the land—destroyed these individuals who have dared to rebel against God and His anointed ones [i.e., the Hasidim].[47]

R. Avigdor's complaint, that the law no longer permitted Jewish scholars to settle the Jews' affairs unilaterally, was a cause for celebration among the Hasidim. Hasidic traditions note that following the second and third partition of Poland, the Russian authorities outlawed use of the *herem*, and the Mitnagdim were no longer able to ban the movement, as they had in the past. Official scrutiny of communal actions made such activity virtually impossible.[48]

The Hasidic tradition relates that the new policy against use of the *herem* was adopted in 1794, not 1795. If correct, the 1795 *ukaz* reiterated a policy adopted a year earlier, after the second partition of Poland. The earlier Hasidic dating would also help shed light on an important historical event—the publication of the first Hasidic book in Russia.

R. Shneur Zalman of Liady's halakhic manual *hilkhot talmud torah* was first published in 1794 in Shklov, with a letter of approbation from its communal rabbi, R. Chanokh Henekh Schick.[49] The circumstances surrounding this publication are shrouded in mystery. The book was issued anonymously, without indicating the author's identity, in the city which had been the citadel of Mitnagdism. The very same R. Chanokh Henekh Schick had signed the anti-Hasidic ordinances of the *va'ad medinat rusiya* seven years earlier. Hasidic tradition contends that R. Chanokh Henekh's opposition to the movement dissipated during the intervening years, but this does not explain the apparent inaction of the *va'ad medinat rusiya* and the "Sages of Shklov" to prevent the book's publication.[50] The only plausible explanation is that Shklov's Mitnagdic circles no longer had the legal or moral authority to prevent the publication of Hasidic literature on their territory, beginning in 1794. If so, the publication of R. Shneur Zalman's book in Shklov was a demonstrative act in which the Hasidim were exercising, and thereby celebrating, their newly acquired freedom in the Mogilev province.

At about this time, in 1794 or 1795, Hasidism began to spread in the Mogilev province. In the absence of a coordinated, enforceable ban, individuals no longer feared openly identifying with the movement. By March 1796, there were Hasidic *minyanim* in Shklov, Orsha, Chaus, Dubrovna, Kopys, and other communities in the Mogilev province.[51] Shklov itself soon became a major center of Habad Hasidism, and was home to some of R. Shneur Zalman's closest disciples and followers. According to one tradition, the Shklov Hasidim were, in fact, "the loftiest of all."[52]

Mitnagdic rabbinism remained a strong religious and ideological trend in Shklov and the Mogilev province as a whole. The circle of disciples of the Vilna Gaon, which coalesced around R. Benjamin b. Shlomo Zalman Rivlin, continued to flourish. But after the *ukaz* of

1794 (or 1795), the Mitnagdim lost their monopoly over Jewish religious life in the Mogilev province which they had held for some twenty-two years.

In the late 1790s, the Hasidic-Mitnagdic conflict in Russia entered its final phase. With free use of the *herem* no longer permitted by law, the Hasidic camp became more aggressive and ambitious, while the Mitnagdim grew bitterly desperate. The main battlefield shifted to Vilna—acquired by Russia in the third partition of Poland in 1795—where the Hasidim mounted an organized effort to topple the Mitnagdic-led kahal. The kahal responded by issuing an anti-Hasidic *herem* in October 1797, in violation of the Imperial decree of 1794 (or 1795). The Hasidim immediately complained to Tsarist officials that the kahal had acted in violation of Russian law, by exercising unauthorized powers. The authorities upheld their complaint, and the Hasidic presence in Vilna was legitimized. A cycle of denunciations and counterdenunciations ensued, and culminated with the Mitnagdim informing on R. Shneur Zalman to the central Russian government in St. Petersburg. This, in turn, led to R. Shneur Zalman's arrest and brief imprisonment in 1798 and 1801.[53]

Meanwhile, in the "land of Russia" itself, an unfriendly truce prevailed between the two camps. Tensions and polemics between the "Sages of Shklov" and local Hasidim persisted. In Shklov itself, the division was so intense that even after Hasidic conventicles functioned within the community, Hasidim were buried in a separate plot within the communal cemetery, probably at the insistence of certain Mitnagdim.[54]

But the violent life-and-death war was over. Like it or not, there was little the local Mitnagdim could do to supress the movement, now that the *va'ad medinat rusiya* had been stripped of its civil powers. In 1804, the de facto coexistence which prevailed in Shklov and elsewhere was enshrined in Russian Imperial legislation. The Imperial "Statute Concerning the Jews" issued in that year, under Tsar Alexander I, stipulated that all Jewish communities were required to permit both Hasidic and non-Hasidic congregations to function, under the umbrella of a single, unified kahal. In the same year, 1804, R. Shneur Zalman paid his first official visit to Shklov.[55]

CHAPTER 2

From Byelorussia to Prussia:
The Odyssey of Rabbi Barukh Schick

The name of Rabbi Barukh Schick of Shklov (1744–1808) has survived in historical memory thanks to a few lines in the introduction to one of his books, a Hebrew translation of Euclid's *Elements*, in which he related remarks made to him by the Vilna Gaon in February 1778 in support of the study of science. "I heard from his holy tongue," wrote Schick, "that for every deficiency of knowledge a man has in the sciences [*hokhmah*], he will have ten deficiencies of knowledge in the science of the Torah; for Torah and science are closely related. And he commanded me to translate everything possible of the sciences into our holy tongue . . . in order to spread knowledge among our people Israel."[1]

These words played a pivotal role in immortalizing the Vilna Gaon as an advocate of the sciences, and a forerunner of the Haskalah. During the nineteenth century, Russian Maskilim cited them in order to lend a rabbinic stamp of approval to their program to reform Jewish education and culture. Traditionalists responded by offering more restrictive interpretations of the Gaon's words to Schick.[2]

The Maskilim and historians who quoted these famous lines focused their attention on interpreting their message, and neglected to take a close look at the messenger. Schick's personal odyssey was frequently ignored or glossed over. He was occasionally depicted as R. Elijah's loyal disciple (a flattering but baseless characterization), and rarely was much attention paid to the fact that he had spent a year in Berlin, in the company of Moses Mendelssohn, Naftali Hirtz Wessely, and David Friedlander, shortly before his audience with R. Elijah.[3] Yet an awareness of this fact leads one to raise questions about Schick's motives and reliability. Did he approach R. Elijah with a hidden Maskilic agenda? Was his account of the Gaon's words accurate or a self-serving distortion?

Schick's story deserves to be examined in its own right as well. A Byelorussian rabbi who traversed the distance between Berlin and Vilna in the late eighteenth century, and who was exposed to the intellectual ferments surrounding Moses Mendelssohn and the Vilna Gaon, merits close scrutiny. It has usually been assumed that these two great arenas of Jewish intellectual history were cut off from each other. Schick's story indicates that there was a degree of contact and even intellectual traffic between the Berlin and Vilna circles. In addition, the story of a Byelorussian rabbi who went to Berlin, saw the Haskalah circle firsthand, and then returned home somewhat changed, promises to shed light on the cultural division which was emerging at that time between Maskilim and traditionalists. Schick's reaction to the Haskalah—which was neither one of total embrace nor total rejection—draws attention to the variety of modes in which traditional rabbis approached modernity.

A Practitioner of Rabbinic Science

Barukh Schick was born in Shklov in 1744, into a distinguished family of Byelorussia's rabbinic elite. His father, R. Jacob, served as Shklov's communal rabbi for some twenty years, and was, according to contemporaries, a respected Talmudist and halakhic authority. R. Barukh's uncle, his mother's brother, was the noted R. Arye Leyb Ginzburg, the *Sha'agat arye*, widely viewed as the most outstanding halakhist in eighteenth-century Poland-Lithuania after the Vilna Gaon himself. In a society where social status was closely connected with family pedigree, Barukh Schick's relation to the *Sha'agat arye* was of particular importance. The Ginzburg family was also the predominant force in the Byelorussian rabbinate, with members of this clan holding the office of provincial rabbi for "the land of Russia" throughout the eighteenth century, and others serving as communal rabbis in several local towns.[4]

Schick's early life history was that of a young man following in the footsteps of his family. He studied the Talmud under his father's tutelage in Shklov, then moved to Minsk in 1760, joined the exclusive *shivah keruim* society (open only to scholars and communal leaders), and began to rise up its ranks. In 1764, Schick was granted *semikha* (ordination) by R. Avraham Katzenellenbogen of Brest-Litovsk (Brisk), and eventually served as a *parnas* and *dayyan* of the Minsk community.[5] One has here a typical biography of a scholar rising up the ladder of rabbinic and communal leadership, thanks to his learning, kinship ties, and connections.

But there is one feature of Schick's early life which appears to be atypical for someone of his rabbinic background and Polish-Lithuanian milieu—his study of scientific disciplines, and his involvement in composing Hebrew books of science. According to Schick, these activities began during his years in Shklov and Minsk. In the introduction to his first book, he reminisced:

"I said I shall be wise," and I prepared my books of science, "but it was far from me" (Eccl. 7:23). For when I composed two or three pages, the city burnt down, and all my books and tools were destroyed. Later on, I had a bit of prosperity, and I continued to collect "words of understanding and wisdom of the times" (I Chron. 12:32). Then the burden of sustenance fell upon me, and I in my anguish arranged the little that I had of scientific books and decided to elucidate that which a man needs to know regarding himself, his body, and composition.[6]

Several details in this testimony correspond to events in Schick's life during his years in Minsk during the 1760s. After beginning to compose a work of science, his books were devoured in a local fire—an allusion to the great Minsk blaze of 1762, which destroyed the synagogue of the *shivah keruim* society and other buildings in the Jewish quarter.[7] Shortly thereafter, he was married and assumed the burden of supporting a family, an event which must have taken place during his Minsk years. Despite these obstacles, he was able to compose his first work, devoted to human anatomy and physiology, subsequently published under the title *Tiferet adam* (The Splendor of Man; Berlin, 1777).

In a second brief testimony, written during his stay in Berlin, Schick dated his involvement in science to an even earlier stage of his life—his childhood years in Shklov.

When I was still in the home of my father, the famous rabbi and scholar, and we used to study together the Talmud with the commentaries of Rashi,

Tosafot, and codes, day and night, my soul longed to lift up the crown of Israel, and to translate books into the Hebrew language on every discipline and science. But the vicissitudes of time overtook me, and these thoughts of mine came to an end . . . due to my dislocation from one home to another, and from one city to another.[8]

One may justifiably wonder whether Schick conceived of his unprecedented project of translating books from all scientific disciplines into Hebrew at age sixteen or younger. Schick may have been projecting his current designs in Berlin back into his childhood in Shklov. But there is no reason to doubt his contention that his study of science began in Shklov during the 1750s; the point is, in fact, corroborated by internal evidence from his early treatises.[9]

Anatomy and lunar astronomy, the subjects of Schick's early works, enjoyed venerable traditions as objects of rabbinic study and creativity. Anatomy was an essential part of medical education, and had attracted the interest of numerous rabbi-physicians, ever since the days of Shabbetai Donello and Maimonides. In addition to its practical application in the medical profession, anatomy was viewed by rabbis who were themselves physicians as a valuable tool for instilling an awareness of God in one's consciousness. The human body was God's greatest creation, and examination of it served to strengthen one's religious sensibility, argued Donello, Joseph Ibn Aknin, Meir Aldabi, and numerous others. They invariably cited Job 19:26, "from my flesh I behold God," as the proof text for their contention that study of the human body was a sacred activity.[10]

The tradition of astronomical study among rabbis was just as strong. Calculating the exact time of the lunar phasis, which marked the beginning of the new Hebrew month, was considered by many to constitute fulfillment of the biblical commandment to "sanctify the moon." Ever since Maimonides' epoch-making treatise on *Hilkhot kidush ha-hodesh*, scores of rabbis had studied the relevant mathematical and astronomical calculations, in order to determine the moment of the new moon's "birth." Lunar astronomy was thus regarded as a legitimate specialty in the field of halakhah, and generated a small library of rabbinic works and commentaries.[11]

Both these traditions were inactive in eighteenth-century Poland. Lunar astronomy—a popular discipline among Polish rabbis in the sixteenth and early seventeenth centuries—fell into general disuse after the great deluge of 1648–57; and human anatomy thrived among Italian rabbi-physicians for a lengthy period of time, but was never popular among Polish rabbis, who rarely complemented their rabbinic studies with a medical education.[12] Schick's originality lay in his turning to these spheres of inquiry, which were dormant in his time and place.

Dormant, but not delegitimized, medicine was a respected and honored profession among Polish Jews in the eighteenth century, with several of the finest and brightest young men journeying to Padua or Frankfurt to obtain a medical education. Moreover, the Spanish-Italian tradition of rabbi-physicians was embedded in history and viewed with distant respect, and astronomy was considered a discipline which was sanctioned by the rabbinic tradition. In theory, it remained a legitimate intellectual option. And a few eighteenth-century Polish rabbinic authors pursued it in practice as well—R. Solomon of Chelma, R. Israel of Zamosc, R. Jonathan of Ruzhany, and R. Elijah, the Vilna Gaon himself.[13] Schick's study of these disciplines was not commonplace for his day and age, but there was nothing deviant or rebellious in it. It evidently did not hinder his rise to positions of prominence, such as *dayyan* and *parnas* in the Minsk Jewish community.

A perusal of Schick's early works provides an interesting glimpse of his scientific workshop and thinking before his exposure to the West. On the whole, these works follow in the tradition of medieval rabbinic science—their content is essentially premodern, they cite rabbinic literature as a source of scientific wisdom, and they are prefaced by religious rationales for the study of their respective disciplines. But within these traditional parameters, there are some novel and surprising features worthy of note.

1. *Scientific Content.* Schick's anatomy followed Galen, apparently oblivious to Harvey's discoveries on the heart and blood circulation, which revolutionized the study of the human body. His astronomy was Ptolemaic, without so much as an allusion to the Copernican theory of a heliocentric planetary system. In their naïveté regarding scientific developments which had occurred more

than 150 years earlier, Schick's works were truly a throwback to the Middle Ages. A number of his predecessors in the sixteenth and seventeenth centuries had displayed a keen awareness (if not an enthusiastic embrace) of the theories of Harvey and Copernicus.[14]

One cannot ascribe Schick's scientific backwardness to his ignorance of Latin. Schick knew Latin (although just how he learned it remains unclear) and used Latin literature in his works. In his anatomy, he cited the work of Girolamo Cardano (1501–76), a professor of medicine at Pavia University, and in his astronomy he referred to François Viete's (1540–1603) *Canon Mathematicus* and to Euclid's *Elements*, a work which, as already mentioned, he later translated from Latin into Hebrew.[15] Indeed, Schick prided himself on his Latin scholarship, and took to task earlier authors on astronomy for "lacking the necessary learning from books in foreign tongues, such as Euclid and others." This was indeed an apt critique of the rabbinic astronomy practiced in sixteenth- and seventeenth-century Poland, whose luminaries drew their knowledge exclusively from medieval Hebrew writings and translations.[16]

Linguistically, Schick was up to the task of obtaining an accurate picture of the state of knowledge in these fields. If Schick's science was severely antiquated, it was due to his remoteness from the centers of European science. Schick based his knowledge upon the few Latin writings which reached him in Byelorussia, and the latter were, it seems, hopelessly outdated.

One can only speculate as to how Latin manuscripts reached Schick's hands. A number of young Lithuanian Jews traveled to Padua, Italy, to pursue a medical education, and it is likely that they brought scientific writings back to Lithuania after their course of study.[17] One such medical student, Yekutiel Gordon of Vilna (known for his membership in the mystical-messianic circle of R. Moshe Hayim Luzzatto), resided in Shklov during the 1730s and 1740s, and practiced medicine there. He may well have been the conduit through which the writings of Cardano, Viete, and Euclid reached Shklov.[18]

In a few instances, Schick's scientific information was relatively advanced. He was aware of the invention of the microscope and its use in biological research (begun by Malpighi in 1660), and he knew of the discovery of the lymphatic system (made by Rudbeck in 1653).[19] But these were minor details, compared to his ignorance of Harvey and Copernicus.

2. *Rabbinic Sources*. In keeping with the tradition of rabbinic science, Schick mined classical rabbinic literature as a repository of scientific wisdom. His astronomy relied heavily upon Maimonides' *Hilkhot kidush ha-hodesh*, and his anatomy invoked the Bible, Talmud, and Zohar as authorities.[20] The utilization of the Zohar in this capacity was innovative and requires some explanation.

A recurring theme in the Zohar and medieval kabbalistic literature is the notion that the Divine *sefirot* correspond—in one sense or another—to the limbs of the human body. It was commonplace for the Zohar to refer to different *sefirot* in anthropomorphic terms, as the supernal brain, eyes, liver, and so forth. The sefirotic realm itself was frequently referred to as *Adam 'elyon*, "supernal man." Most post-zoharic kabbalists, rejecting as they did the anthropomorphic conception of God, were eager to stress that the correspondence between the human limbs and the *sefirot* was purely symbolic. But however allegorized or minimized, the idea of correspondence between the "supernal image" and the human image was part and parcel of the kabbalistic tradition.[21]

This doctrine allowed Schick to employ the anthropomorphic sections of the Zohar as reliable statements of human anatomy; indeed as the most reliable statements of all, since he viewed the Zohar, in accordance with tradition, as the product of Divine revelation to R. Shimon bar Yohai in the second century. Consequently, Schick's discussion of the lungs quoted an excerpt from the *Raya mehemna* section of the Zohar which dealt, in symbolic language, with the sefirot of *hesed* and *din*; his discussion of the kidneys cited a passage from *Tikune zohar* elucidating the relation between *netzah* and *hod*; he derived information on the structure of the brain from the Zohar's discussion of *keter*, and so on.[22] In doing so, Schick did not empty these passages of their theosophic meaning. On the contrary, in keeping with the doctrine of correspondence, he accepted them as accurate anatomy and truthful theosophy at one and the same time.[23]

3. *Religious Rationales*. Schick's adherence to the Zohar, and more generally to Kabbalah, also came to the fore in his apologia

for the study of anatomy. Besides invoking the time-honored rationale that study of the human body heightened one's awareness of
and reverence for God, he adduced a kabbalistic argument as well,
based on the very same zoharic doctrine of the "supernal image."
Offering a new exegetical twist to Job 19:26, he claimed that anatomy was key to apprehending the mystery of God himself.

Within [man] are bound and hidden the clues to the mystery of God, as it is
written, "from my flesh I behold God."[24]

[God] created man in His likeness and image, so that [man] might attain
from his very self the mysteries and knowledge of the Creator, as it is
written, "from my flesh I behold God." We have therefore undertaken to
explain man's structure and composition, and the composition of his limbs,
so that the initiated [ha-maskil] may delve into their hidden meaning,
which is concealed and spiritual.[25]

Here Schick employed the doctrine of the supernal image in the
opposite direction as beforehand. If each sefirah was analogous to a
human limb, then study of the human body could provide the
initiated kabbalist with valuable insights concerning the sefirot. He
would be able to translate his knowledge of anatomy into Kabbalah, and read the Zohar's anthropomorphic sections with deeper
mystical understanding. "Each and every organ intimates a deep
mystery," Schick claimed. Hence the need for the comprehensive
study of anatomy.[26]

This line of argumentation was not totally new. Schick drew
much of it from R. Moshe Hayim Luzzatto (known by his acronym
Ramhal), the great Italian kabbalist, ethicist, and author. Luzzatto
had expounded upon the theme of the "mystery of the body" in the
introduction to his commentary on the Idra Rabba section of the
Zohar. Invoking Job 19:26, and citing the Zohar's statement that
man should "know himself, who he is, and how his body has been
arranged," Luzzatto concluded that "there are things which one
should understand concerning the sefirot by virtue of man."[27] It
was left to Schick to take his argument to its logical conclusion,
and claim that a systematic exposition of human anatomy was of
theosophic import.

Schick's introduction to Tiferet adam referred in passing to "the
manuscript commentary on the Idra by Rabbi Hayim Luzzatto."

This is noteworthy, since Luzzatto's treatise was unpublished at the time, and manuscripts of the latter's works were copied and disseminated in Eastern Europe by none other than Yekutiel Gordon, the former Padua medical student who resided in Shklov in the 1740s. Our discovery of Ramhalian influence on Schick leads us to Gordon as intermediary. This lends strength to our earlier suggestion that Gordon was the courier who brought Latin scientific manuscripts to Shklov.[28]

Schick's kabbalistic rationale for the study of anatomy is noteworthy for substantive reasons as well. It is a vivid illustration of the fact that Kabbalah and science were not necessarily polar opposites in traditional Jewish thought; preoccupation with the one did not preclude acceptance and study of the other. Rabbinic minds such as Schick's (and that of greater luminaries, such as the Vilna Gaon) constructed intellectual *modi vivendi* in which Kabbalah and science were harmonious, complementary, and even reinforced each other. The student of science was not by definition a rationalist.

While Schick's study of science was atypical for his milieu, his allegiance to Kabbalah indicates the extent to which he shared the traditional modes of thinking of his time. Kabbalah dominated Jewish religious thought in eighteenth-century Eastern Europe,[29] and Schick, a product of its rabbinic elite, was no exception. His originality notwithstanding, Schick's thinking was very much that of an eighteenth-century Polish-Lithuanian rabbi. The basic contours of his early works were set by the rabbinic tradition of science: his interest was confined to areas with strong rabbinic traditions of study, and he rationalized the study of these disciplines in terms of their advancing traditional religious values—whether the elucidation of *Hilkhot kidush ha-hodesh* or the enhancement of one's kabbalistic knowledge. There is no merit in viewing Schick in his pre-Berlin years as a forerunner of the Jewish Enlightenment, or Haskalah.

Encounter with Berlin

The last-known record of Schick's residence in Minsk hails from 1773, when he was sold a seat on the eastern wall of the *shivah keruim* society's synagogue, an indication of his continued high status within that exclusive group. He next surfaced in Berlin in late 1776. The intervening years are a mystery.[30]

Schick's journeying westward and his residence in Berlin were in themselves nothing out of the ordinary. During the second half of the eighteenth century, thousands of Polish-Lithuanian Jews migrated westward, to Prussia and other German states, as a result of the political and economic disarray in which Poland found itself. Although entry into Berlin was restricted and somewhat difficult, some Polish Jewish peddlers, *melamdim*, and wealthy merchants made their way through the city's gates. In addition, there were those scholars and intellectuals who came to Berlin and became part of the circle of enlightened Jews surrounding Moses Mendelssohn. These included Isaac Satanov and Solomon Dubno in the 1770s, and Solomon Maimon and Menahem Mendl Lefin in the 1780s.[31]

One is tempted to add Schick's name to this list of emigrés turned Maskilim, but there are several respects in which Schick differed from the latter. First, Schick was not an immigrant at all. He journeyed westward for the limited purpose of collecting advance subscribers for his scientific writings to finance their publication.[32] After obtaining subscribers in a number of Polish and German towns (Zlotowo, Lissa, Schwerin), Schick had the good fortune of encountering the Jewish community of Berlin, which was singularly supportive of his literary ventures. But he was nothing more than a visitor in their midst. His stay there lasted less than a year, and he returned to Byelorussia after successfully publishing his books.

Secondly, Schick did not come to Berlin as a young man in search of truth and wisdom, as did Maimon and Lefin. He was a bona fide member of the East European rabbinic elite—an ordained rabbi, a *dayyan*, and the scion of a prestigious rabbinic family. All these factors impinged upon the relations between Schick and the Berlin circle during his stay there. They also provide a context for understanding why Schick's Berlin experience had a moderate rather than a revolutionary impact upon him.

His first contact appears to have been with the rabbi of the Berlin Jewish community, R. Hirschl Levin, and the latter's son R. Shaul, then rabbi of the neighboring Frankfurt on the Oder. Both father and son greeted him warmly, and composed letters of approbation for his *Amude ha-shamayim-tiferet adam*. R. Hirschl encouraged Schick to continue publishing scientific treatises, and assisted him in initiating his second literary venture—the preparation of a printed edition of Isaac Israeli's *Yesod 'olam* (Foundation of the Earth), a classic of medieval Hebrew astronomy—by sharing two manuscripts of the work from his private library. It is also likely that R. Hirschl introduced Schick to the notables of the Berlin Jewish community, including the circle of enlightened Jews surrounding Moses Mendelssohn.[33]

By 1777, the time of Schick's arrival, the Mendelssohnian circle was firmly established. Marcus Hertz, David Friedlander, Isaac Satanov, Solomon Dubno, and Naftali Hirtz Wessely had all settled or resettled in Berlin. They, along with several others, constituted a well-defined and distinct social circle, which met frequently in Mendelssohn's home. Moreover, they had by then developed their distinctive outlook on the need to introduce reforms in Jewish culture and society. In 1777, Mendelssohn and Dubno were at work on their joint Bible translation and commentary, known as the *Bi'ur*, a project which undertook to spread knowledge of "pure German" among Jews, and instill in them an aesthetic appreciation of the Bible. David Friedlander was in the midst of organizing the Freischule, a school which would combine secular disciplines and European languages with a reformed Jewish religious curriculum. Schick encountered the circle during the heady early days of its efflorescence, and, one should add, before it clashed in public with the rabbinic authorities of the time.[34]

As far as one can judge, Schick's reception by the intellectual and social elite of the Berlin Jewish community was more than cordial—it was warm, outgoing, even effusive. A group of *parnasim* and prominent citizens became his patrons, and hired him to tutor their sons in mathematics. They and the Mendelssohnian circle rallied around Schick's project to publish *Yesod 'olam*, and provided him with material support. In just over a month, Schick had the necessary funds to publish a volume which was a work of typographic craftsmanship—with four different typefaces on the title page, diagrams within the body of the text, clear printing, and durable paper. This magnificent edition could only have been made possible thanks to considerable financial resources.[35]

The list of advance subscribers to the volume was virtually a who's who of the Berlin Jewish community. It included Moses Mendelssohn himself, Daniel Itzig (then head of the community), four of Itzig's sons, including Isaac Daniel Itzig (soon to be co-director of the Freischule), David Friedlander (who purchased five copies— for himself and his four brothers in Königsberg), R. Shaul Levin (whose name was placed at the head of the list of subscribers), and eight parnasim of the Berlin community. R. Hirschl Levin provided a warm letter of approbation, which was endorsed by the full rabbinic courts of Berlin and Frankfurt on the Oder. Finally, Naftali Hirtz Wessely, the poet laureate of the Mendelssohnian circle, contributed a special poem in praise of Schick and his enterprise.[36]

It is clear that the Mendelssohnian circle viewed the publication of Yesod 'olam as an important literary event. It was, in fact, the very first publishing venture they entered into as a group. Why so much fanfare and enthusiasm for the work of a virtual stranger, a passing visitor? What great attraction was there in a Hebrew book of Ptolemaic astronomy that its publication should be transformed into a sort of public cultural manifestation?

To a certain extent, the commotion surrounding Schick may have been due to condescending curiosity on the Berliners' part. The sight of an Ost-Jude from the farthest corner of Eastern Europe, who had mastered the mathematical sciences was something astonishing and exotic for them. (They would be similarly surprised by Solomon Maimon's incisive philosophic thinking when the latter arrived in Berlin a few years later.) Schick (and later Maimon) did not fit their image of Ost-Juden as "ignorant of languages, dignified behavior and matters of science," an image based largely upon the peddlers and melamdim whom they saw in their midst. A Polish Jew who wrote books of astronomy and mathematics was cause for amazement. Surely such a person deserved their charitable assistance.[37]

But the organized and public show of support for Schick's edition of Yesod 'olam was unquestionably more than an expression of paternalistic benevolence. It is safe to conclude that the Berliners took Schick under their wing because they saw great promise in him as an agent of positive change among the Jews of Poland-Lithuania. Schick intended to return to his homeland and distribute his books there, and the Berliners hoped that he would be able to generate interest in science among East European Jews, particularly among the rabbis. As a rabbi, *dayyan*, and scion of a great rabbinic family, he was in a unique position, they hoped, to introduce scientific studies into the rabbinic curriculum. This would be an important step forward, and could pave the way for a broader, more comprehensive reform of the Jews in Eastern Europe. If Talmudists began to study science, then the spirit of science and reason might eventually spread into other spheres of life as well.

This reconstruction of the Berliners' thinking is admittedly speculative. But it is the most plausible explanation for the outpouring of support which Schick's *Yesod 'olam* project elicited from the enlightened Jews of the city.

The hopes which the latter placed on Schick were expressed in Wessely's laudatory poem to him, which read, in part:

Arise Barukh, and plow through your land,
Cause fruits to blossom from your garden of reason,
The generous ones have watered your dry soil,
Now give your voice to the cause of wisdom.

The fortresses of the arrogant shall not stand forever,
In due time their iron bolts shall be broken,
Your shield of wisdom is eternal, your fruit—everlasting,
You and your supporters will not expire.

Woe unto the fools who chase after nothingness,
The man of reason is in their eyes a misleader,
Blessed is the man who hearkens to instruction,
Who is a friend of the wise and a companion of the knowing.[38]

To suggest that the Mendelssohnian circle embraced Schick as someone who could begin the process of reforming East European Jewish culture does not mean that Schick's own goals were identical to theirs. Schick's "agenda," if one may call it that, was restricted to science. Theirs was much broader, including reforms in the spheres of language, dress, manners and morality, economic activity, and, ultimately, social rapprochement with enlightened Gentiles and political emancipation. Schick's frame of reference was squarely within the rabbinic tradition. In the introduction to his edition of *Yesod 'olam*, his central argument was that the mathematical sciences were indispensable for understanding various commandments of the Torah. The Berliners' frame of reference was largely that of the European Enlightenment. But their differing goals and outlooks did converge on this one point—the study of science—and the Berliners were eager to support any project which would expand the Jews' intellectual horizons beyond their conventional parameters.

Schick and the Berliners could not help but be aware of the differences between them. The Berliners must have found him sorely lacking in a number of areas. His range of interests was too narrow, since he was evidently indifferent to matters of philosophy, aesthetics, Hebrew grammar, and the humanities. He lacked fluency in German, and probably could not read German literature. In their terms, Schick could hardly have been considered a man of culture. This evaluation is precisely the one which is found in a passage of Wessely's pamphlet *Divre shalom ve-'emet* (Words of Peace and Truth), written five years after Schick's visit. Wessely's description of Polish rabbinic scientists who visited Berlin matches Schick to a tee. It is quoted here in full.

We have seen among our Polish brethren who have come to this city great Torah scholars, who studied geometry and astronomy in their homeland by themselves, without the aid of a teacher. They knew the depths of these sciences, to such an extent that Gentile scholars marveled at their reaching such a level of knowledge without a teacher. They studied the few books which were written by scholars of our nation, such as *Yesod 'olam* by Isaac Israeli and *'Elim* by Joseph of Kandiah. If these people had mastered one of the foreign languages, they would have learned much more in less time, because of the many books written on these sciences by Gentile scholars, in an orderly fashion and a pure language understandable to beginners. The books which they studied, however, were not written for beginners, and are not written in an orderly fashion. They also did not know anything of the natural sciences, since nothing is written about them in Hebrew. Needless to say, they did not know geography and history, even though the latter are much easier than the deep sciences which they studied, because there are no Hebrew books to study about them. Even in those sciences which they mastered, they could not organize their words and communicate well to others, because of their stuttering language. From all of this we see what a great misfortune it is if the youths do not study one of the foreign languages grammatically, such that they can speak it clearly, and can read any book or letter written in it.[39]

Wessely's reference to *Yesod 'olam* leaves little doubt that he had Schick in mind when composing this portrait of Polish rabbinic scientists. The upshot of Wessely's remarks was to stress the indispensability of fluency in a modern European language (actually German) in order to become educated and cultured. He cited Schick as a negative example of someone whose scope of knowledge was extremely narrow, and who was unable to communicate his knowledge logically and effectively because of his lack of fluency in German. Schick was hardly a model of the new type of Jew the Berlin Maskilim envisioned.

But despite their ideological and cultural differences, Schick and the Berliners found it useful, for their own separate purposes, to ally themselves with each other. Schick was able to publish his books, and the Berliners were able to gain a modest foothold in Eastern Europe for their program of cultural reform. Their common interest in disseminating scientific knowledge among the Jews did, in fact, set both of them apart from the Ashkenazic Jewish culture of their time.

Schick left Berlin for Poland in the fall of 1777. But before moving on to assess the impact which his Berlin experience had upon him, it is worthwhile to pause and consider the converse as well. What impact, if any, did his visit have on the Mendelssohnian circle? Clearly, the visit must have been a memorable event that left a lasting impression if Wessely referred to it years later in *Divre shalom ve-'emet*. But did it have any concrete effect on the Berliners' thinking and activity?

With the aid of hindsight, one can say that Schick's visit aroused a lasting interest among members of the Mendelssohnian circle in the problem of reforming Polish Jewry. Their exposure to Schick, with his unique mixture of progressiveness and backwardness, heightened their awareness of the opportunities and difficulties involved in altering the complexion of the vast Jewry to the east. The topic remained in their consciousness after Schick's departure, and their interest in it resurfaced periodically, in the form of publication projects designed to advance Polish Jewry's reform. To a greater or lesser extent, these publications were modeled after *Yesod 'olam*.

In 1784, Mendelssohn, Friedlander, and a group of enlightened Jews hired Solomon Maimon to translate select works into Hebrew "in order to enlighten the Polish Jews still living in darkness," as Maimon recalled in his autobiography. The group considered various prospective books which would further this goal, ranging from Basnage's *History of the Jews* to Reimarus's *Natural Religion*, but finally agreed on composing a mathematics text in Hebrew, based on the Latin writings of Wolff. Maimon recorded with some bitterness that after spending several months composing his translation, the group withdrew its financial commitment to the volume, claiming that it was too expensive and unprofitable.[40]

Five years later, in 1789, the Berlin Freischule press managed to bring a similar project to fruition. It published Menahem Mendl Lefin's *Moda le-binah* (Announcer of Wisdom), a volume consisting of letters on the natural sciences and a discourse on health translated from a popular medical manual. Lefin, a native of Podolia, undertook the project during his stay in Berlin (1780–83), at the suggestion of Mendelssohn, who intended it for "our brethren the children of Israel in the land of Poland." Mendelssohn composed a fund-raising letter for the volume in 1785 (shortly before his death) in which he stressed the need for Hebrew discourses on medicine "in Poland, which is without a single reliable physician and is full of incompetents and fakes."[41]

It is noteworthy that both these projects sought to initiate the reform of Polish Jewry through the medium of books of mathematics and natural science (including medicine) rather than through works of philosophy, ethics, history, or a textbook of German. In their choice of subject matter, these projects followed in the footsteps of *Yesod 'olam*.

Aftermath: A Conservative Reformer

The years following Schick's stay in Berlin were his most active and productive ones. In the course of just a few years, he published a manual of preventative medicine, *Derekh yeshara* (The Straight Path; The Hague, 1779), a translation of the first six books of

Euclid's *Elements*, *Uklides* (The Hague, 1780), and a translation of a British work on algebra, geometry, and trigonometry, *Keneh hamidah* (The Tool of Measurement; Prague, 1783). Schick spent these years residing in Minsk, although he did venture westward to Prague in 1783.[42]

A perusal of these writings reveals that Schick was not converted into a Maskil—in any meaningful sense of the term—by the year which he spent in Berlin. He did not come to espouse Haskalah positions on the need to alter Jewish language, manners, moral behavior, economic activity, social relations, or even elementary schooling. Indeed he remained profoundly indifferent to these concerns, which formed the matrix of Haskalah ideology. Schick's sphere of interest continued to be limited to science, and primarily to mathematics. But this is not to say that he remained completely unchanged by his Berlin experience—his activity was transformed and intensified, and his mode of thinking underwent certain changes.

Before Berlin, Schick was an isolated practitioner of rabbinic science; afterward he was an active crusader for the dissemination of scientific wisdom. He was imbued with an urgent sense of mission that contributed toward his prolific output during these years. In addition to his published works, he completed and announced the imminent publication of three volumes—the concluding second volume of *Uklides*, a treatise on triangles, and a collection of medical remedies—whose appearance in print was prevented by a lack of funds.[43] Much as the Berliners had hoped, Schick engaged in a one-man literary campaign to spread scientific knowledge among his brethren in Poland and Russia.

This intensified literary activity was complemented by an aggressive pursuit of supporters and allies among the great rabbinic authorities of the day. One of Schick's first steps after returning to Poland was to meet with the Vilna Gaon—a meeting which took place in February 1778, roughly six months after the publication of *Yesod 'olam* in Berlin. It is likely that Schick hoped to obtain a *haskamah* from the Gaon for one of his books, or a written public pronouncement on behalf of the study of science. The latter would have been the most effective means by which to gain the attention of rabbinic scholars throughout Lithuania and beyond. If this was

Schick's goal, he was to be disappointed by the outcome of their meeting. R. Elijah did not issue a *haskamah* or public statement (in his lifetime, R. Elijah gave a total of three letters of approbation), although he did express some words of encouragement which Schick eagerly publicized in his introduction to *Uklides*.[44]

Four years later, in 1783, Schick journeyed to Prague with an apparently similar intention—to enlist the support of its chief rabbi, R. Ezekiel Landau, who was equal to the Vilna Gaon in his standing as a rabbinic authority. There Schick published *Keneh ha-midah*, along with Landau's remarkably brief *haskamah* (all of ten lines), which praised the book in rather guarded language.[45] Once again Schick had journeyed a considerable distance in order to engage the support of a rabbinic luminary, only to receive a favorable, but less than enthusiastic, response.[46]

What transformed Schick from a cloistered scholar of the sciences to an activist on behalf of their dissemination? The answer appears to lie in a new development in Schick's thinking which may be attributed to his stay in Berlin; namely, his deep distress and concern about the Jews' inferiority in the sphere of scientific learning.

The topic of Jewish inferiority, absent from Schick's early works, was first mentioned in his introduction to *Yesod 'olam* and assumed greater prominence in his post-Berlin writings. Schick claimed in the introductions to *Uklides* and *Keneh ha-midah* that the Jews' ignorance of science had led to their being mocked and derided by Gentiles. In *Uklides*, he lashed out at unnamed "enemies of wisdom" and claimed that the latter had brought great harm to the public image of the Jews.

They are the ones who have caused the children of Israel to sin against the sciences, and have stricken them with the plague of blindness. They have thereby made [the children of Israel] a mockery and disgrace in the eyes of the nations.[47]

A few lines later he returned to the topic a second time: "The name of heaven is disgraced among the Gentiles, who abuse us by saying that we are a foolish nation, not a wise one."[48]

Toward the end of the introduction, Schick asserted that Jewish honor could be restored by disseminating scientific wisdom among rabbinic scholars. He now professed that this was in fact his chief intention in publishing Hebrew books of science such as *Uklides*. His professed goal was

to remove the boastful arrogance of the tyrants, the multitude of nations who roar at us like the sound of great waves, "where is your wisdom?" thus leading to the desecration of God's name.[49]

Although these sentences are couched in stereotypic rabbinic phrases regarding the sanctification of God's name *(kidush ha-shem)* and a "wise and knowing people" (Deuteronomy 4:6), it would be wrong to dismiss them as only so much rabbinic rhetoric. The topic of Gentile mockery was raised three separate times in the course of the introduction to *Uklides*, clearly more than one would expect for the utilization of a standard rabbinic theme, and the same "standard theme" was totally absent from Schick's pre-Berlin works. The claim of Gentile mockery should be taken seriously, as a matter of deep concern to Schick.

Moreover, we know from Wessely's account in *Divre shalom ve-'emet* that Schick did indeed meet with German scholars, who "marveled at [his] having reached such a level of knowledge without a teacher." It is likely that this "marveling" at Schick's geometry and mathematics was coupled with a heavy dosage of condescension and amusement at his antediluvian knowledge of the natural sciences. If so, then Schick may well have experienced "the mockery of the Gentiles" firsthand! In any event, it was certainly a topic he heard much about from the Berlin Maskilim, who were exceedingly sensitive about the subject of the Jews' ignorance of science and other branches of culture.

Schick's phrases regarding "the mockery of the Gentiles" reflect the personal distress which he experienced in Berlin upon his discovery that he and his coreligionists were considered to be ignorant and backward in many spheres of knowledge. This must have come as a jolting realization for Schick. In eighteenth-century Eastern Europe, Jews lived predominantly among a peasant population and were, on the whole, more culturally advanced than their Gentile neighbors. When it came to literacy and mathematical ability, Jews in Shklov or Minsk were heads above most local townsmen and peasants. But in Berlin, Schick, a scholar who had devoted years of study to the sciences, was considered backward and ignorant. This was a case of acute culture shock.

For Schick, the intellectual inferiority of Jews, and specifically of rabbis such as himself, in the sciences was not so much a social problem (as it was for the Berlin Maskilim) as a religious one. It reflected negatively on Judaism, and led observers to the conclusion that Judaism itself was somehow inferior. He voiced this concern in the following terms

The Gentiles abuse us and say that we are a foolish nation, not a wise one. They consequently slander the words of our sages, and say that whoever studies them becomes divorced from the norms of civility and from nature [yibadel mi-hok ha-medini ve-teva 'olam].[50]

Here Schick was echoing in his own terms the vilification of the Talmud practiced by adherents of the European Enlightenment. Enlightenment thinkers perennially blamed the Talmud for the Jews' obscurantism, backwardness, and separatism. It was, they asserted, a compendium of superstitions, nonsense, and lies which had perverted the Jews' thinking and character. In order to enlighten the Jews and render them worthy of emancipation, they would first have to be drawn away from the pernicious influence of the Talmud.[51]

Schick cared little about the Jews' emancipation or enlightenment, but he could not remain indifferent to the defamation of the Talmud. In particular, he was disturbed by the charge that "whoever studies [it] becomes divorced from . . . nature"; that is, that in its content and spirit, the Talmud was inimical to science. This struck at the very essence of his personal being as a rabbi, and as a rabbinic scientist. Schick responded to the charge with an impassioned defense of the Talmud, claiming that it was a veritable treasure house of science.

Such was not the way of our sages. No mystery, discipline, or science eluded them. This is evident from many statements in the Talmud, made in just a few words. Such as the statement in tractate Berahot [58b], "if comets passed through the galaxy of Orion, the world would be destroyed"; and the magnifying glass of Rabbi Gamliel [Eruvin 43b]; and all the matters of animal wounds (trefot) in which they were highly expert, such as the wound which, "if salves are applied, [the animal] will survive" [Hulin 54a], as opposed to those wounds which it would not survive.[52]

On a more basic level, Schick's entire campaign to spread scientific learning among rabbinic scholars was motivated by a desire to respond to the Enlightenment's assault on the Talmud. For in the final analysis, the charge that the Talmud was a pernicious, obscurantist force could not be refuted by mere textual arguments, but by living examples of Talmudists who were also devotees of science. As long as the symbolic representatives of Talmudic Judaism, the rabbis, remained ignoramuses in these matters, Judaism's name would continue to be scarred. Schick's intensive program of publication and propaganda on behalf of science, following his visit to Berlin, was driven by an apologetic urge to disprove the slanderous charges against Judaism and the Talmud that he had encountered in the West. His transformation from a scholar into an engaged activist was thus a direct result of his exposure to the Enlightenment, his being profoundly troubled by its view of Judaism, and his desire to refute that view to the best of his ability.

Since the issue at stake was, according to Schick's understanding, a religious one ("what is the nature of Judaism?"), his efforts were directed at reforming the intellectual profile of the rabbinic elite, which was the living embodiment of the Talmudic tradition. The reform of Jewish elementary education, a major concern of Mendelssohn, Wessely, and Friedlander in the 1780s, was not on Schick's agenda. This is reflected in the content of Schick's books, which were designed not for Jewish schoolchildren, but rather for sharp Talmudic minds. They moved rapidly from basic principles to complex and difficult theorems, challenging their readers at every step of the way.

In the introduction to *Uklides*, Schick's apologetic concerns shared the limelight with the traditional argument that knowledge of the sciences facilitated and enhanced the elucidation of hallowed texts. (This was the gist of the remarks Schick quoted from the Vilna Gaon, that "for every deficiency of knowledge in the sciences, one will have ten deficiencies of knowledge in the science of the Torah.") But in his introduction to *Keneh ha-midah*, published three years later, there was no such balance between religious and apologetic arguments. Without making so much as an allusion to the religious or halakhic benefits to be gained from the study of science, he addressed himself solely to its apologetic importance, as a means by which the public image of Judaism would be rehabilitated.

> In these times, "science" serves to increase the honor of the Torah. It renders Torah scholars honorable and esteemed in the eyes of the nations and princes. I have therefore decided to come to the aid of Israel and to lift up the fallen crown of Judah.[53]

To sum up this point, Schick did not become a Maskil after Berlin, but he was, nonetheless, substantially affected by his exposure to the enlightened view that Judaism was obscurantist. His response was two-pronged. On the one hand he argued that the rabbis in the time of the Talmud were deeply involved in the study of science, and at the same time he devoted himself fully to disseminating scientific learning among contemporary rabbis and Talmudists. By responding to the enlightened critique of Judaism, and unconsciously internalizing a small portion of its worldview, Schick moved beyond the self-contained parameters of rabbinic science. He became a *rav maskil*, a rabbi who was himself, to a certain degree, influenced by the attitudes of the Enlightenment.

There were other noteworthy changes in Schick's writings following his visit to Berlin. One was related to their scope and content. Schick's major treatises in his post-Berlin years were devoted exclusively to mathematics, with the natural and biological sciences conspicuously absent. Gone were anatomy and astronomy; in their place came geometry, algebra, and trigonometry. Why this sudden narrowing of purview?

As we suggested earlier, Schick discovered in Berlin that his knowledge of the natural sciences was inferior and backward, compared to that of Gentile scholars. In the purely mathematical disciplines, the gap between him and German scholars was considerably narrower. Wessely had taken note of this discrepancy: on the one hand, Gentile scholars "marveled" at Schick's level of knowledge in geometry; on the other hand, he "did not know anything of the natural sciences."[54] In Berlin, Schick reached much the same conclusion; and in his subsequent works he "retreated" to the disciplines where his knowledge was on firmer ground.

A second change in Schick's writings related to the sources he utilized. After Berlin, he discontinued his previous practice of drawing scientific data from the Talmud, Zohar, and Maimonides. Instead he undertook a project of translating foreign scientific works into Hebrew. Rather than combining the scientific wisdom available in classical rabbinic sources and non-Jewish ones, he now dropped the one and relied exclusively on the other. This shift is attributable to Schick's discovery that the scientific information contained in his rabbinic sources was somewhat problematic, a discovery which was an integral part of the culture shock he experienced in Berlin.

Schick's failure to utilize the Zohar is particularly noteworthy. The latter was as replete with mystical mathematics (i.e., numerology) as it was with mystical anatomy, but Schick refrained from mining the Zohar for math as he had once done for anatomy.[55]

In general, Schick's connection with Kabbalah weakened after his stay in Berlin. He did not preface *Uklides* or *Keneh ha-midah* with a kabbalistic mystique of numbers—a theme with a long tradition—akin to his mystique of the human body in *Tiferet adam*. Kabbalistic arguments for science were now part of his past. Schick alluded but once in his introduction to *Uklides* to a passage from the Zohar, and in the context of his argumentation it carried little weight.[56] The decline in the position of Kabbalah in Schick's thought was likely the result of assaults on it by enlightened Jews in Berlin, who viewed Kabbalah as superstitious and nonsensical.

In sum, Schick's exposure to Berlin brought on key changes in his works of science as such. Their scope and content were narrowed to mathematics alone. Non-Jewish treatises displaced rabbinic literature as a source of information, and the rationales presented for the study of scientific disciplines underwent a marked transformation. The kabbalistic mode of rationalization disappeared; the halakhic-talmudic rationale receded in importance, and a new apologetic rationale assumed a preeminent position. These changes in purview, sources, and rationale constituted a move away from the tradition of rabbinic science, in the direction of modern European science.

The case of R. Barukh Schick is a rare instance in which the indigenous rabbinic tradition of science and the Berlin Haskalah encountered each other face-to-face. These two intellectual currents should not be confused with each other, but neither should it be overlooked that they did share, in the context of eighteenth-century Ashkenazic Jewish culture, certain points of convergence. As a result of their shared interest in science, Schick and the Berlin circle were able to collaborate on a project of mutual interest.

Schick's story indicates how the two trends could mutually influence each other. Although he remained deaf to most of the Haskalah's message, particularly to its social and political goals, Schick was deeply affected by the enlightened critique of rabbinic Judaism as obscurantist and antithetical to science. In the specific area of science, Schick was transformed into a crusader and reformer. This is an instance of Haskalah ideology being internalized in a fractured, fragmentary form.

Schick's campaign to introduce scientific learning among rabbis and Talmudists was motivated, to a considerable extent, by apologetic concerns, that is, a desire to defend rabbinic Judaism against its enlightened detractors. His apologetic stance was predicated upon a partial, if unconscious, acceptance of their value system. In this respect, Schick may be seen as a paradigm for a certain type of traditionalist rabbi combining science and Torah primarily as a demonstrative apologetic act, in order to prove that Judaism is "wise and understanding." In the minds of such rabbis, the issue of science was divorced from both theology and broader social and political concerns.

CHAPTER 3

New Social and Cultural Horizons

During the first years after Russia's annexation of eastern Byelorussia, several of the territory's largest estates were confiscated from their Polish and Lithuanian landlords, who refused to take an oath of allegiance to the Empire, and granted by Empress Catherine the Great to Russian officials and dignitaries. Among the recipients of Catherine's largesse were her close personal companion and political adviser Count Grigorii Potemkin (1739–91), who received the Krichev district in January 1776, and Major-General Count Semion Gavrilovich Zorich (1745–99), who received Shklov and its estates in September 1777. Zorich, a celebrated hero of the first Russian-Turkish war, was Catherine's romantic "favorite" at the time of this acquisition.[1] As these two Russian aristocrats became involved in administering and developing their Byelorussian estates, their relationship with the local Jews grew more immediate and complex. Zorich and Potemkin brought the Jews of Shklov and its surroundings into direct contact with Russian life and institutions, and, as a result, their social and cultural horizons were broadened and transformed.

Zorich's Court and the Transformation of Shklov

Semion Zorich's tenure as the Empress's romantic companion was predictably short-lived. Catherine terminated their liaison in 1778, and, in a parting expression of gratitude, presented him with treasure chests of jewels and 200,000 rubles in cash. She also asked him to leave St. Petersburg. Faced with few alternatives, the jilted general settled on his Shklov estate.

The move from the royal court to Shklov was a depressing step downward for Zorich. Instead of the pageantry, high society, and refined culture of the capital city, he found himself in "a typical Polish town stinking of zhids," in the blunt description of one Russian aristocrat.[2] In an effort to make the best of the situation, he decided to use his recently acquired wealth to create a little St. Petersburg of his own in Shklov. In a few short months, he succeeded.

Zorich took up residence in the old castle on the outskirts of town, along with several close associates from his years in the military and at court. On November 24, 1778, he hosted his first banquet and masquerade ball—a grand celebration in honor of the anniversary of Catherine's coronation. Elaborate evenings of this kind soon became the trademark of Zorich's court at Shklov, which attracted Polish magnates, Russian aristocrats and officials, as well as foreign visitors en route to Moscow and St. Petersburg. All were welcome to stay as Zorich's guests, for an evening, a week, or even longer.[3]

Christian Julian Schlegel, a German traveler who visited Zorich's court in 1780, expressed great enthusiasm for its refined ambiance and distinguished society:

One barely believes one's own senses. After traversing a hundred miles of morass, forest, and backwardness [Unkultur] in every conceivable respect, . . . one begins to doubt whether one will ever encounter people of refined heart and spirit again. One then arrives at a place which contains a multitude of people from distant corners of Europe, who have brought here the culture of the lands where they once dwelled; the culture which renders them the choice inhabitants of the earth. Here they edify themselves and cultivate their souls in their leisure time.[4]

Zorich's castle featured a beautiful stone facade, an ornamented dance hall, a drawing room with wide sofas, a social hall with tall glass doors, and an exquisite flower garden. The daily program of recreation and entertainment began at 5 P.M., when cannon shots announced that dinner was to be served. The guests assembled for a meal prepared by French and Russian chefs, which concluded with a glass of Hungarian wine. After dinner, coffee was served in the social hall, game tables were set up, and the guests either played or strolled in the flower garden. Many of them left for their quarters to take a brief nap, and returned to the castle between 8 and 9 P.M. for a full evening of dance and games. A late meal was offered at midnight, followed by more dancing and games. The guests retired for the night some time between 2 and 3 A.M.[5]

Contemporaries were struck by the heterogeneous makeup of the guests and residents at Zorich's court. "One found here people of every class, rank, and nationality . . . Frenchmen, Italians, Germans, Serbs, Greeks, Moldavians, and even Turks." A visitor from St. Petersburg expressed his pleasure at having made the acquaintance of some Polish ladies, whose morals and manners he found quite interesting and exotic.[6] The castle served as a retreat for the Russian and foreign European elite, to escape from the surrounding "barbarians" and enjoy each other's company in pleasant surroundings. Their common language of discourse was French.[7]

For the entertainment of his entourage and guests, Zorich constructed a theater house, and established two standing theater troupes, for drama and ballet, respectively, with an orchestra and choir. The theater's dramatic repertoire consisted of French operas, Russian tragedies, improvised comedies, and pantomime. The ballet company was, according to many observers, on a professional level comparable to that of the Imperial Ballet in St. Petersburg. Indeed, following Zorich's death and the liquidation of his estate, fourteen of its dancers were accepted into the ranks of the Imperial Ballet.[8]

The theater contributed a great deal to the cosmopolitan ambiance in Shklov. Its artistic directors were all imported from abroad: the choir director was "of the Polish nation"; the conductor of the orchestra was German—Joseph Ludwig Stefan, a graduate of the Königsberg Academy, who had, inter alia, studied philosophy with Immanuel Kant; and the ballet was directed by Paulo Barcanti of Florence, Italy. Foreign musicians, vocalists, and theater companies commonly visited Shklov and performed there while en route to St. Petersburg, where they were engaged by the Imperial opera house. On the other hand, the regular performers in Shklov's theater and ballet were not from such lofty social backgrounds; most of them were local peasants, Zorich's serfs, who were especially selected and trained by the foreign artistic directors.[9]

One of the most spectacular events in the history of Zorich's court was the visit by Empress Catherine and her entourage in May

1780. The Empress stopped off while en route to Mogilev, where she met Emperor Joseph II of Austria, and returned to Shklov a few days later together with her royal guest. Zorich constructed triumphal gates at the town's entrance in honor of her visit, and the Empress made a majestic appearance in Shklov's central square to greet its inhabitants. On her return visit with Joseph II, the two monarchs were treated to an evening of pantomime at the theater, a masquerade ball and banquet, followed by fireworks.[10]

Although Zorich himself was "a limited person, without any education," as Catherine once noted in her diary, his social aspirations and cultural pretensions prompted him to establish educational institutions at his court.[11] He founded a dance school for girls, which drew its students from among the local Byelorussian peasantry and trained them for the ballet. The girls studied dance with an Italian headmaster, Mariodini, and were given classes in French, Russian reading and writing, and mathematics with a French governess. The dance school served as a vehicle for social mobility for its most talented students. According to Schlegel, "those girls who surpass the others in their studies are drawn into the general's high society. When a former peasant girl excels in ballet, she is invited to the ball and dances in the same row with the most distinguished women."[12]

More important was the Shklov Nobility Academy (blagorodnoe uchilishche) created and financed by Zorich, a school for the male children of Russian and Polish aristocrats. Officially a military academy (it was also referred to as the Shklov kadetskii korpus), most of the school's curriculum was devoted to the arts and sciences. Its program of instruction included languages (French, Italian, German), mathematics (algebra and geometry), Russian grammar and composition, the humanities (history, geography, catechisms of the Catholic and Orthodox faiths) and the fine arts (dance, music, painting, fencing, horseback riding). Affiliated with the Academy were a library (over a thousand volumes, most in French), a scientific laboratory, and an art gallery. In 1780, two hundred students were enrolled in the school; the figure later rose to three hundred. Most of its graduates assumed positions in the Russian civil service and military.[13]

The Shklov Nobility Academy was the first non-ecclesiastical school in Byelorussia, and combined features of the military academies of St. Petersburg and the philanthropic schools of Central and Western Europe. The Western composition of its faculty and administration was quite striking. The school's first headmaster was a Frenchman, Timolean Alfonse Galien de Salle-Morant, a self-proclaimed protégé of Voltaire with broad interests in the arts and sciences. (In his spare time, he conducted scientific experiments in the Academy's laboratory and composed comedies for the local theater.) In 1793, half of the Academy's fourteen teachers were foreigners.[14]

The Western colony in Shklov also included foreign masters, who were engaged by Zorich to manage his industrial enterprises. His shipbuilding factory, which produced canoes, boats, and frigates, was headed by a Greek, Dersakli; his tannery was run by a Swedish master, Erich Holtz; and Zorich's rope and cable factory was administered by the Englishmen David and George Frasier.[15]

The rapid growth of Zorich's court and its institutions transformed life in Shklov. It injected European high society, culture, education, and technology into a predominantly Jewish commercial town. The coexistence of a large aristocratic court alongside and, indeed, in the midst of a sizable Jewish community was itself an unusual phenomenon. In the eighteenth century, these two worlds met only on their peripheries. Jewish residence was prohibited or severely restricted in the great capital cities of Europe— Paris, Berlin, Vienna, Warsaw, and St. Petersburg—and only exceptional Court Jews had intimate, everyday contact with the lifestyle and culture of the aristocratic elite.

But in Shklov, these two worlds met face-to-face. According to a study commissioned by the general governor of the Mogilev province in the 1790s, 80 percent of the town's total adult population of 2,381—or 1,884—consisted of Jews. Given the town's small dimensions, Jews and aristocrats could hardly avoid each other. The Nobility Academy, with its library and laboratory, was located in the same town square as the synagogue and yeshiva. The theater and dance school were likewise in the center of town. Jews could not fail to observe, almost daily, the students of the Academy in their military uniforms, and the various dignitaries on their way to and from the theater.[16] Foreigners and aristocrats were likewise forced to come into contact with Shklov's Jews; as Schlegel noted—or rather complained—the only place a visitor could lodge was in the home of a Jew.[17] There were numerous opportunities for social observation and interaction between the two groups.

Zorich's court and Shklov's Jewish commercial economy became closely intertwined. Zorich required a perpetual flow of imported luxury items to support his lavish lifestyle, and used Jewish merchants as his agents, bankers, and purveyors. According to local traditions, he actively assisted Jewish merchants in bringing contraband goods into Russia without the payment of duty. This, coupled with the town's location in relation to Russia's newly drawn borders, made Shklov into the commercial hub of Russian Jewry. According to one contemporary estimate, the Shklov kahal collected twice as much in commercial taxes as the second richest kahal in the vicinity—the neighboring provincial capital of Mogilev (4,000 rubles versus 2,000 rubles).[18]

As we shall see, Shklov's preeminent Jewish merchants were closely associated with Zorich's court, and became, through it, drawn into the social orbit and business world of Russian officialdom. Jews from other social strata may also have gained entry to the court's social and cultural life—one of the dancers in the Shklov ballet company was a Jewess named Elena Yankelevich.[19] In the final analysis, all segments of Jewish society—whether they were directly involved with the court or not—confronted its culture and institutions, and were forced to adopt a stance toward them.

There are signs that part of the Jewish middle class was attracted by what it saw, and consciously imitated the court's manners and lifestyle. The phenomenon was described by R. Judah Leyb Margoliot, a preacher and scholar who resided in Shklov in the 1780s:

The rebellious ones have grown numerous, those who wish to establish new societies similar to evening study groups *(mishmarim)*. They are forcefully confronted: "Is not the practice of our ancestors adequate? Why do we need these innovations?" How are they not ashamed and their faces not reddened by their drinking of tea and coffee, and the women's jewelry which they hang from their necks! A plague is spreading in the house of Jacob— luxurious vessels, five sets of garments, and the sound of music as in the

tavern. They separate the young boys from God's Torah to teach them
French and mathematics. They add to the practices of their forefathers,
and deviate from them with ever greater strength. The Torah dons a sack-
cloth, for it has been diminished.[20]

The patterns of behavior observed by Margoliot were clearly
modeled after those at Zorich's court. Groups of "rebels" conducted
social gatherings in the evenings for their entertainment and edification. (Margoliot could only conceive of these salon-like gatherings as something similar to evening study groups.) The participants
wore elaborate garments and jewelry, drank tea and coffee, and
listened to music. In addition, they gave their children a European-
style education, with tutoring in French and mathematics.

The New Social and Political Elite: Notkin and Zeitlin

The greatest degree of acculturation and social mobility was attained by the town's Jewish commercial elite. For this social upper
crust, Zorich's court was the gateway to business relationships,
social ties, and political influence with the Russian ruling class. As
they worked and mingled with high-ranking Russian officials, they
adopted the Russian language and made the cosmopolitan court
culture of St. Petersburg their own. The most outstanding representative of this social type was Natan Nota b. Hayim, known in
Russian as Nota Khaimovich Notkin.

Born in Mogilev, Notkin was active in commerce and mon-
eylending before the partition of Poland, providing loans and other
financial services to Polish magnates. He was recognized for these
activities by King Stanislaw Augustus Poniatowski, who bestowed
upon him the title "Royal Court Adviser," thereby making it possible for him, a Jew, to own real property. Shortly after the Mogilev
region came under Russian control, he moved to Shklov and proceeded to become one of Zorich's main contractors.[21]

In the early 1780s, Notkin's main business ties were with Central
Europe. In 1780, he was sent by Zorich to Dresden to purchase
porcelain in anticipation of Empress Catherine's visit to Shklov. An
anecdote regarding that journey, told by a Russian contemporary,
speaks volumes about Notkin's perceived prestige and influence.
Notkin was charged duty twice for transporting the porcelain

through Prussia, both upon entering and leaving the kingdom's borders. He complained about this double taxation to King Frederick II, and the latter responded in a personal note to the "Honorable Shklov merchant Notka" that "if you did not wish to pay duty twice, you could have purchased the porcelain from my factory in Berlin."[22]

Notkin was a frequent visitor at the Leipzig fairs, and his absence from the 1785 fair was noteworthy enough to be recorded by officials, along with its reason: He was engaged at the time as a field supplier for the Russian military.[23] Given his frequent journeys to Germany, and his extraordinary wealth and business contacts, it was natural for Notkin to find his peer group among the wealthy Jewish merchants and Maskilim of Berlin. He was a subscriber to their journal, Ha-me'asef, in 1784–85, and purchased four advance copies of one of their publications—an edition of the Psalms with Mendelssohn's German translation and Bi'ur. Notkin himself became a proponent of moderate acculturation, and reportedly educated his children in a European manner, arranging for them to be taught Russian, Polish, and French.[24]

Notkin's association with the Berlin circle probably went back to his 1780 journey through Prussia. In that year, the Jews of Shklov and Mogilev commissioned Naftali Hirtz Wessely to compose Hebrew poems in honor of the Empress's visit to their region. The Hebrew verses and their German translation by Mendelssohn were published in Berlin in two separate pamphlets—one on behalf of the Shklov Jewish community, and the other on behalf of the Jews of the Mogilev province at large. The arrangements for their composition and publication were probably made by Notkin.[25]

The focus of Nota Khaimovich's commercial affairs shifted gradually from Central Europe to Russia proper. His relationship with Zorich became strained in 1783, when the general became embroiled in a scandal regarding the issuance of false promissory notes, and sought to lay blame for the forgeries on Notkin and other local Jews. But Nota Khaimovich found a new patron in Count Grigorii Potemkin, who also owned sizable estates in the Mogilev province, not far from Shklov. Potemkin, Russia's viceroy of the South, engaged him as a contractor to transport goods down the Dniepr river to the territories of New Russia. Notkin played a crucial role as a purveyor to the military in the 1787 war with Turkey, delivering fodder and provisions to the army and navy. He undertook dangerous supply missions which other contractors were afraid to attempt, and loaned the government treasury 200,000 rubles—a debt which he seems never to have fully recouped.[26]

Having established his Russian patriotic bona fides, Notkin took the bold step of settling after the war in Moscow, a city which had not seen Jews within its limits in more than a century. He resided in the ancient capital city in 1788–89, issued promissory notes to state business concerns (including the *imperatorskii vospitatelnii dom* and the *imperatorskii fabrikantskii kontor*), and established a partnership with the Moscow merchants Shoshinin and Ikonov.[27] His financial success produced intense resentment among Muscovite merchants, who complained that he and other Byelorussian Jews residing in Moscow were engaging in dishonest dealings. The Muscovites lodged a formal complaint to the municipal authorities, charging that the Jews "caused tangible harm and obstruction" to local commerce by importing contraband goods, clipping coins, and other deceptive practices. They singled out Notkin as the most egregious culprit.

One of their people, the Byelorussian *zhid* Nota Khaimovich, better known by the name Notki[n], used various tricks and forgeries to obtain credits, and deceived many local merchants into giving him goods on credit, whose value was 500,000 rubles. He took the goods to a certain place known only to him, and then took them secretly out of Moscow and smuggled them out of the country, leaving behind destruction in the homes of many kind merchants. Many of them were left impoverished, with their wives and children, without any sustenance, bereft of their property and credits.[28]

The complainants demanded that the Jews be expelled from the city of Moscow. Their complaint made its way to the Council of State, where it was endorsed by Count A. R. Vorontsov, and led eventually to the issuance of an Imperial *ukaz* on December 23, 1791, denying Jews the right to reside and register as merchants in cities outside of Byelorussia. The decree was the first to place severe restrictions on Jewish residence in Russia, and was the cornerstone for the later creation of the Pale of Jewish Settlement.[29]

Despite his rude reception in Moscow, Notkin did not retreat to Shklov or the territories of the Pale of Settlement. In 1797, he used his personal influence and connections to take up residence in St. Petersburg, despite the legal prohibition then in force on Jews residing outside of Russia's western provinces. Notkin lived in the capital city under the personal protection of General Procurator Aleksei Borisovich Kurakin, who was asked by Zorich to extend his assistance, in light of Notkin's "distinguished service to the fatherland."[30] A number of other Jews, most of them merchants from Shklov and Mogilev, also resided in St. Petersburg on a semi-secretive basis, under the protection of Russian officials. As Empress Catherine had noted in a letter, "they are tolerated, in violation of the law; we pretend as if they aren't noticed." Notkin was, however, the first well-known Jewish personality to reside openly in the capital, thereby creating tacit public acknowledgment of a Jewish presence in St. Petersburg.[31]

Notkin spent the final years of his life shuttling between St. Petersburg and Shklov. In Byelorussia, he and his sons managed an estate with 225 serfs in the village of Ostrov, on behalf of a certain Russian Admiral Deribas. He also developed an extended, if uneasy, relationship with Count Gavriil Derzhavin, the poet and Minister of Justice, who was dispatched to Shklov in 1799 to settle a complex legal dispute between Zorich and the Jewish community. Notkin submitted to Derzhavin a proposal on the reform of the Jews' economic condition, and was subsequently invited by the latter to serve as a consultant to the State Committee for the Organization of Jewish Life (1802–4). But the sharp differences between their outlooks led to the deterioration of their relationship, and Notkin drew closer to another Committee member, Count Viktor Pavlovich Kochubei, whose views were more compatible with his own.[32]

Notkin's life story is characterized by a remarkably extensive level of involvement with the highest echelon of Russian officialdom. He moved from one aristocratic patron to another—from Zorich to Potemkin, to Kurakin, to Derzhavin, to Kochubei—and spent most of his mature years in parts of the Russian Empire where there were no organized Jewish communities. While doing so, Notkin developed the necessary linguistic skills, social graces, and worldly knowledge to work and live in a Russian milieu, and left many Imperial officials favorably impressed. Zorich wrote of him, in a private note to Kurakin, that "although a Jew, he is a very rewarding person," and Derzhavin confessed in his memoirs that he had never encountered a Jew who was as wise, practical, and educated as Notkin.[33]

Notkin's illustrious career propelled him into the role of serving as the foremost political leader of Russian Jewry. Numerous legends were told about his activities as *shtadlan*, in which he utilized his personal contacts in St. Petersburg to rescue Jews in distress. According to popular memory, "the name of Nota the *shtadlan* was mentioned with awesome respect, not only in the Mogilev guberniia, but in all Jewish towns in Russia. He acted as a sort of exilarch *(nasi)*; in all difficult political situations, he was dispatched to St. Petersburg." Among his documented accomplishments were securing the release of R. Shneur Zalman b. Barukh from his second arrest in 1801, and averting the expulsion of Jews from the Smolensk province in 1803.[34]

In keeping with his high social standing as "exilarch," Notkin married off his son Shabbetai to the daughter of Byelorussia's foremost rabbinic authority, R. Arye Leyb Ginzburg, the *Sha'agat arye*.[35]

Notkin, his brother, and son, were among the ten founding wardens of the St. Petersburg Jewish Burial Society, created in 1802. The establishment of the society, and its acquisition of a burial plot, was an act of communal affirmation which required great diplomatic skill, given the fact that Jews were officially banned from living in the city. It is unlikely that the purchase of the plot could have been transacted without Notkin's personal involvement. Notkin himself died in St. Petersburg, and was laid to rest in the society's burial plot, in 1804.[36]

An interesting analogue to Notkin's biography is provided by the life of his friend and associate, Joshua Zeitlin (1742–1821). A native of Shklov, and a descendant of its most famous family, Zeitlin was more deeply rooted in rabbinic learning and piety than Notkin, having studied in his youth in the yeshiva of the *Sha'agat arye* in Minsk. In most respects, his rise to prominence closely paralleled Notkin's: his entrée into Russian high society came via Zorich's court (his brother being Zorich's import/export agent in Riga); his international affairs brought him into association with the Berlin

Jewish community; and he acted as a contractor for Potemkin in the Russian-Turkish war, thereby gaining fame and recognition in the Empire's ruling circles. But Zeitlin's rabbinic training left an indelible imprint on his personality, and he represented a unique blend of rabbinic and Russian culture.[37]

As a man seeking to bridge the traditional religious world of his youth with the Western and Russian worlds he encountered in his maturity, Zeitlin was attracted to the circle of the Berlin Haskalah. He is reported to have frequented Mendelssohn's home during visits to Berlin, and to have been engaged by the ideas to which he was exposed there. Some time in late 1780s, he married off his younger daughter to the nephew of the Berlin chief rabbi—a young Galician scholar named Abraham Perets (1771–1833), who lived at the time in the Prussian capital. Following the marriage, Perets moved to Shklov, where he and his father-in-law continued to maintain ties with Berlin. Zeitlin and Perets purchased eight advance copies of Mendelssohn's German translation of the Psalms (published in 1791), and Perets personally underwrote publication of one of the Berlin Haskalah's more controversial works—the collection of forged responsa *Besamim rosh* (The Incense of Rabbi Asher), issued by his first cousin Shaul Berlin (in 1793).[38]

Zeitlin was the first Jewish notable in Russia to combine acculturation and involvement in Russian affairs, with deep rabbinic learning and piety. His rabbinic scholarship was not eclipsed or concealed during the years of his association with Potemkin, as a contractor involved in the effort to develop cities and roads in New Russia. Zeitlin's great-grandson, the Hebrew writer Shai Hurvitz, offered the following portrait based on family traditions:

He walked with Potemkin like a brother and friend. . . . He also received from the Empress an adorned uniform, as a mark of honor, with gold stripes and shining buttons, and a sword attached to its belt. He would wear this uniform when he traveled with his comrade, Count Potemkin, to review the roads he had paved and the glorious buildings he had erected. He would ride on a majestic horse alongside Potemkin, and during the time that the latter accepted various petitions from officials and the masses, the sage R. Joshua Zeitlin would accept written halakhic queries from rabbis and scholars on matters of ritual law and *'agunot*. He would get down from his horse and compose halakhic responsa in a kneeling position, and then continue on his journey.[39]

As a crowning reward for his loyal service to Russia, Zeitlin was issued the title "court adviser" *(nadvornii sovetnik)* and was thereby formally entered into the ranks of the Russian aristocracy. In Hebrew, he was referred to as *Ha-sar Zeitlin*, Lord Zeitlin. The Empress also awarded him an estate in the Mogilev province, called Ustye, with over nine hundred serfs and a magnificent palace.[40]

Following Potemkin's death in 1791, Zeitlin entrusted his commercial affairs to his son-in-law, Perets, and retired to his Ustye estate. There he adopted the lifestyle of a Russian aristocrat, establishing a court which was similar to Zorich's in its grandeur and luxuriousness, "with a beautiful landscape, gardens and vineyards. . . . He sat in his palace in the manner of the great noblemen, with a great multitude of rooms full of wealth and precious items." But in marked contrast to the courts in Shklov and St. Petersburg, there was no social frivolity, mingling of the sexes, or theatrical/musical entertainment at Ustye. Ustye was a Jewish court, and its ambiance was cerebral and pious. Instead of the theater and games, it featured "libraries for books—old and new, ancient and precious— and for manuscripts in halakha and Kabbalah; a large *bet midrash* (house of study and prayer), glorious in its holiness, with ancient Torah scrolls from Turkey, written on deer-parchment, and valuable holy vessels made of silver, gold and precious stones."[41]

Taking a leaf out of Russian court culture, Zeitlin became a patron of Hebrew letters in Russia, inviting select scholars and authors to live and write, at his expense, in Ustye. In the 1790s, he sponsored two scholars: R. Barukh Schick, who returned to the Mogilev province of his youth, and R. Menahem Mendl Lefin (1741– 1819), a well-known advocate of Jewish social and cultural reform, and a popularizer of science and medicine. Both Schick and Lefin had spent time in Berlin, in the society of Mendelssohn and the Haskalah circle. Amidst Ustye's serene surroundings, Schick continued his mathematical studies, and Lefin composed his moral guidebook, *Heshbon ha-nefesh* (Self-Examination; Lvov, 1808), based, in part, on the writings of Benjamin Franklin.[42] Lefin also served as a tutor for Zeitlin's grandson, Hirsh Perets (b. 1790).[43] In choosing these two men as the recipients of his largesse, Zeitlin expressed his identification with the Mendelssohnian Haskalah and the ideal of moderate acculturation.

But Zeitlin's commitment to acculturation was combined with an abiding support for traditional rabbinic scholarship. He helped finance the establishment of the Volozhin yeshiva in 1803, and issued a circular letter calling upon fellow philanthropists to come to the aid of its founder, R. Hayim of Volozhin. In later years, he sponsored R. Menahem Nahum of Chaus and R. Eliezer of Slonim as scholars-in-residence at Ustye, who composed Talmudic commentaries and novellae during their residence there. The latter were followed by Shklov's foremost Talmudist, R. Benjamin Rivlin. Zeitlin's own sole literary enterprise was a commentary on the *Sefer mitsvot katan* (Small Book of Commandments), a medieval French halakhic code.[44]

An admirer of both Moses Mendelssohn and the Vilna Gaon, Zeitlin offered financial support to disciples of both men, in the apparent belief that their teachings were fundamentally compatible.

While representing this original combination of involvements—in Russian affairs, Haskalah, and traditional rabbinic culture—Zeitlin was recognized as one of the foremost social and religious leaders of Russian Jewry. Although he held no official communal title or office, important questions and problems were routinely brought before him: "Every embittered and troubled person, every rabbi with a question of ritual or civil law, the judges and their litigants—all came to his gates." Meetings on pressing communal affairs were reportedly held at Ustye, and Zeitlin's advice was solicited on overturning various anti-Jewish decrees.[45]

Zeitlin seems to have represented an embryonic new "ideal type" for East European Jewry—a leader who combined the values of Torah, wealth, and piety with worldliness, loyal service to the state, and moderate acculturation.

Other Personal and Literary Contacts with the West

Although separated from Berlin and Paris by hundreds of miles, Shklov's Jewish merchants were linked to the West through extensive commercial ties, and traveled widely across Europe. Notkin and Zeitlin were the most celebrated examples, but they were by no means exceptional in this respect. A local scribe noted in a letter to the Jews of Bukhara that "most of its [Shklov's] inhabitants are merchants from the children of Israel who journey to the end of the earth to bring from there all sorts of merchandise." Anecdotal evidence supports this image of broad transcontinental mobility. Count G. Zanovich, a Russian aristocrat closely associated with Zorich, mentioned in a letter that he had recently met a "Byelorussian zhid," Isaac Khaimakovich, known to him from St. Petersburg (!), during a visit to Berlin. Khaimakovich asked him to take back to Russia some deeds which he had procured in Königsberg, since he was about to travel across France and Germany in connection with his business affairs, and would not return home for some time.[46]

Aspiring intellectuals and rabbinic authors also ventured westward. One of the more interesting travelers was Elias Ackord of Mogilev (b. 1757), who migrated to Prussia in 1778 to study medicine in Königsberg and Berlin. Upon being certified as a physician by the Berlin College of Medicine in 1783, he settled in Warsaw, established a medical practice there, and participated in the public debate regarding the legal status of the Jews in the waning Polish Commonwealth. Ackord published a German translation of an anonymous Polish pamphlet entitled The Jews, Or On the Necessary Reform of the Jews in the Republic of Poland, to which he added his own comments in support of the author's liberal position on the Jewish question. He endorsed the author's calls that Jewish legal disabilities and discriminatory taxes be eliminated, and that the Jews relinquish their social, juridical, and linguistic separatism. Exhibiting a keen affinity with the German Aufklärung, Ackord referred enthusiastically to the model set by Moses Mendelssohn, and to the noble ideals of "our eternally immortal Lessing." He proposed the establishment of Jewish elementary schools with Polish as the language of instruction, noting "I have seen a living example of this in Berlin." Such schools would do much more, Ackord contended, to draw Jewish youth away from the Talmud than state censorship of Jewish books, a measure proposed by the pamphlet's author.[47]

Ackord subsequently returned to Russia, and was certified to practice medicine there in 1788. He served as a military physician at a field hospital in Kiev and in the town of Vasilkov.[48]

Another traveler from Russia to Prussia was R. Moshe b. Eliezer

Kerner (born ca. 1766), a rabbinic scholar who resided in the Shklov district for nearly a decade, from 1786 to 1796, teaching and writing philological-exegetical notes on the Pentateuch. Kerner, who was close to Nota Notkin, corresponded with Naftali Hirtz Wessely on questions of Hebrew language, and praised the latter's works profusely: "The Lord endowed him with extraordinary wisdom to interpret the Biblical text using his pure reason, according to the simple meaning. Elevated individuals such as him are indeed few." Upon completing an exegetical treatise on the first three verses of Leviticus 19, Kerner set out for Berlin, at Notkin's suggestion, and published his work there in the "Orientalische Buchdruckerei," the Hebrew press sponsored by the circle of Maskilim.[49]

For the peripatetic merchants, intellectuals, and rabbis mentioned above—Notkin, Zeitlin, Khaimakovich, Ackord, Kerner, and R. Barukh Schick—Berlin was a key destination, where they were exposed to European culture and Enlightenment ideas. But the traffic between Berlin and Shklov also went in the opposite direction. Haskalah literature and at least one exponent of Jewish enlightenment made their way eastward from Prussia to the Mogilev province. The first volume of the Pentateuch with the *Bi'ur* and Mendelssohn's German translation (1780) listed three prepublication subscribers from Shklov, and five others from the neighboring towns of Mogilev, Dubrovna, Bykhov, and Chaus. (There were, significantly, no subscribers to the *Bi'ur* from the heavily Hasidic Polotsk province.) *Ha-me'asef*, the periodical organ of the Berlin Jewish enlightenment, which began publication in 1783–84, had five subscribers in Shklov, more than in any other East European city, including Vilna.[50]

Ideas were spread by living exponents, not only by books. A German Jewish merchant, Jacob Hirsch of Breslau, settled in Byelorussia in 1776, in a period when Western know-how and influence were welcomed by Catherine the Great. Hirsch negotiated an agreement with the Russian authorities which gave him ownership of eight villages in the Mogilev province, along with 792 bonded serfs, free of charge. In return, he promised to train local apprentices in the art of sheep grazing and the production of high-quality wool.[51]

In 1783, Hirsch approached the Russian authorities with a plan for the sweeping reform of Jewish education in Russia. Troubled by the Jews' ignorance, which was the cause of "the terrible and lowly state of my unfortunate people," and inspired by the educational provisions of Joseph II of Austria's Edict of Toleration (1781), he laid out the following proposal: All Jewish *heders* in the Mogilev province should be placed under the supervision of the Imperial Commission for the Construction of Elementary Schools, and their curriculum should be altered to conform to its requirements. "All that is required is to give proper form and order to these schools and to their instruction of Torah, . . . and to teach correct morality, as well as various useful, necessary arts and sciences, which are required of members of human society." A large model school should be established in the provincial capital of Mogilev.[52]

Hirsch noted that he could find some teachers for the schools locally, in Russia, and that he could invite others from Germany, "through the agency of the learned Moses Mendelssohn." While asking for government authorization and funding, he stressed that there was considerable local support for his proposal:

I have consulted on this project with the most prominent members of my religion in the Mogilev province, and I can count on their support. . . . Many wealthy Jewish merchants have promised me that they would not refrain from contributing two hundred rubles each, as a first donation, if such schools were established.[53]

The reform of Jewish education, one of the central ideas of the Berlin Haskalah, was thus propagated in the Mogilev province as early as 1783—by a German Jewish expatriate, who claimed that his proposal enjoyed a considerable degree of local support.

It is difficult to determine the extent to which the broad European horizons of Shklov's Jewish elite filtered down to the plebian elements of the community. Oral traditions speak of a yawning social gap between the town's wealthy and poor Jews. Nonetheless, interest in Western know-how and ideas did come to the fore in local popular literature. A Yiddish medical and business manual published in Shklov in 1795, as the first of a planned series, announced proudly on its title page that it was based entirely upon foreign literature: "A booklet in which you will find curious, necessary, and useful things on how to keep one's health and make a living, extracted from new authors from foreign lands: Berlin, Vienna, Danzig, Leipzig, Paris and etcetera [sic], translated into our language, so that all can read it and derive utility from it."[54] The prominent display of the names of European cities was intended to indicate the booklet's up-to-date, reliable content. Even for the readers of a Yiddish pamphlet, the West was a lure and an authority.

The 1780s were the decade in which the social and cultural horizons of the Shklov Jewish community expanded most rapidly, as the town became an outpost of modern Europe in the backwater of Byelorussia. The presence of Zorich's court, the growing involvement of Jewish lay leaders in Russian affairs, and the complex of ties between the Mogilev province and the Mendelssohnian circle in Berlin—all of these forces rendered Shklov the first Jewish community in Russia to grapple with the questions of enlightenment and emancipation. The merchants were the first to confront questions on the relationship between Jewish and Gentile culture; but the intellectuals and rabbis were not far behind.

CHAPTER 4

Ideological and Literary Ferment

In eighteenth-century Eastern Europe, the contours of Jewish literature mirrored the religious values of Jewish society. Literary creativity in Hebrew fell overwhelmingly into three broad categories—
halakhah, homiletics, and Kabbalah. Only at the turn of the nineteenth century did Hebrew authors appear in Eastern Europe who
challenged traditional beliefs and values, and called for the reform
and renewal of Jewish culture. They produced works whose subject
matter, form, ideas, and style were a bold departure from traditional Jewish literature.

The most famous pioneer of Haskalah literature in Eastern Europe was Menahem Mendl Lefin (1749–1826), who produced numerous works of social criticism, popular science, philosophy, and satirical fiction during the course of his colorful career. Lefin, who was
active as author and publicist in Berlin, Warsaw, and Shklov (at
Zeitlin's Ustye estate), settled in Brody in 1806, and served there
as literary and intellectual mentor for a generation of Galician
Maskilim.[1] As we shall see, analogous works of instructional and
artistic literature were produced in the Shklov-Mogilev region at
the time, by two less famous early Maskilic authors, Naftali Hirtz
Schulman and Hayim Avraham Katz.[2]

Naftali Hirtz Schulman: The Quest for Cultural Reform

Naftali Hirtz Schulman was born in Stary Bykhov, a town some
eighty versts (forty miles) south of Shklov, along the banks of the
Dniepr. The son of a rabbi, Schulman developed an intense interest
during his youth in the study of Maimonides' *Guide to the Per-*

plexed. Fascination with this work was often the first step in the intellectual emancipation of East European *maskilim* from the fetters of tradition. The *Guide* was not a popular work in seventeenth- and eighteenth-century Poland, and was never printed there. Indeed, the only Ashkenazic editions during those centuries were Jesnitz, 1742, and Berlin, 1791–94, edited by the *maskil* Isaac Satanov. Traditional Polish Jewish society viewed Maimonides' treatise with respectful apprehension, as a profound but potentially dangerous work which could "lead astray those who are straighthearted in their path of faith, and perplex those who study it."[3] Young *maskilim*, on the other hand, found in the *Guide* on attractive rationalist worldview on miracles, prophecy, human free will, and the purpose of the Torah's commandments. Perhaps even more important, young rebels discovered in Maimonides' treatise a universalist realm of discourse, whose participants included not only the sages of Israel, but also Plato, Aristotle, and numerous Muslim philosophers.[4]

During a sojourn in Vilna in the 1790s, where Schulman served as a tutor for the children of wealthy families, he openly challenged the traditional taboo on public study of the *Guide*. He presented *shi'urim* (lectures) on Maimonides' treatise to a group of laymen in the old Vilna synagogue *(kloyz-yashan)*, an act which aroused the indignation of some communal leaders. The latter protested to the Vilna Gaon, R. Elijah, and urged him to ban the classes. But the Gaon, himself no adherent of rationalist philosophy, emphatically refused to do so, saying: "The Rambam [Maimonides] wrote it, and I will prohibit studying it?! May I only sit in his company in paradise!"[5] The controversy foreshadowed future confrontations between "obscurantist" and "enlightened" camps in the Vilna community.

Schulman also focused his intellectual energies on the mastery of Hebrew grammar and philology, which were conspicuously neglected by East European rabbinic authors. His studies in this area likewise came to the attention of the Vilna Gaon, who reportedly "tested" his grammatical skills in a private audience. Schulman's most grandiose philological project was a Hebrew-Aramaic dictionary of "all the words in the Targum, Babylonian Talmud, Jerusalem Talmud, Zohar, Midrash, and books of Kabbalah and philosophy."

Although never published, the work circulated in manuscript during the nineteenth century.[6]

From these pursuits, it is clear that Schulman challenged the boundaries of Jewish literary culture in Eastern Europe, seeking to push them back in accordance with the new model set by the Berlin Haskalah. Philosophy and grammar were important facets of the new Hebrew literature cultivated by Mendelssohn, N. H. Wessely, Isaac Satanov, and the editors of Ha-me'asef. Schulman disseminated these disciplines—and the intellectual-aesthetic values they represented—in the Russian Empire.[7]

In 1797, Schulman settled in Shklov, where he continued to serve as a melamed for children and a teacher for adults—without arousing any of the opposition he had encountered in Vilna. He made his literary debut there, as the editor of a new edition of Mikveh yisra'el (The Hope of Israel), a booklet by R. Manasseh Ben Israel of Amsterdam (1604–57) on the discovery of the ten lost tribes of Israel among the American Indians. The innocuous booklet appeared at first glance to be a diversion from Schulman's Maskilic cultural agenda. In his editor's preface, he adopted a pious pose and contended that his purpose was to console and strengthen his brethren with the good news that the kingdom of the ten lost tribes had been discovered. God had not forsaken the people of Israel; the Messianic ingathering of exiles would yet come to pass.[8]

But the religious rhetoric was merely a mask for more worldly concerns, which were alluded to by Schulman in his preface. Unlike earlier works on the discovery of the lost tribes, such as the medieval travelogues of Eldad the Danite and Benjamin of Tudela, Mikveh yisra'el provided a guide to the New World of America and the Caribbean. It offered a detailed geography and ethnography of the Western hemisphere, whose lands and peoples were unknown to most East European Jews in the late eighteenth century. Schulman recognized that the book could serve as a useful introduction to modern geography:

For in these times, all the corners of the earth have been discovered by the peoples of Europe, who circled the globe from end to end and found numerous lands, faiths, and peoples, whose laws are different from each other. . . . I tasted a bit of this book and my eyes were illuminated; I studied it and comprehended it. For it is based upon the new geography whose truth is known and whose foundation is firm.[9]

By introducing East European Jews to the New World, Schulman not only broadened their intellectual horizons in a substantive manner, but also raised by implication the question of "Gentile wisdom," its validity and significance. Ben Israel's *Mikveh yisra'el* was based upon the testimonies of authors and discoverers, ranging from Plutarch and Pico to Aries Montano and Fransisco de Rivera; its references to the Bible, Talmud, and rabbinic literature were understandably few and far between. If such a booklet was nothing extraordinary or controversial for the Jews of seventeenth-century Holland, in late eighteenth-century Eastern Europe it was a literary sensation. No Hebrew book ever printed in Poland or Russia was as replete with citations of Gentile literature and as skimpy on rabbinic material. Schulman accentuated this feature by prominently displaying a list of its sources in two columns—"Hebrew books" and "books of the nations"—with the latter outnumbering the former, sixty-five to twenty-three.[10] The message was unmistakable: there was a vast realm of Gentile wisdom and science, unknown to East European Jews, with which they needed to become familiar.

For Schulman, *Mikveh yisra'el* was a vehicle for arguing for the legitimacy and validity of knowledge originating from outside the rabbinic tradition. In eighteenth-century East European Jewry, this idea was by no means a forgone conclusion. The discovery of the New World was itself disputed by obscurantists, who argued that since the American continent was not mentioned by the prophets and Talmudic sages, it did not, and could not, exist. Aaron Halle Wolfsohn, a central figure in the Berlin Haskalah, relates that he encountered a Polish rabbi who refused to believe in the existence of America. When Wolfsohn presented testimonies and evidence, the rabbi accused him of being a heretic and exclaimed: "Can you find a single reference to America anywhere in the Bible?"[11]

Mikveh yisra'el also included information on the populated lands in the southern hemisphere, a matter which was rejected with equal fervor. Not only were there no Scriptural references to Brazil or Peru, but the existence of such lands contradicted traditional

Jewish Bible exegesis. Maimonides and other sages had interpreted the verse "for He has founded it [the earth] upon the seas" (Psalms 24:2), as meaning that the earth's lower half was immersed in water, with its upper half floating above the surface. In this case, common sense seemed to concur with tradition. How could people live "opposite the bottoms of our feet"?[12]

Schulman did not address the religious issues raised by the New Geography, other than to note that its "truth [was] well-known" and its "foundation [was] firm." But his edition of *Mikveh yisra'el* implicitly caste doubts on the sufficiency of the rabbinic tradition in the area of geography. And the book provoked a reaction on the part of those who vocally rejected the New Geography and ridiculed it. R. Hayim Avraham Katz, an enlightened preacher and author in Mogilev, reported:

I have seen wise and God-fearing people in our land who are full of mockery upon hearing of the discovery of America and the populated lands opposite the bottoms of our feet. They say, "how is it possible to believe something of this kind, which contradicts the axioms of reason?" And despite all of our strenuous efforts, we are unable to open their closed hearts, remove from it their idea on this matter, and explain to them that it is actually nothing but a figment of their imagination.[13]

Following in Schulman's footsteps, subsequent Maskilim also used the discovery of America as an effective device to argue for openness to non-Jewish science and culture. Works on the discovery of America became a minor genre of early Haskalah literature. Its most notable representatives were Moshe Frankfurter-Mendelsohn's *Metsi'at ha'arets ha-hadasha* (The Finding of the New Land; Altona, 1807), Hayim-Chaikl Hurwitz's *Tsofnas pa'aneah* (The Revealer of Secrets; Berdichev, 1817), and Mordechai Aaron Günzburg's *Gelut ha-arets ha-hadasha* (The Discovery of the New Land; Vilna, 1823). All sought to broaden the intellectual horizons of East European Jews by exposing them to the New World, and impressing upon them the importance and legitimacy of Gentile advances in human knowledge.[14]

Schulman's second literary venture was also a new edition of a classic, in which he cloaked his reformist message in a pious garb. In 1804, he reissued Benjamin Mussafia's *Zekher rav* (Great Remembrance; first edition: Amsterdam, 1638), a moralistic treatise in rhymed meter praising the marvels of God and His creation. Mussafia's work was notable less for its content than for its literary tour de force: it was written using every single word (or verbal root) in the Hebrew Bible. Schulman exploited this feature to transform *Zekher rav* into a tool for advancing Bible study, and the acquisition of German.

Schulman's edition included a running linear translation of Mussafia's text into "pure German" in Hebrew characters; above the linear translation was a reference to a biblical verse where the word (or verbal root) appeared (see illustration in insert). At the end of the volume, Schulman appended an index of Hebrew words and roots, which referred the reader to the appropriate page and line in Mussafia's text. Schulman explained the purpose of these innovations as follows: *Melamdim* would study *Zekher rav* with their young students, memorizing each Hebrew word along with its German translation. Once this process was complete, study of the Bible would be greatly facilitated; students would recognize the biblical words and instantly recall their German equivalent. They would be able to study entire books of the Bible in a short period of time.[15]

In his introduction, Schulman pressed for the reform of Jewish elementary education, urging that greater attention be paid to the study of the Bible. He criticized the *melamdim* who rushed their students hastily from one stage of learning to the next. Students learned only the first few verses of the weekly *sidrah* (Torah portion), with excessive rabbinic homilies and commentaries. Before long, the Pentateuch was abandoned altogether, and replaced by study of the Talmud, and the dialectics of the medieval *Tosafot* and the *Maharsha* (R. Shmuel Edels, 1555–1631).

Schulman cited as an alternative "the wonderful order of study among the Sephardim," and quoted at length the glowing description of the Sephardic Talmud Torah in Amsterdam by R. Sheftl Horowitz (1561–1619). At the Amsterdam school, students studied the entire Pentateuch from beginning to end, then all the Prophets and Writings, before advancing to the Mishna, and finally, at a later age, to the Talmud. Schulman urged his contemporaries to break with their ingrained conservatism and to follow this practice. "I ask the communities to gather in every single town, and to appoint a *melamed* who will teach students the entire Bible from beginning to end."[16]

Had Schulman stopped at this point, his educational reform plan would have been only slightly different from that proposed by the sixteenth-century rabbi R. Judah Loew of Prague (1525–1609) and some of his disciples, such as Horowitz. R. Judah Loew had argued for the more methodical and systematic study of Judaism's sacred texts. There was nothing necessarily Maskilic about such a proposal.[17]

But Schulman went further. He criticized Talmud-centered education per se, and asserted that Jewish children were deprived of a much-needed moral education.

The boy is bereft of both learning and ethics *[limud ve-derekh erets]*. As for training the boys in virtuous character traits and proper conduct, this is not to be found in our land, except among a select few.[18]

The distinction between Judaism and ethics was a leaf taken out of the ideology of the Berlin Haskalah. In suggesting that the exclusive focus of Jewish elementary education on the Talmud was detrimental to the moral development of Jewish youths, Schulman echoed a central theme of Naftali Hirtz Wessely's manifesto *Divre shalom ve-'emet* (Berlin, 1782).[19]

In addition, Schulman argued for altering the language of Bible translation in the *heder*. He urged *melamdim* to use his "pure German [linear] translation" of Mussafia's biblical Hebrew, and attacked the Yiddish spoken by his contemporaries as "a garbled tongue." "It is part Polish, part Russian, part other languages, and many words whose origin is unknown to us." His edition of *Zekher rav* was intended to correct this linguistic deformity by teaching basic proper German to children in the *heder*.[20] In using the Hebrew Bible as a springboard for the study of German, the project was evidently inspired by Mendelssohn's famed translation of the Pentateuch.

Acquiring fluency in German was a difficult undertaking for the Yiddish-speaking Jews of Lithuania and Byelorussia. Solomon Maimon, a native of Niesviezh who migrated to Prussia in the 1780s, had continuous difficulties mastering the rules of German grammar, pronunciation, and spelling. Even attaining a passive reading knowledge of literary German was not an easy task, as is evident from the case of R. Manasseh of Ilya, an early nineteenth-century Lithuanian Maskil who was never able to bridge the linguistic gap between Yiddish and German, despite his strenuous efforts, and remained cut off from German literature, philosophy, and science throughout his life.[21] Schulman sought to bring down this language barrier by beginning the instruction of German at the earliest age, in the *heder*, by employing it in the traditional word-by-word translation of the Bible.[22]

Schulman's edition of *Zekher rav* could, of course, be used not only by *melamdim* and children, but also by adults, who could consult the linear translation to "correct" their "garbled tongue" and study basic German. And thanks to the index of words and verbal roots at the back of the volume, an adult with basic knowledge of Hebrew could look up the Hebrew word of his choice and find its German equivalent—in other words, use the book as a Hebrew-German dictionary. Schulman was clearly aware of this fact. In his introduction, he announced that he planned to publish a Russian linear translation of Mussafia's text as well. A Russian translation would have been totally unsuitable for children in the *heder*; how could they learn one foreign language (biblical Hebrew) by using a linear translation in a second, even more foreign language (Russian)? But adults with knowledge of Hebrew could use the running translation as a Hebrew-Russian dictionary. Schulman, who according to the Vilna Maskil Samuel Joseph Fuenn, was "one of the first [Jews] who knew the Russian language well," conceived of *Zekher rav* as a tool for linguistic Germanization and/or Russification.[23]

Schulman's program of educational reform was thus three-pronged: ascribing the highest priority to study of the Bible, paying attention to moral-ethical training, and teaching the rudiments of "pure German." All three proposals were derived from the educational program of the Berlin Haskalah, and reflected the influence of Wessely's *Divre shalom ve-'emet*.

Conspicuously absent, however, from Schulman's educational program was an explicit call for the study of the sciences and worldly disciplines in the *heder*. Schulman was probably too cautious to propose such a radical break with tradition. He was not as bold and provocative as his literary mentor, Wessely. But advocating the acquisition of worldly knowledge by adults was another matter. Schulman addressed the topic obliquely in his edition of *Mikveh yisra'el*, and directly in an appendix to *Zekher rav*, where he announced his plan to publish a weekly Hebrew newspaper in Shklov. Noting that many Jews "in each and every city" were eager to broaden their knowledge and "attain [intellectual] perfection," but were hindered by "a lack of books and information," he described the envisioned periodical as a vehicle for disseminating worldly knowledge:

I will publish each week the news *[hidushim]* happening all over the world, including translations of the most necessary items from the newspapers of Hamburg, St. Petersburg, and Berlin, and news from the books of wisdom. Merchants will be able to read about wars and commerce, and the lovers of wisdom will be able to read about the sciences and other news. Every person who has a piece of correct news will inform me of it, and I will inform each and every city in which we [Jews] reside under the protection of the Tsar, may his glory be uplifted. We will thus disseminate among our people the grammar of various languages, mathematics, geometry, geography, natural science and other matters.[24]

The abortive periodical, which never appeared in print, apparently because of a lack of financial backing, was Schulman's most explicit and ambitious enlightenment project. It was a self-conscious vehicle for bridging the gap between the insulated world of Russian Jewry and the political, scientific, and cultural world of Western Europe.

Schulman's designs to reform Jewish education resurfaced several years later, when he resided once again in Vilna. Having curried favor with Tsar Alexander I by composing a trilingual (Hebrew-Russian-German) hymn in honor of the birth of his daughter, Grand Duchess Elizabeth, Schulman managed to obtain a government permit to establish schools for Jewish youth which incorporated Russian language instruction. He opened such a school in Vilna (according to one account in 1820) and "began to blow the spirit of the Haskalah among the youth." But this first modern Jewish school in Lithuania was short-lived. Local zealots, fearing "that if their sons will understand the language of the land, they will abandon the Torah," denounced Schulman to the governor-general of the Vilna province. They accused him of corrupting the youth, and disseminating the idea of political insurrection. The governor-general rescinded Schulman's permit and ordered him to leave Russia at once. Exiled from his native land, he settled in his beloved Amsterdam, the home of Manasseh Ben Israel and Benjamin Mussafia, where he lived out the remainder of his years.[25]

It is no exaggeration to say that Schulman was the first Russian Maskil—a man who propagated Jewish enlightenment and cultural reform through various literary and educational projects, and who attempted to establish the institutions to advance this cause, a periodical journal and a network of schools. His ambitious designs were ultimately frustrated, due to insufficient financial support in the first case, and aggressive opposition by zealots in the other. Nonetheless, Schulman transposed Wessely's ideas to Russia, and modified them, by placing knowledge of Russian on an equal footing with German. In doing so, he pioneered the effort to free the Haskalah movement of its Germano-centric tendency, and reorient it toward civil and cultural integration with Russia.

Hayim Avraham Katz: The Discovery of Aesthetics and the Imagination

In the same year that Schulman made his literary debut, 1797, an extraordinary book was published anonymously in Shklov—a Hebrew drama on the biblical story of Joseph, entitled *Milhama ba-shalom* (War against Peace). Written by the communal preacher of Mogilev, R. Hayim Avraham b. Arye Leyb Katz, the book was the first Hebrew drama composed in Eastern Europe, and constituted an unusual foray into imaginative literature by an Ashkenazic rabbi.[26]

The book's ground-breaking quality was signaled by the fact that Katz was at a loss for an appropriate Hebrew word for "play" or "drama" to define the genre of his work. He referred to it as a *mahberet* (booklet), perhaps in an oblique allusion to its generic similarity to the *Mahbarot* of Immanuel of Rome (ca. 1261–1328), a classical work of imaginative narrative poetry in Hebrew. The best Katz could do was characterize his work as "the story of Joseph and his brothers in a rhetorical booklet, in the form of debate" (*sipur yosef ve-ehav be-mahberet halatsi'it 'al derekh ha-vikuah*).

In his introduction, Katz offered an apology for belletristic literature in general, and for his own dramatic writing in particular. Citing Scripture, medicine, and the works of Maimonides, he argued that excessive intellectuality brought on depression, and that, for the sake of one's emotional equilibrium, wisdom had to be coupled with "things that amuse one's heart." Although such amusements were objectively trivial compared to the "Sea of Wisdom," it was necessary, for the sake of one's well-being, to suspend one's awareness of their triviality, and imagine that they were intrinsically meaningful. "A man may exert his imaginative power, attach his soul to a falsehood and treat it as if it were true, if the hour requires it." Katz legitimized belletristic literature, and for that matter all leisure activity, as a healthy and necessary form of emotional escape.[27]

The preacher from Mogilev confessed that he had learned this lesson from his own bouts of depression. He had turned to creative writing as a satisfying amusement, because most forms of social amusement were considered unbecoming for a person of his rank, and elicited public scorn. Recognizing that he was endowed with a God-given gift for language and rhetoric, and that his work as preacher had trained him to present his ideas in parables and stories, his decision to engage in creative writing came to him quite naturally.

I turned to composing words of pleasantness which are sweet to the tongue of a reader. For I said, "may my couch console me; in my bed will I find relaxation at my time of need." I therefore decided to compose a little booklet with my pen, and not to desist from loving it until I could call it my daughter.[28]

Katz's introduction reveals the internalization of strikingly modern concepts: the recognition of art as an autonomous realm of meaning, and its appreciation as a vehicle for personal self-expression and self-realization. Katz reconciled these ideas with his traditional religious worldview by conceding that, in the final analysis, art was a trivial diversion from the realm of ultimate and absolute meaning—God and Torah. In another context, Katz used a similar tactic to embrace modern science and reconcile it with tradition. He argued that the new geography's discovery of America and the southern hemisphere was factual, but that in the final analysis, the matter was of trivial importance. "Even if such knowledge has a certain degree of utility, it does not relate to the soul of the Israelite nation, or to spiritual life. Not regarding such matters does scripture say 'for it [The Torah] is your life' " (Deut. 30:20).[29] In Katz's case, openness to artistic and scientific pursuits was accompanied by their compartmentalization and ultimate devaluation.

In the case of art, the compartmentalization was not absolute. Katz admitted that he could not totally cast aside "wisdom" in pursuit of "amusement" in his dramatic writing. He simply could not find any comfort and pleasure in a style of writing which was utterly trivial. He therefore integrated philosophic-religious sections into his "booklet," which discussed God as creator, Divine providence, love and fear of God, the revival of the dead and so forth, in the form of a debate between the Egyptian wisemen and the children of Jacob.[30] In Katz's conception of literature, the distinction between Truth and Art, "wisdom" and "amusement," was not absolute.

Milhama ba-shalom re-enacted the Joseph story from beginning to end, drawing upon the biblical narrative, rabbinic Midrash and *'agadah*, classical exegetes, and the medieval *Sefer ha-yashar*. The rabbis of Shklov, who offered their letter of approbation to Katz's volume, praised it as a work of biblical exegesis, which helped resolve difficulties in the text by elaborating upon the commentators' words. But in fact, *Milhama ba-shalom* was a work of art, and not of exegesis. It weaved together select themes from its various sources to construct a plausible and internally coherent plot. Katz discarded certain famous rabbinic *agadot* which were too fantastic or supernatural for his taste, and he chose between *agadot* which were mutually contradictory. A drama had to follow a single storyline and could not present alternate versions of an event, as could a commentary.[31]

But Katz went considerably beyond recasting select rabbinic material in dramatic form. He created original dialogues, scenes, subplots, and characters which were not based on any of his sources. He composed an original work of fiction, without any compunctions that this might constitute a "desecration" of the biblical text.

Many of Katz's imaginative additions were designed to fill in gaps in the biblical narrative, and construct a more coherent story. In the scene in which the brothers sold Joseph to the Midianites, the brothers explained that the young man they were selling was a domestic servant who had been born into their household, and who had recently begun hallucinating that he was their brother. They hoped that by living in a new environment, away from their home, he would recover from his malady.[32] This addition helped address obvious questions left unanswered by the biblical account: Had not Joseph protested to the Midianites that he was being sold by his brothers? How did the brothers respond to his charge?

Katz also created scenes and characters purely for the sake of their dramatic effect. Joseph, as viceroy of Egypt, told his unknowing brothers of two recent dreams, not mentioned by the Bible or Midrash, which were a veiled parable of his sale into bondage. This was a device to heighten the irony of the encounter between them. A totally new figure was introduced to the Egyptian royal court: Belis, the waiter, Joseph's loyal servant, who befriended the brothers and consoled them during their imprisonment. Characters who were scarcely mentioned by the Midrash were freely developed. Joseph's Egyptian wife 'Osnat was shown quarreling with her husband, as he ordered her to prepare a lavish meal for the Hebrew visitors. Yohni and Mamrei, the heads of the Egyptian sorcerers, engaged Isaschar in an extended conversation on Judaism's doctrines of faith, and became convinced of its philosophic truth.[33]

At certain points, *Milhama ba-shalom* digressed from its biblical plot altogether, with the heroes telling folktales and parables, some of which were of obviously non-Jewish provenance. When first brought before Pharoah, Joseph recounted the story of Chomethius of Macedonia, a physician who left his homeland, lost his possessions, and was mistaken everywhere for a poor beggar, instead of the medical genius that he was.[34] Such tales and parables served as dramatic relief from the play's familiar biblical plot, and are further evidence that the play's primary purposes were entertainment and edification, not exegesis.

One of the striking features of *Milhama ba-shalom* was its insistence on realism. The play broke with those Midrashic traditions that injected fantastic, miraculous elements into the Joseph story. Katz eliminated, for instance, the legendary dialogue between Jacob and a wolf which had allegedly devoured his son, or the amazing feats of physical strength displayed by the brothers in Egypt. Even the stories told about kings of India, ancient wisemen, and doctors were realistic didactic narratives. Katz avoided wonder tales, which were commonplace in eighteenth-century Yiddish chapbooks and in the Hasidic stories of his time.[35]

An even more impressive artistic feature was the author's ability to empathize with his characters—even with Joseph's brothers as they sold him into slavery, and with Potifar's wife as she sought to seduce him. Katz used the dramatic genre to provide psychological insights into their thoughts and motives, and to portray them as misguided—rather than purely evil—figures. Judah and Shimon expressed anger and a sense of betrayal for being slandered before their father by Joseph. To their mind, Joseph was a talebearer, a self-serving scoundrel who sought to alienate their father from them. Had not their father Jacob taught them that slanderers should be put to death? This presentation of the brothers' side to the story was a novel departure from the black-and-white approach of the rabbinic sources, and Katz drew attention to this aspect in his introduction.

The entire reason for the brothers' persecuting him was that their hearts deceived them into believing that he was the opposite of a righteous person [tsadik]. May the reader therefore not consider it strange to find them speak of him as a "traitor" or "evil person." The truth came unto them later on, that he was righteous.[36]

Potifar's wife, Zeliha, also emerged in a more ambivalent light. She cried out to Joseph for help, desperate to bear a child, after years of barrenness from her elderly husband. Although aware that her proposition to lie together was considered sinful, Zeliha believed that God would understand and even approve of her action. She denied the existence of absolute good and evil, and espoused a philosophy of moral relativism: "For everything there is a season, and a time for every purpose. Just as there is no good thing which does not become bad at a certain time, there is no bad thing which

does not become good at its time." In her desperate effort to per-
suade Joseph, Zeliha promised that she would not have sexual relations with any other man, and would marry him after her husband's
death, thereby attenuating the sin. In Katz's play, she became a
thinking and suffering character, rather than merely the embodiment of temptation.[37]

A few words should be said about the technical features of Katz's
drama. Although *Milhama ba-shalom* was not formally divided into
acts and scenes, it had its own equivalent structure. The play was
divided into two parts: "The Course of Events" *(tokhen ha-'alilot)*,
which took the story from its beginning until Benjamin's departure
for Egypt, and "The Open Rebuke" *(tokhahat megule)*, which featured the extensive philosophic debates between the brothers and
the Egyptian sorcerers, as well as the final confrontation and recon-
ciliation between Joseph and his brothers. The beginning of new
scenes was marked by an introductory sentence, in large bold typeface, which related the background and setting of events in biblical
verses or Katz's own words. Katz offered extensive stage directions
of voice, movement, and gesture, which were also printed in bold
typeface, so as to distinguish them from the the dramatic text
printed in cursive. Katz exhibited considerable interest in stage
technique; his work was by no means a bare-bones symposium, "in
the form of debate."

How is one to explain the sudden appearance of such a sophisti-
cated dramatic work, for its time and place, as *Milhama ba-shalom?*
Katz did not place his work in any literary tradition or historical
context, but he must have had certain models of dramatic writing
before him, which served as his points of reference. Unfortunately,
they cannot be identified with absolute certainty.

The tradition of Yiddish *Purim-shpiln* certainly exerted some
influence on Katz's enterprise. The Joseph story was a popular
theme of Purim folk plays, second only to the Esther story itself,
and this living theatrical genre helped determine Katz's choice of
plot. But otherwise, *Milhama ba-shalom* had little in common with
the traditional *mikhires yosef shpil*. The latter was a light melo-
drama in rhymed Yiddish verse, and lacked the emotional intensity,
or psychological sophistication of Katz's play. Katz's dialogue in
lofty biblical Hebrew endowed his work with a classical and epic

quality totally unlike the light, folksy, almost frivolous tone of the *Purim-shpil*.[38]

There is even less basis to believe that Katz used the Hebrew dramas of late eighteenth-century Germany as his literary models. Although dramatic writing flourished among authors associated with the Berlin Haskalah, such as Menahem Mendl Bresslau (*Yaldut u-vaharut* [Childhood and Youth], Berlin, 1786), Samuel Rommanelli (*Ha-kolot yehdalun* [The Voices Cease], Berlin, 1791), and Joseph Ha-'efrati (*Melukhat sha'ul* [Saul's Kingdom]; Vienna, 1794), these works were artistically worlds apart from Katz's. Rommanelli's and Ha-'efrati's dramas were written in highly formalized rhymed verse, using ornate language, while Katz's play used realistic Hebrew speech as found in biblical narratives. Rommanelli's and Ha-'efrati's great artistic strengths were poetic technique and imagery, whereas Katz focused on character construction and dramatic plot development.[39]

It stands to reason that Katz's foray into drama was influenced, at least in part, by the active theater culture at Zorich's court in Shklov. Katz was no stranger to the town; he lived but a few miles away, in Mogilev, and maintained close business ties with his father-in-law, a resident of Shklov.[40] Any occasional visitor to the town would have seen its active theatrical establishment, and heard about its repertoire of tragedy, comedy, opera, and ballet. Katz must have been challenged, either consciously or subconsciously, by the Shklov theater to attempt a Hebrew drama which would entertain its imagined audience, while remaining within the didactic and religious parameters of a traditional Jewish sensibility.[41]

With *Milhama ba-shalom*, Katz took Hebrew writing in Eastern Europe in an altogether new direction. Although it had no immediate imitators or followers, his work went on to be a best-selling chapbook in Yiddish translation, which was considered an early example of Maskilic didactic prose.[42]

CHAPTER 5

Struggles for Emancipation

Prosaic Requests, Poetic Appeals

In the spring of 1787, Empress Catherine stopped off in Shklov while en route to Kiev, and received ten leaders of its Jewish community in an official audience. After the formalities and niceties, such as kissing the Empress's hand, the leaders, who must have included Notkin and Zeitlin, submitted a petition requesting that Jews no longer be referred to in official parlance by the derogatory term *zhidy*, and that they henceforth be called by the more lofty biblical term *evrei* (Hebrews). Catherine agreed, and issued a directive to that effect. The Hamburg *Staats- und Gelehrte Zeitung*, which reported the event, explained that the change of terms was adopted because the monarch wished "to remove, as much as possible, all external signs of contempt toward the Jews," and "the name 'Jew' is usually connected with humiliating ideas."[1] And indeed, from that point on, *evrei* became the standard term used in Imperial decrees and legislation.

Enlightened Jews celebrated the directive as an important act elevating the Jews' social status. More than a decade and a half later, the Russian Jewish writer Judah Leyb Nevakhovich paid tribute to Catherine for its issuance: "The Jew's earlier name . . . which was a disgrace and insult, passed on and was no more. He was called a Hebrew ['*ivri*,] as a sign of honor and beauty."[2]

This incident reveals the Westernized mentality of Shklov's Jewish leaders, who followed the example of their acculturated counterparts in France and Germany in this respect. The latter dissociated themselves from the word "Jew," and began to identify themselves as "Israelites," in the belief that a change of terminology was a necessary step on the path to social acceptance. Traditional Jews, who had no ambitions of integration and social acceptance, did not worry about the negative connotations that the word "Jew" carried in Gentile parlance. Only modernized, emancipationist Jews did.[3]

Beyond this incident, little else is known about the Shklov community's political contacts with the Russian authorities in the 1780s. While Shklov was the uncontested religious and cultural center of the Jews in the Mogilev province (the title pages of Hebrew books printed in the provincial capital referred to it as "Mogilev, which is adjacent to Shklov"), it may not have played a lead role in the external politics of Russian Jewry until the time of that audience. In part, this may have been due to its anomalous legal status. As a private town under Zorich's personal jurisdiction, Shklov was not subject to many of the administrative laws and decrees issued in St. Petersburg. Its Jews were not incorporated into the Imperial system of municipal administration which was established in 1783, as were those of Mogilev and Polotsk, and the power of its kahal to adjudicate civil cases was not curtailed by Imperial statute in 1786. In Shklov, the word of Zorich was law, and the political relationship that mattered most was the one with the general-turned-landlord.[4]

The relationship with Zorich was a complex and increasingly troubled one. Popular memory records repeated incidents of harassment, persecution, and capricious action, which led Notkin and Zeitlin, the rising stars of the communal elite in the 1780s, to intercede with Potemkin on the community's behalf. Potemkin repeatedly came to the Jews' protection, and Zorich relented, since he could ill-afford to disregard the entreaties and warnings of Catherine's closest adviser and confident. The relations between Zorich and the Jewish community deteriorated considerably after Potemkin's death (in 1791), and reached a nadir in 1799, when the Jews submitted a full-blown complaint and lawsuit against Zorich to the Russian Senate.[5]

Notkin and Zeitlin began to play an active role in Russian Jewish politics on the national level only after the 1787 war with Turkey, during which they distinguished themselves as military purveyors. Once their relationship with Potemkin and other members of the

Russian political elite was firmly secured, they assumed the role of Jewish political leaders. Much of what they did was traditional *shtadlanut*, averting expulsions and acts of persecution through petitions and personal intercessions. Of greater note is the fact that in later years, they and their associates addressed the broader issue of the legal and social status of the Jews in Russia, and promoted the cause of Jewish integration and emancipation.

The first political pamphlet to emanate from the Shklov Jewish community was written in the form of a poem submitted in honor of Paul I's assumption of the Imperial throne, in 1796. The community seized upon the moment of transition in Russian governance to articulate its political goals and aspirations:

As a father has compassion on his children,
So may our king have compassion on all the
inhabitants of his lands,
May there be one law for all.

May hatred among men,
And oppression of one's brethren because of
differences of faith,
Not be seen or heard in his day.

May every man who fears the Lord,
And observes the laws of the "Doctrine of Man,"
Who is loyal to his king and kingdom,
Who works with all his might for the benefit
of the state—

May every one who carries the burden of the land,
Also eat of its fruit and be satiated by its goodness,
And sit peacefully in the shade of enlightened
laws, established for all eternity. . . .

Lord, You who know the heart of every man!
It is known to you that we have always been
faithful to the kings and princes ruling over us,
And that we faithfully swear allegiance to our
master, King Paul Petrovitch, and his son the successor.

Therefore, Lord our God, may our king's heart
be kind unto us.

For a prince such as he, who walks in Your path
to do justice and kindness,
Knows that we are all children of one Father.

In his justice, may he make our law and lot in
his kingdom,
Equal to the law and lot of all the nations.[6]

These poetic words were uttered at a time when Russian Jewry was
the object of several recently introduced discriminatory measures,
such as the Pale of Settlement (1794), double taxation (1794), and
the renewed expulsion of Jews from the villages (1795). The poem
constituted a plea for civic equality, based upon the political doctrines of enlightened absolutism: The Jews contributed toward the
welfare of the state, adhered to basic moral norms, and were loyal
to their fatherland (a term used in the poem's accompanying German translation). They therefore merited equal treatment with
other subjects. The poem prayed for universal brotherhood, and for
the elimination of religious enmity and intolerance. In voicing
these enlightened sentiments, it referred obliquely to the Jews' pre-
carious social position.

At the time of the poem's writing, Russian political circles were
not inclined to accept its assertions of the Jews' civic virtue, or to
entertain proposals that their legal status be equalized with that of
other subjects. If anything, official thinking about the Jews was
turning increasingly hostile. A 1797 memorandum by the provincial
governor of the Minsk *guberniia*, Zakhar Karneev, on the causes of
the recent famine in his province, emphasized the destructive role
played by the Jews in the rural economy, and urged that they be
forbidden to lease liquor franchises or run inns. When the Russian
Senate reviewed Karneev's report, it accepted his analysis and ordered him to stop the Jews' "ruination of the peasants." Whereas
Karneev also drew attention to other factors, and laid some blame
at the feet of the Orthodox church, the Senate was more single-
minded in its explanation:

The peasants of the Minsk province are mired in extreme poverty not so
much because of the frequent drought there, but rather because the landlords engage Jews for various leases and inns, and the latter cause the

peasants' impoverishment by giving them alcoholic beverages on credit or in exchange for their pawning essential items. The peasants are thereby rendered incapable of managing their domestic economy.[7]

Spurred by Karneev's report, the Senate asked the governors of other provinces to submit their views on the Jewish question, in what was the first official survey of Imperial officials on the subject. The responses were universally unsympathetic in their assessment of the Jews' role in society, and in their prescription of restrictive measures.[8]

"The Defender of His People": Nota Notkin's Reform Projects

Nota Khaimovich Notkin entered the official discussion of the Jewish question at this tense and rather inhospitable moment, with a 1797 memorandum addressed to General Procurator Aleksei Kurakin, and submitted for consideration by the Tsar. In it, Notkin drew attention to the Jews' own acute poverty, examined its causes and harmful consequences, and made specific proposals for its alleviation.

Notkin's memorandum attributed the Jews' growing poverty to the restrictive legal measures taken against them in recent years: the prohibition on their trading in the cities of inner Russia, the expulsions of Jews from their long-standing places of residence in the villages, and the imposition of double taxation. These measures had caused thousands of Jews to lose their livelihoods, and had put tremendous financial burdens on the kahals. Inter alia, Notkin acknowledged that the Jews' economic hardships had also produced negative consequences for society at large. Jews had become increasingly concentrated in the leasing of taverns and the sale of alcohol, an activity which was not "useful to society," and many of them failed to pay taxes to the state treasury because of their financial plight.[9]

To address this crisis, Notkin proposed, first, the overall "equalization of [the Jews'] taxes with that of members of other religions," and second, an ambitious government program of retraining and resettlement. Specifically, he advocated the creation of Jewish colonies in the territories of New Russia along the Black Sea, which would engage in animal husbandry (the breeding of cattle and sheep), crafts (the manufacture of cloths, ropes, and sails), and farming (including the planting of trees and vineyards). As an incentive for Jews to resettle in the south, colonists should be exempted from all state taxes for a number of years, following which they should be allowed to pay their taxes in kind, in the form of agricultural and industrial products. The colonists would eventually become full-fledged owners of their enterprises, with the right to sell them freely. Notkin was confident that the project would attract foreign (Jewish) investment, and would actually increase the treasury's income from Jewish taxation.[10]

Perhaps the most interesting feature of Notkin's memorandum was its deft use of contemporary absolutist and physiocratic ideas. The stated goal of his colonization plan was to render the Jews "good and useful citizens in society, and punctual tax-payers to the treasury." To achieve this goal, their lives needed to be rearranged so that they could "have sustenance from the labor of their hands" and engage in "useful work." Notkin accepted much of the late eighteenth-century criticism of Jewish involvement in the production and sale of alcohol, although his explanation of its causes and his prescription for its reform differed from that of Russian contemporaries. Following in the tradition of C. W. Dohm and Moses Mendelssohn, Notkin argued that the Jews were capable of economic reform, if only productive avenues of employment were opened up to them. His proposal to create Jewish agricultural and industrial colonies bore the influence of a similar effort undertaken by Joseph II of Austria in 1786.[11]

Notkin's memorandum was the first contribution by a Jew to the political debate on the Jewish question in Russia. Although neither Kurakin nor Tsar Paul responded in writing to his proposals, Notkin continued to be actively involved in the debate in subsequent years, when it assumed greater urgency and intensity.

In June 1800, the Senate dispatched Count Gavriil Derzhavin on his second official tour of Byelorussia, this time to investigate the shortage of bread in the region, and instructed him to pay special attention to the activities of the Jews, "who are a major cause of the peasants' ruination there." Derzhavin's report or "Opinion" (the full title was "The Opinion of Senator Derzhavin Regarding the Avoidance of Grain Shortage in Byelorussia by Curing the Mercenary Trades of the Jews, and Regarding Their Reform, and Other Things") was a comprehensive Judeophobic tract. It presented a demonic image of the Jews, as the eternal enemies Christ and of mankind, as dishonest and avaricious parasites, and as an inherently criminal, immoral people. His concrete proposals to the Senate regarding the reform of the Jews' legal status were as follows: the abolition of the kahal and its replacement by a governmental "Protector of the Jews" in charge of their affairs; abolition of the Jews' right to vote and be elected in municipal elections; the forced deportation of "unnecessary Jews" from the villages, where they distilled and sold alcohol, to agricultural colonies in New Russia. He urged that the ban on Jewish residence in inner Russia be maintained and, indeed, strengthened, and that Jewish proselytizing activity be prohibited, as well as the employment of Christian servants by Jews.

Derzhavin also proposed strict state control over Jewish culture: outlawing traditional Jewish dress, requiring the education of children above age twelve in Russian state schools, strict censorship and control over the publication of Hebrew books, and a ban on importing such books from abroad. The "Opinion" was guided by a vision of isolating the Jews, restricting their harmful activities, and closely policing all aspects of their lives.[12]

Shortly after Derzhavin submitted his "Opinion," Tsar Paul died, and his report was left in limbo. In November 1802, the recently crowned Tsar Alexander I ordered the formation of the State Committee for the Organization of Jewish Life, whose task was to draft new, comprehensive legislation. The Committee consisted of Derzhavin (then Minister of Justice), Count Viktor Kochubei (then Minister of Internal Affairs), Mikhail Speranskii (then Assistant Minister of Internal Affairs), Count V. A. Zubov, and the Polish counts Adam Czartoryski and S. O. Potocki. In a sign of openness, Committee members were permitted to select deputies from among the "most enlightened Jews" to serve as advisers to the Committee, and Notkin was invited by Derzhavin to serve in that capacity. In his letter of invitation, Derzhavin acknowledged Notkin's "zeal on behalf of the general good, and useful propositions for the Jewish people, which have reached the attention of His Imperial Highness."[13]

Some historians have concluded from the letter that Notkin and Derzhavin were on close friendly terms at the time, and that their relations soured only after the Committee's proceedings began. This seems unlikely, since Derzhavin's Judeophobic views were well known from his "Opinion." Derzhavin probably considered Notkin's appointment politically prudent, if not inevitable, since he was the foremost Jewish political leader, and had written a well-known memorandum on the Jews' economic reform. Derzhavin had no reason to fear that Notkin's opinions, as opposed to his own, would carry the day, since the Jewish deputies served only in an advisory capacity.[14]

One of Notkin's first actions following his appointment as deputy was to draw the Committee's attention to the fear and anxiety which its very creation had generated among Russian Jewry. He wrote to Count Kochubei—and not, interestingly enough, to his official "sponsor" Derzhavin—to advise him that the Jews were in a state of panic that the Committee intended to issue harsh decrees against them. In response to Notkin's appeal, Kochubei issued a reassuring circular letter in January 1803, which declared in part:

By the establishment of a committee to oversee their affairs, it was not intended to hinder [the Jews'] position or diminish their essential privileges. On the contrary, through the examination of all circumstances, their better organization and tranquillity are sought.[15]

In May 1803, Notkin submitted a memorandum to the Committee regarding the Jews's "better organization and tranquillity." It offered a blueprint for reform which was diametrically opposed to Derzhavin's "Opinion" and the earlier anti-Jewish pronouncements of the Senate and provincial governors. Indeed, the memorandum can most profitably be read as a point-by-point response to Derzhavin's "Opinion."

Notkin emphatically denied that the Jews were morally defective, and that they were responsible for the ruination of the peasants.

To consider the Jews as the only culpable ones for the poverty of the peasants is without foundation. In many places where there are Jews, peasants live amid plenty, and on the contrary, in other places there are no Jews and the peasants suffer privation. . . . The abuses ascribed to the Jews are mostly unsubstantiated, and if there are abuses, they come solely from poverty. Therefore, in order to utilize the Jews for the benefit of the state and themselves, it is necessary to ward off their poverty.[16]

Notkin spoke out against the proposals to restrict the Jews' economic activity, noting that they would only aggravate Jewish poverty, and bring harm to other elements of society as well. If Jews were prohibited from leasing gentry properties and were expelled from the villages (as Derzhavin and others had suggested), one hundred thousand Jewish men, women, and children would be left homeless. Who would feed them? And if there were no Jewish inhabitants on gentry lands, the peasants would be deprived of an efficient way of disposing of their produce and purchasing finished goods. Scores of inns and taverns would be closed down, thereby hampering travelers in need of food and lodging, and harming the transport of goods.

In response to Derzhavin's proposal to forcibly deport large numbers of "unnecessary Jews" to agricultural colonies in the south, Notkin retreated from his own earlier enthusiasm for colonization. It would be enormously expensive to resettle and feed masses of Jews in New Russia, and to train them in agricultural work "to which they are unaccustomed and not inclined." He contended that the idea of turning the Jews into a people of farmers was "absurd," and that it was foolhardy to impose upon them the socioeconomic structure of other peoples. "It is impossible for everyone to lead the exact same kind of life."

Notkin proposed, instead, that government efforts concentrate on large-scale retraining of the Jews in crafts and light industry in their local dwelling places. Each Jewish community in the Empire would be required to establish its own factories, with the assistance of private Jewish capital and state funding. Poor Jews would be assigned to the factories as workers, and the factories themselves would be considered common communal property. As in his 1797 proposal, Notkin suggested that taxes be collected from the Jews in kind, in the form of industrial products, and he called once again for the elimination of the Jews' double taxation. He paid lip service to the idea of agrarianization by proposing that those Jews who

were interested in becoming farmers should be granted vacant Imperial lands in their province of residence and given technical assistance. But clearly Notkin placed his greatest hope on the prospect
of industrialization, not agrarianization.[17]

Notkin's 1803 plan for the Jews' economic reform was not only
more realistic than its 1797 predecessor, but also more ambitious.
The earlier document had envisioned that the colonies along the
Black Sea would serve as a socioeconomic safety valve, to absorb
the Jews' excess population; it freely conceded that most Jews
would neither move south nor change their occupations. The later
project, on the other hand, proposed a mechanism for the radical
occupational transformation of Russian Jewry as a whole, without
the traumatic and costly endeavor of large-scale resettlement.

The 1803 memorandum did not limit itself to economic affairs,
and included proposals for the reform of Jewish political institutions
and culture as well. Notkin's ideas were clearly intended as an
alternative to the harsh measures advocated by Derzhavin. Instead
of abolishing the kahal, he suggested a system which would have
merged Jewish self-governing bodies with the Imperial administration. Commissions of Jewish deputies would govern Jewish affairs
in each province, under the supervision of the provincial governors.
A governmental guardian, with direct access to the Tsar, would
supervise Jewish affairs on the Imperial level. Notkin's system envisioned the preservation of a curtailed, but still significant, level of
Jewish civil autonomy. Tax funds would be raised from the Jewish
population by the state apparatus, and not the kahal, but the funds
raised would be handed over to the Commissions of Jewish Deputies, who would disburse them as they saw fit—subject to the
guardian's approval. The construction of factories, for instance,
was to be planned and implemented by the Commissions of Jewish
Deputies, but the plans would be subject to approval by the
guardian.

Notkin's apparent goal was to devise a system in which Jewish
autonomous bodies and the state apparatus worked in close cooper-
ation with each other, rather than at cross-purposes. Reforms would
be implemented by the Jewish leadership, and not imposed from
above by the state.

This system was to be applied to the reform of Jewish education as well. The Commissions of Deputies would establish public schools in all communities, which would teach Russian and other languages to Jewish children. Notkin did not develop his school plan at any length, but his remarks that the new schools would admit "both rich and poor children" and that they would ensure that Jews not "entrust their children's education simply to anyone at all" suggest that he envisioned the elimination of the privately run *heders* and communal *talmud torahs* and their replacement by the new schools. On the other hand, Notkin insisted that schooling needed to remain an internal Jewish affair. In a jab at Derzhavin's proposal that Jewish children above age twelve be required to attend general state schools, he noted: "it is pointless to expect that Jewish parents would willingly entrust their children to Christian schools, in order to teach them Russian."[18]

Notkin believed that the spread of the Russian language among the Jews should be advanced through a system which encouraged enlightened self-interest, rather than through compulsion. Competent Jews who were proficient in Russian should be admitted into the Russian civil service and granted positions in the state ministries, with all the associated ranks and privileges. Notkin's proposal, if enacted, would have created a broad social class of privileged, acculturated Jews similar to himself. The opportunity to obtain a government post would serve as an incentive for Jews to master the state language. Notkin avoided any reference to prohibiting the use of Hebrew in contracts and business records, as was proposed by Derzhavin.

In sum, Notkin offered a vision of the Jews' integration into the Russian state and society, which preserved a degree of their communal autonomy and avoided direct interference by the state in their religious and cultural affairs. Reform could be implemented benevolently, through cooperative action by Jewish leaders and the Imperial authorities, and by opening up new professional and economic opportunities to the Jews.

Conspicuously absent from Notkin's 1803 memorandum to the State Committee was a call for the outright abolition of the Pale of Settlement. Political realism probably prevented him from proposing that Jewish merchants be allowed to reside and trade freely in Moscow and St. Petersburg. Notkin remembered well the public uproar which his own residence in Moscow had created a decade earlier, and must have realized that, given the unfavorable political atmosphere on the Jewish question, it would not be useful to raise such a proposal. Instead, he advanced the more limited proposal of admitting qualified Jews into the Russian civil service. The latter would, by definition, have been entitled to hold state positions in the capital cities and to reside there with their families. But since induction to the "table of ranks" was a privilege controlled by the Imperial court, and awarded on an individual basis, there was no danger that Moscow and St. Petersburg would be flooded with Jewish migrants.[19]

Notkin's memoranda of 1797 and 1803 represented the emergence of a new voice in the political debate surrounding the Jews in Russia—that of the enlightened Jewish reformer. Notkin's point of view differed from that of the established Jewish communal leadership. The kahal leaders, rabbis, and Hasidic *tsadikim* did not share his desire to reform the Jews' education, culture, and position in Russian society; they sought instead to prevent any and all incursions into the Jews' communal autonomy, religious culture, and economic activity. Following the establishment of the State Committee, they anxiously dispatched deputies to St. Petersburg, in accordance with a provision in Alexander's decree on the Committee which permitted them to do so, and the latter used bribes and stalling tactics to thwart the Committee's efforts to reach decisions and draft legislation. Compared to the established Jewish leadership, Notkin could be considered an ally of the Imperial authorities' effort to reform the status of Russian Jewry.[20]

Perets and Nevakhovich: The Quest for Social Acceptance

Notkin was not the only enlightened Jew invited to serve as a deputy to the State Committee; he was apparently joined by Abraham Perets, R. Joshua Zeitlin's son-in-law, who was by then a wealthy, well-connected resident of St. Petersburg in his own right. Although Perets's formal appointment by the Committee is not documented, there is no doubt that he exerted behind-the-scenes influence on its proceedings. Derzhavin complained in his memoirs that Committee member Mikhail Speranskii was "totally devoted to the *zhids*, on account of the well-known merchant Perets." And the enlightened Jewish writer Judah Leyb Nevakhovich, who published the apologetic pamphlet "The Lament of the Daughter of Judah" (Russian 1803, Hebrew 1804) in conjunction with the Committee's deliberations, dedicated its Hebrew edition to Notkin and Perets—suggesting that both acted in the capacity of Jewish deputies.[21]

Perets became a frequent visitor to St. Petersburg after his father-in-law's retirement from active business affairs in 1791, and he settled in the capital around the time that Notkin did, in 1797. With the help of his father-in-law's riches and connections, he established himself as a successful contractor and court purveyor, and secured lucrative state contracts for the construction of ships and the purchase of Crimean salt. In recognition of his financial services to the state, he was awarded the title *komertsii sovetnik* by Tsar Paul I in 1801, and officially entered into the ranks of the Russian civil service.

Perets's extensive business dealings were complemented by an active social life among the St. Petersburg elite. His home was, in the words of one contemporary, "an open house which hosted the entire city," and he developed close friendships with Count I. P. Kutaisov (Paul's favorite), E. F. Kankrin (later Minister of Finance), and especially with Mikhail Speranskii. The Perets-Speranskii friendship was a cause célèbre in Russian high society, as gossip abounded about the Deputy Minister's fraternizing with a Jew. Russian opinion about Perets's character ranged widely. Derzhavin despised him as a parvenu and accused him of having bribed his way to financial and social success. Others were more accepting. "The contractor Perets is a *zhid*, but a kind and truly noble person" observed N. Grech, a Russian contemporary.[22]

Perets attained a higher degree of social integration into Russian court society than had Notkin and Zeitlin before him, and at a much earlier stage in his life. Unlike his predecessors, his interest in Jewish cultural and communal affairs waned after his move to St. Petersburg. Indeed, until his apparent appointment to the State Committee, Perets did not use his high-placed connections to intercede on behalf of Jewish concerns, as Notkin and Zeitlin had done. It is telling, that he, the richest and socially most prominent Jew in the capital, was not one of the wardens of the St. Petersburg Jewish Burial Society, the city's only Jewish communal institution, which was established by Notkin and others in 1802. Perets satisfied his social and cultural needs outside the parameters of the Jewish community. After settling in St. Petersburg, he never returned to Byelorussia.[23]

Perets's growing alienation from Jewry had a poignant personal dimension to it. His wife Feygele did not move to St. Petersburg with him, but chose instead to stay behind at her father's Ustye estate, perhaps sensing that she would find no place for herself in the capital. Husband and wife grew increasingly estranged from each other, and a battle arose between Perets and Zeitlin regarding custody over the couple's son, Hirsh (b. 1790). The boy remained in Ustye, under Zeitlin's supervision, and was educated in Jewish and general disciplines by private tutors, including the Maskil Menahem Mendl Lefin and a Russian aristocrat named Siniavskii. Only after his bar mitzvah, in 1803, did Hirsh move to his father's household in St. Petersburg. At Zeitlin's insistence, Hirsh set out in the accompaniment of his teacher, Lefin, who could serve as a much-needed role model for the combination of tradition and enlightenment. But upon their arrival in the capital, Lefin was replaced by a teacher of Abraham Perets's choosing—a Swiss named Loran. The latter provided the youngster, who was now called by his Russian name Grigorii, with a thorough European education of languages, arts, and sciences, including the works of Voltaire and Adam Smith. No Hebrew tutor was hired.[24]

Abraham Perets's involvement with the State Committee on the Jews, probably as Speranskii's Jewish deputy, was his only foray into Jewish politics. There is no firm information on the positions that he (or, for that matter, Speranskii) took during the Committee's deliberations, since most of its records were later destroyed in a fire. Russian Jewish historians have considered Speranskii, the great Russian liberal and reformer, to have been an ardent Judeophile, and have attributed to him an anonymous, liberal-minded entry in the Committee's journal, which called for "as few restrictions as possible, and as much freedom as possible." If this attribution is correct, it begs the question of Perets's role in the development of Speranskii's thinking.[25]

A more visible role in the debate on the Jewish question was played by Perets's friend and protégé Judah Leyb Nevakhovich (1776–1831). A native of Letishev, in Vohlyn province, Nevakhovich settled in Shklov in 1790 or 1791, and resided there under Perets's patronage. He devoted himself to mastering Russian speech, grammar, and literature, and reportedly tutored his Galician-born patron in these areas. The beauty and profundity of Russian literature affected him deeply, a fact which he acknowledged in the following Hebrew-language testimony.

I, Judah Leyb b. Noah, a child of the Hebrews from the province of Vohlyn, came to dwell under the shade of the wings of Russia. I turned my heart to study and examine the pleasant style of the language of this land, where Judah resides securely. I descended into the garden of its authors and scholars to collect roses—and the branches of their ideas blossomed before me.[26]

Nevakhovich moved to St. Petersburg along with Perets, and continued to enjoy the latter's patronage there. He served as a government translator of Hebrew documents, rendering the petitions and written testimony of R. Shneur Zalman b. Barukh into Russian, during the Hasidic master's second arrest and imprisonment, in 1801.[27] More importantly, he embarked upon a career as a Russian author and playwright, and eventually attained a moderate level of success in that area.

Nevakhovich's public literary debut was his 1803 pamphlet, "The Lament of the Daughter of Judah" (*Vopl dshcheri iudeiskoi*), an impassioned plea to Russian society to cast off its prejudice and discrimination against the Jews. *Vopl* was a landmark literary event, the first book written by a Jew in Russian, and it was eloquently composed in the sentimentalist style of the times, popularized by author Nikolai Karamzin.

The book's emotional duality was presaged in its introductory letter of dedication to Count V. P. Kochubei. On the one hand, Nevakhovich declared his burning love for the Tsar and the Russian fatherland, and his deep admiration for Russia's military prowess and the dawn of its internal renewal. On the other hand, he expressed his depression at the sight of his Jewish brethren, wallowing in sorrow and being rejected by the hearts of their compatriots.[28]

The booklet vacillated between the conflicting emotions of Russian patriotism and Jewish pain, without fully reconciling the two.

Nevakhovich began his pamphlet by celebrating the spirit of progress which had guided Russia since the dawn of the eighteenth century, under Peter the Great, and which was now reaching new heights under Alexander I. He declared his "joy and pride that I can call the Russians my compatriots," and noted with delight that they had "seen the rays of enlightenment, and adopted the spirit of tolerance."[29]

This patriotic enthusiasm also pertained to Imperial policy regarding the Jews. Nevakhovich recalled the suffering which Jews had endured, in the form of blood-libels and student disturbances *(schuler-gelauf)*, in pre-partition Poland, "in the times when Jews did not yet have the joy of being Russian subjects," and he praised Russia for eradicating those abuses.

Only the omnipotent ruler of Russia, Empress Catherine the Great, could lighten the lot of this people, which had previously been the plaything of others' caprices. Under the peaceful protection of the Russian ruler, this persecuted people rested from its previous oppression, and began to feel the full scope of its former misfortune.[30]

Nevakhovich developed the theme of patriotism and gratitude toward the Tsarist Empire in an separate essay which he appended to the *Vopl,* entitled "Feeling of a Loyal Subject on the Occasion of the Establishment by Alexander of the State Committee for the Organization of Jewish Life." The essay glorified the Russian nation for its "gigantic, unfathomable strides as it marches toward moral and political perfection." While conceding that other nations had preceded Russia with advances in science and knowledge, Nevakhovich contended that Russia had preceded all others in the area of tolerance and love of fellow men. Foreigners and members of other faiths were freely admitted into its realm and treated respectfully, in a policy initiated by Peter the Great and continued by Catherine.[31]

Turning specifically to the Jews, Nevakhovich noted that they enjoyed full freedom of religious worship in Russia, that the derogatory appellation *zhid* had been discarded and replaced by the more respectful *evrei,* and that they participated in the institutions of municipal governance, as voters and as elected magistrates. He exclaimed his admiration for the Imperial policy of beneficence toward the Jews.

I will never, never cease praising the kindnesses which the Russian king-dom has poured upon us, the neglected and forsaken the people of Judah. All these graces are engraved in the depths of my heart with unerasable letters. And I will loudly announce them to the nations, as much as my modest strength allows my weak and mortal self to do so.[32]

Comparing Russia with other countries, he derided the French Republic for its hypocritical proclamations of liberty: "A liberty which costs thousands of victims, a liberty which brings with it almost uninterrupted strife, a liberty which is unsettled by the slightest blow of the vicissitudes of fate." In Germany, which boasted of its advancement and enlightenment, Jews "weep and sigh" for being denied permanent rights of residence and trade. "They plead for mercy, to use the rights of ownership, the rights of a subject, the rights of man and the rights of nature."[33]

The essay "Feeling of a Loyal Subject" concluded with an appeal to the Jews of Russia to appreciate their fortunate lot: If our perse-cuted and martyred ancestors could rise from the grave, and would compare their times with ours, they would rejoice with us in our salvation. They would teach us to express our gratitude, and would join us in a prayer of thanksgiving to God for the beneficence of Russia, "the most praiseworthy and meritorious part of mankind."[34]

Nevakhovich's "Lament" did not cry out against the political mistreatment of the Jews in Russia, since he did not believe there was any. It did not ask for the elimination of the disabilities which so troubled Notkin. Instead, it decried the social ostracization of the Jews, and the popular prejudices and biases held against them by Russians. "The very word Jew (*iudei*) produces strange and unor-dinary grimaces in both its utterer and listener. The very word has become abusive, contemptuous, insulting, and frightening for children and the simple-minded."[35] Speaking in the name of reason and tolerance, he asked his Russian compatriots to cast off their blind adherence to inherited biases, and to investigate the subject of the Jews fairly, with an open mind.

Nevakhovich responded to the claim that Jews were, as rejectors of Christ, unworthy of respect and compassion from Christians by quoting passages from Moses Mendelssohn's *Jerusalem*, which argued that a person's religion should not effect his social or civil status, so long as he observed the norms of civil peace and well-being. And he asked rhetorically in a Mendelssohnian vein: "If we repudiated our law in order to attain equal rights, would we thereby render ourselves more dignified?" Religious differences per se were not legitimate grounds for hostility or social exclusion.[36]

The pamphlet then lunged into an assault on the reliability of the sources which perpetuated anti-Jewish prejudices. Foremost among these were the unlettered masses (Russian: *narod*, Hebrew: *hamon*). As a rule, the masses almost never witnessed firsthand the things about which they prattled, and invariably distorted the reports which they heard. Their tales passed orally from person to person, until they bore little or no resemblance to the truth. Nevakhovich did not hide his antiplebeian bias, or, for that matter, his disdain for the French model of republican government. The masses were not to be trusted or believed.

Literary characterizations of the Jews were equally subject to challenge and criticism. Authors could be deceived by their sources, and occasionally exaggerated or fabricated their stories to attract their readers' curiosity. Nevakhovich noted that there was no internal consistency to the accusations against the Jews which one found in books. One author accused the Jews of witchcraft, the next—of atheism, and the next—of superstition. Nevakhovich drew attention to two recent admirable exceptions whose works offered fair and sympathetic depictions of Jews—Nikolai Karamzin's *Notes of a Russian Traveler*, and Ephraim Gotthold Lessing's *Nathan the Wise*.[37]

The *Vopl* called upon Russians to reject their biased sources of information on the Jews, and look upon the latter independently, with fresh eyes and open minds. An honest examination would reveal a people with many virtues.

Oh Christians! You who dwell together with [the Jews] in one land. You must certainly see that good deeds are just as holy to them as they are to you. Notice closely! But with what sort of eyes do you gaze at them? You look for the Jew in the man. Look, rather, for the man in the Jew, and you will certainly find it! If you will only notice, you will see among them a multitude of people who keep their word of honor. You will see a multitude of compassionate people, who give a helping hand to the poor; not only to their own poor, but also to those of other peoples. You will see that many of them magnanimously forgive insults. You will see in them the qualities of gratitude, temperance, and reverence for elders. You will see how sincerely they adore people of other faiths who deal with them kindly, and how reverent they are of the Tsar.[38]

If negative traits were to be found among some Jews, surely a whole nation should not be judged based on the behavior of corrupt individuals. The most honorable Jews were afraid of Christians, and avoided contact with them, due to the centuries of persecution which they had suffered at their hands. Consequently, Christians usually had dealings with the more corrupt elements of the Jewish community.

Nevakhovich conceded that certain depravities were common among the Jews. But he argued, following in the footsteps of Mendelssohn and Dohm, that these traits were themselves the result of long-standing persecution. Moral qualities were not inherent to nations and individuals, but were the outgrowth of education and experience. They were subject to modification and change. In those lands where Jews enjoyed rights and liberty, such as England, Holland, and Prussia, their moral character was outstanding, and admittedly superior to that of their brethren in lands of oppression.[39]

Jewish moral shortcomings could not be laid at the feet of their religion, whose teachings were virtuous. Judaism did not teach enmity toward Gentiles; one of its central ideas was that every person, whether of the Jewish faith or not, was capable of achieving perfection. Judaism commanded that one pray for the welfare of the monarch; it taught that the law of the state was binding upon all, and it prohibited the evasion of taxes and duties. "I swear, that a Jew who truly observes his religion cannot be an evil person or a bad citizen." To bolster this point, Nevakhovich provided a Russian translation of the *Yigdal* hymn, as a specimen of the Jewish liturgy and a summary of Judaism's basic doctrines.[40]

Nevakhovich then entered into a discourse on the purpose and inherent limitations of punishment as a means of social control, and concluded that a people's moral qualities could not be improved through their collective punishment. Such action was cruel and unjust, since it involved inflicting pain on innocent persons. Collective punishment for unspecified misdeeds was also ineffectual and counterproductive, since it would generate bitterness and resistance among the punished group. The only way to improve the morals of a people was to eliminate the external causes which had led them to engage in harmful behavior. In the case of the Jews, the causes were clear—hostility and discrimination from their neighbors.

Nevakhovich concluded his pamphlet with an expression of faith and hope in the Russian people:

I know that changing one's heart and ideas are among the most difficult things on earth. It may demand a century of labor. But I also know that the undertakings of Russians always attain the speediest and almost incredible success. The spirit of the North seeks out great things, and it will establish a shining, new era, in which the manner of thinking about the abused and tearful daughter of Israel will be transformed.[41]

"The Lament of the Daughter of Judah" could not fail to impress its readers as an eloquent work of apologetics. Its author was clearly well versed in the literature of the French Enlightenment, as was evident from his theoretical excurses on moral development, the conflict between prejudice and reason, the uses and misuses of criminal punishment, and other subjects. The pamphlet was punctuated by rich allusions to Russian and world history. As an apologia for the Jews, the work was by no means narrowly construed. It examined the Jewish issue from a broad philosophic and historical perspective.

Precisely these features created certain problems for Nevakhovich when he set out to translate *Vopl* into Hebrew. He found it difficult to render his emotionally laden Russian style and philosophically abstract discourses in Hebrew. Nevakhovich also could not presume the same level of general knowledge among his Jewish readers as he had among his original Russian audience. Literary allusions were therefore explained in copious footnotes, and an introductory essay was added to the Hebrew version, on the history of religious conflict in Europe, the emergence of the idea of tolerance, and the history of Russia from the time of Vladimir the Great until the present.[42]

The Hebrew version of "The Lament of the Daughter of Judah" claimed that it was intended as a manual of Jewish apologetics for those who wished to plead their people's case before Russian officials.[43] But with the help of its notes and introductory essay, it also served as a vehicle for educating Jewish readers about the society in whose midst they lived, and about select ideas of the European Enlightenment. The book's Hebrew version was as much a Haskalah tract as a work of Jewish apologetics.

CHAPTER 6

Rabbinic Accommodation

One striking feature of the Shklov Jewish community in the late eighteenth century is the conspicuous absence of rejectionism toward enlightenment and acculturation by its rabbinic leadership. There were no calls by the rabbis of the community to beware of Gentile science and languages, of rationalism and heresy. While the Maskil Naftali Hirtz Schulman encountered staunch opposition in Vilna (in the 1790s, and again in the 1810s), he published his Maskilic works freely in Shklov, with letters of approbation from the town's communal rabbis.[1]

Indeed, the Shklov community's recognized social and political leaders—Notkin and Zeitlin—were themselves strongly identified with the cause of enlightenment and moderate acculturation. Zeitlin's ties to Berlin and Notkin's proposals for Jewish reform notwithstanding, their relations with Shklov's religious leadership were warm and cordial. Local rabbinic personalities accommodated themselves, to a greater or lesser extent, to the new cultural climate in their community, and did not engage in frontal resistance or opposition. Some of them openly advocated and engaged in the study of science and worldly disciplines themselves.

The willingness of the Shklov rabbinic elite to accommodate acculturation and enlightenment merits close analysis and explication.

The Legacy of the Vilna Gaon

As Shklov developed into as a Jewish economic, political, and cultural center in its own right—during the post-partition period—the

Vilna Gaon played a dominant role in guiding the development of its rabbinic culture. R. Elijah's ties with the "sages of Shklov" were forged in the spring of 1772, when he endorsed their decision to wage war against the Hasidic movement, and led the Vilna community and others into the fray. From that point on, the relationship between the two communities grew and flourished.

The Gaon's teachings were transmitted in Shklov by his close colleague and disciple (and distant cousin), R. Benjamin b. Shlomo Zalman Rivlin (1728–1812). Rivlin, whose father had once represented "the land of Russia" on the va'ad medinat lita, spent many years in Vilna studying with R. Elijah. He then returned home to Shklov and established a yeshiva (according to one report—in 1772), in which the convoluted casuistics of pilpul were rejected in favor of the Gaon's more disciplined and text-critical method of Talmudic study. Besides serving as a center for advanced Talmudic learning in Russia, Rivlin's yeshiva also became a center for transmitting R. Elijah's religious and philosophical worldview.

Writing after R. Elijah's death, the Gaon's sons paid tribute to Rivlin as a loyal and industrious disciple of their father:

> It is he who built the praiseworthy city of Shklov in its place. [Its sages] adopted and took upon themselves many of his [the Gaon's] practices regarding methods of study and the paths of proper observance of the commandments.[2]

Rivlin also adopted his mentor's style of leadership: he assumed no official communal office. He was not the communal rabbi of Shklov—a post held for many years by his brother in law, R. Issachar Ber b. Judah Leyb (d. 1790)—but was rather a private scholar, who headed his own Talmudic academy. Despite his lack of official title, Rivlin's religious authority by far surpassed that of the communal rabbi. He was the guiding spirit behind the anti-Hasidic takkanot issued by the va'ad medinat rusiya in 1787, and of the overall campaign against Hasidism in the Mogilev province.[3]

During the height of the Vilna Gaon's influence in Shklov, in the 1780s, his teachings were also disseminated there on a popular level by his brother, R. Avraham b. Shlomo Zalman (1742–1807), who served as the town's communal preacher. Little is known about

R. Avraham's activity in Shklov, though one can presume that he preached the transcending value of *talmud torah*, a subject which he immortalized in his treatise *Ma'alot ha-torah* (The Virtues of the Torah; Vilna, 1824). Most important of all was the symbolic significance of R. Avraham's presence in Shklov, which solidified and institutionalized the bond between the Shklov community and R. Elijah of Vilna during a crucial transitional period.[4]

Under Rivlin's influence, numerous scholars from Shklov and the Mogilev province became devotees of the Gaon, and sought to be admitted into the latter's exclusive circle of disciples in Vilna. Only a few of them succeeded; foremost among them were the brothers R. Simha Bunem b. Barukh Bendet (d. 1808) and R. Menahem Mendl b. Barukh Bendet (d. 1827), both of whom studied with R. Elijah during his old age. R. Menahem Mendl subsequently returned home to Shklov and, like Rivlin, reportedly headed a yeshiva.[5]

R. Menahem Mendl played a key role in arranging the publication of the Gaon's writings and teachings following his death. R. Elijah's sons and the rabbinic court of Vilna—which issued a ban against publishing purported teachings of the Gaon without obtaining their prior approval—recognized him as the authorized editor and/or publisher of several of the Gaon's works. He proceeded to publish the latter's notes and commentaries on the Book of Proverbs (1798), *Seder 'olam rabah* (1801), the *Orah hayyim* section of the *Shulhan 'arukh* (1803), and Tractate *avot* (1804)—all of which were printed in Shklov—as well as on the Passover Hagadah (1805) and kabbalistic tract *Sefer yetsirah* (1806), which were published in Grodna.[6]

As a scholar in his own right, R. Menahem Mendl was best known as a kabbalist, and composed ten original treatises in that field. He claimed to have had supernal revelations from heaven, as well as from the departed soul of his master, R. Elijah.[7]

Another local scholar who was admitted into the Gaon's circle was R. Israel b. Shmuel (d. 1839), who attended to R. Elijah on his deathbed, during the last days and weeks of his life. R. Israel returned to Shklov after his master's death, and gave *shiurim* there for the next ten years—probably in R. Menahem Mendl's yeshiva. He also assisted R. Menahem Mendl in preparing for publication the Gaon's notes on the *Orah hayyim* section of the *Shulhan 'arukh*

(1803), and edited independently the Gaon's notes on the *Yore de'ah* section (Grodna, 1806).[8]

R. Israel's reputation was first and foremost as a Talmudist, and he inherited from his master a keen interest in those sections of Talmudic literature and halakhah which had been historically neglected by scholars. He composed a commentary on the Tractate *Shekalim* of the Jerusalem Talmud (*Taklin hadetin;* Minsk, 1812), and a discursive code on the agricultural laws of the land of Israel (*Pe'at ha-shulhan;* Safed, 1836). Both works incorporated textual and analytic notes by the Gaon on the relevant tractates of the Jerusalem Talmud, prepared for publication by R. Israel.[9]

Taken together, the circle of devotees and disciples of the Vilna Gaon in Shklov was one of the most intensive and creative centers of rabbinic learning in Eastern Europe in the late eighteenth/early nineteenth centuries. Not for naught was it later referred to as "the Yavneh of Byelorussia."

The Gaon and the Sciences—Through His Disciples' Eyes

One of the ideas transmitted in the Shklov circle was the Gaon's legitimation of the study of science and worldly disciplines. R. Elijah himself composed treatises on the mathematical sciences and Hebrew grammar,[10] and his preoccupation with these disciplines and others was commented upon by several of his intimates. It is worth reviewing their statements, which illuminate the figure of the Gaon himself, as well as the disciples' reception of his ideas.

The first written comment on the subject was by R. Avraham Danziger, R. Elijah's in-law and author of the halakhic code *Haye adam* (Life of Man), in a eulogy written shortly after the latter's death.

The holy temple contained the menorah, which symbolized the Torah. And the seven lights of the menorah symbolized the seven sciences [*hokhmot*], all of which emanate from the Torah. The saintly Gaon was versed in all the sciences. Who was greater than he in grammar, mathematics, and theology [*hokhmat elohut*]? Woe unto us, for we have lost a pure menorah![11]

R. Menahem Mendl of Shklov, writing just a few years later, paid tribute to his master in similar terms:

Who can speak of the limits of his knowledge and his marvels in the sciences, how he knew all of them thoroughly! [He knew] for instance the science of music, which he cited in his commentary to the *Tikune zohar*, and other sciences, on which he left behind treatises. All served as "spices and herbs" for the science of our holy Torah.[12]

These testimonies referred to R. Elijah's non-Talmudic studies as one of the more striking features of his personality, and as further proof of his intellectual greatness. But they did not dwell upon the question of how these studies related to his religious worldview. R. Menahem Mendl's reference to the sciences as "spices and herbs to the Torah" indicates that they served to supplement, enhance, and enrich the "main dish" of his intellectual menu—Torah study, but just how they did so was not specified.

The matter was clarified in a later testimony by R. Israel b. Shmuel of Shklov:

He [the Gaon] said that all the sciences *[hokhmot]* were needed for our Torah and were included in it. He knew them all fully, and would refer to them—algebra, trigonometry, geometry, and music, which he praised greatly. He used to say that one could not know the meaning of the Torah cantilations, the mysteries of the songs of the Levites, and the mysteries of *Tikune zohar* without it.[13]

According to this testimony, the Gaon considered the sciences to be of instrumental value in elucidating the Torah. One could not fully understand Judaism's sacred texts—whether it be the Pentateuch ("the cantilations"), the Psalms ("songs of the Levites"), the Talmud, or the Zohar—unless one was knowledgeable in various worldly disciplines, such as mathematics and music. Indeed since these disciplines were indispensable for the Torah's study, they ought to be considered part and parcel of it.

The same point was underscored in an even later testimony by R. Avraham Simha of Mtsislavl, a nephew of the Gaon's greatest disciple, R. Hayyim of Volozhin. R. Avraham Simha drew attention, inter alia, to yet another area of the Gaon's interest—ancient Jewish historiography.

I heard explicity from the holy tongue of my uncle, the saintly Rabbi Hayyim of Volozhin, that our master [the Gaon] told his son R. Abraham, that he longed for the translation of the sciences from other languages into our holy tongue, and for the translation of the Latin Josephus. For it would enable us to comprehend the intent of our sages in the Talmud and Midrash, who spoke in many places about matters related to the Holy land.[14]

The idea that the sciences could serve as handmaidens to Torah was, of course, not new in itself. The utility of geometry and mathematics for studying various topics in the Talmud (e.g., the laws of *eruv* and *sukkah*) was well-known and widely accepted. In Poland's golden age (1550–1648), entire rabbinic treatises had been devoted to mathematical topics in Talmudic literature, such as R. Jacob Kopelman's *'Omek halakha* (The Depths of Halakhah; Cracow, 1593). Hebrew grammar was also recognized for its instrumental value for Torah study, although it was, in fact, neglected by most Polish rabbinic scholars. But R. Elijah cast the issue much more widely than any of his predecessors. *All* sciences and disciplines— including music and ancient Latin literature, which had never been studied by Polish rabbinic scholars, and had rarely attracted the attention of Sephardic ones—were necessary for the illumination of hallowed texts. The ideal Talmudist needed to be proficient in more than just one or two disciplines; he needed to be a veritable renaissance man. This was the Gaon's novel conceptual breakthrough.

This idea was expressed not only secondhand, by R. Elijah's disciples and followers. R. Elijah expressed it himself, to R. Barukh Schick, when the latter visited him in 1778: "For every deficiency of knowledge a man has in the sciences *[hokhmah]*, he will have ten deficiencies of knowledge in the science of the Torah. For Torah and science are closely related."[15]

The Gaon's statement contained an implicit criticism of those rabbinic scholars, past and present, whose knowledge of the sciences was deficient. This was very much in keeping with the Gaon's critical and independent stance toward earlier rabbinic scholarship: R. Elijah offered his own textual emendations to troublesome Talmudic passages, in utter disregard for the way they had been read by centuries of predecessors; he sharply opposed the popular method of *pilpul*, which generated imaginative analogies and artificial distinctions; and his practical halakhic rulings were based on an independent analysis of the Talmudic sources, and diverged frequently from tradition and precedent—including the ruling of the *Shulhan 'arukh* itself. R. Elijah was a rebel and a revolutionary in the field of rabbinic scholarship. The incorporation of the arts and sciences into rabbinics was one further aspect of his revolution.[16]

While embracing the sciences as an object of study, R. Elijah did not endow them with independent value, and did not view science or reason as the cornerstone of his worldview. He was a staunch opponent of rationalist philosophy, and considered Aristotle a "total heretic . . . who believed that the world operated according to nature." As a committed kabbalist, he chided Maimonides for "not having seen the pleasure-garden," that is, the esoteric teachings of the Kabbalah. Indeed, the Gaon claimed to have had supernatural illuminations from angels and from Elijah the prophet, and told one of his disciples that he was proficient in the esoteric art of creating a golem.[17] The Gaon drew a clear line of separation between reason and theology. Science was a discrete body of knowledge on certain aspects of the material world, and not a method or approach through which to examine *all* of reality.

Just as R. Elijah was no rationalist, he was also no emancipationist or social reformer. He did not envision that the study of the arts and sciences would improve the position of Jews in society or bring about changes in Jewish–Gentile relations. Enlightenment and acculturation were far from his mind, and were not on the agenda of the Vilna Jewish community in his day.[18]

All of this notwithstanding, the Gaon's legitimation of the study of the arts and sciences was a fact, and it assumed broader social significance in Shklov than in Vilna. In Shklov, enlightenment and acculturation were very much on the communal agenda. The rabbis of Shklov grappled with the new cultural and intellectual trends which engulfed their community, and evaluated them through the prism of R. Elijah's words and deeds. It is certainly no coincidence that two of the Gaon's disciples from Shklov (R. Menahem Mendl and R. Israel), and one peripheral associate from Shklov (R. Barukh Schick), drew attention to R. Elijah's study of the sciences, whereas others, such as his sons and his foremost disciple, R. Hayyim of Volozhin, had nothing to say on the subject. In Shklov, the Gaon's words and deeds on science were charged with relevance and meaning.

Following in the Gaon's path, the "sages of Shklov" arrived at a cautious mode of accommodation: They responded favorably to the flourish of science, literature, and wisdom which developed in their midst, but refused to countenance the libertinism and self-indulgence which were characteristic of Russian court culture. They certainly did not envision that science and reason would impinge upon the foundations of religious faith and practice.

R. Benjamin Rivlin: Talmudist and Scientist

R. Benjamin Rivlin himself was the foremost representative of this path of limited, fragmentary accommodation.

In his small volume of novellae on the Bible and Talmud, *Geviei gevia ha-kesef* (The Goblet of Silver; Shklov, 1804), Rivlin gave voice to a religious worldview in which Torah study was the axis and very purpose of human life: The ideal period in a man's lifetime was his youth, when he could devote himself entirely to Torah study, without the distractions of family and livelihood. Subsequent years were a time of "decline." Torah study was superior to all other commandments, including prayer. In a barely veiled attack on Hasidism, Rivlin derided a nameless person "who prattled against me, by saying that his pure prayers were more beloved unto God than Torah." He lashed out at "those who mock Torah students that have not attained the virtuous character traits enumerated by our Sages." There was no mistaking Rivlin's staunch Talmudism and Mitnagdism.[19]

Like his master, the Vilna Gaon, Rivlin's rabbinist outlook was laced with a moderate dose of asceticism. The Torah could only be mastered if one resisted one's material desires, including the lusts for food, drink, wealth, fine clothing, and a good home. Eating and drinking were to be indulged in only as much as was necessary to acquire the energy for Torah study. Subduing and sublimating one's desires was central to the Torah's way of life.[20]

Rivlin encapsuled his combination of Talmudism and asceticism in his citation and interpretation of the following Midrash:

"Give wisdom to the wise" (Daniel 2:21). The verse should have said "Give wisdom to the fools." But the fools meditate on it in lavatories and theaters, and the wise study it in the house of study. (Ecclesiastes Rabbah 1:5)

Rivlin offered the following adumbration: It is pointless for God to give wisdom to those who spend their time in impure places such as theaters and lavatories, devoting themselves to the pursuit of pleasure. Torah and wisdom can only endure in a person who rejects worldly pleasures. Citing Proverbs 21:17, he remarked:

The fool loves two things—joy, and wine and oil. The Talmud, Tractate *berahot*, refers to the human body as a house. . . . One may therefore, by analogy, refer to the body of a person who loves joy as a theater house, and to the body of the person who loves wine and oil as a lavatory. But the body of the wise should be referred to as a house of study.[21]

It is perhaps not coincidental that Rivlin elaborated upon this Midrash, which highlighted the foolishness and vanity of the theater house in contrast to the sanctity of the rabbinic house of study. His words may be read as an oblique reference to the frivolity of Zorich's theater, and a polemic against those Jews who were enamored by its milieu.

Rivlin's pursuit of the rabbinist-ascetic ideal was described by Mordechai Nathanson, who came to know him toward the end of his life. He recalled how Rivlin refrained from eating meat and from drinking wine and alcoholic beverages, even on the Sabbath and holidays, and offered the following portrait of his devotion to Talmudic learning.

He studied all day and all night, with a leaden reed always in his hand, so as to write down his comments in the margins of his books. He used to quote the saying "may the reed be your companion" *(kaneh lekha haver;* a play on Avot 1:6). When he grew tired, we, the residents of the household, would read to him aloud,and he would anticipate the words from memory, while lying on his bed. When he fell asleep and his lips rustled, we departed. And when he awoke, he washed his hands, and returned to his studies.[22]

But Nathanson also recalled that there was a worldly side to Rivlin's personality—his study of the sciences. While heading his yeshiva, R. Benjamin had been a merchant of pharmaceutical goods, and became an expert on botany, minerology, pharmacology, and the natural sciences during the course of his commercial career. Nathanson remarked:

He was an observer of nature, and used to speak about the trees, the stones, all the animals and insects. In the summers, he would take strolls for several hours each day, and collect grasses, roots, and flowers, which he would dry out and make into medicines, according to the science of pharmacology. He knew it well, from the books of Gentile scholars in their language, just as he knew all aspects of the natural sciences.[23]

It is this aspect of R. Benjamin's profile which led to the close association and friendship between him and Joshua Zeitlin. Following his retirement from business and the yeshiva, Rivlin spent his final years on Zeitlin's Ustye estate, as a scholar-in-residence, and it is there that Nathanson—who was Zeitlin's son-in-law—made his acquaintance. Rivlin embodied the combination of Torah and worldly learning which Zeitlin endorsed as an ideal. The two men were a perfect match for each other.

Nathanson related that R. Benjamin practiced medicine, and described how he took his patients' pulse, administered bandages, and prescribed medications. When Zeitlin fell ill, he called for Rivlin, rather than for a professionally trained physician. This combination of the roles of Talmudist and physician was extremely rare and unusual in the East European Jewish milieu. It signified a new social model, in which the mastery of Talmudic and secular learning were joined together.[24]

In scope and sophistication, Rivlin's scientific knowledge actually surpassed that of his teacher, the Vilna Gaon. The Gaon once confessed to his disciples that he had been unable to master the arts of medicine and pharmacology, because they were too time-consuming and would have distracted him from his Torah study.[25] Rivlin was expert in those very disciplines. Moreover, R. Elijah's study of the arts and sciences was limited to works available to him in Hebrew, since he did not read Latin or German. (His enthusiasm for the translation of books of wisdom into Hebrew was, in part, a reflection of his own linguistic limitations.) Rivlin did not suffer from this handicap, and studied, in Nathanson's words, "the books of Gentile scholars in their language."[26]

But in his overall view of the relationship between science and Judaism, Rivlin remained a loyal disciple of the Gaon. He utilized his knowledge of science to elucidate rabbinic texts, and drew upon "the books on the Gentiles" and "the books of nature" to compose *hidushe torah* (novellae), some of which were included in *Geviei gevia ha-kesef*.

The following two items may serve as illustrations of Rivlin's scientific *hidushim:*
(a) The Talmud, Shabbat 152a, relates an exchange between the Emperor and R. Joshua b. Hanania. When the Emperor asked R. Joshua why he had not attended the forum, the latter replied, "the mountain is snowy, it is surrounded by ice, the dog does not bark, and the grinders do not grind." Commentaries on the passage took this reply as a series of metaphorical expressions by R. Joshua about his old age and failing health. As Rashi explained: "The mountain is snowy—my head is white; it is surrounded by ice—my mustache and beard have whitened; the dog does not bark—my voice cannot be heard; the grinders—my teeth [do not grind]." Rivlin offered an alternative to Rashi's interpretation, based on his reading of books of anatomy.

"The dog does not bark." . . . It is difficult to say that the holy voice of our Sages would be referred to with this term. And I found in the books of the Gentiles that the large teeth opposite one's eyes are called "the dog teeth," because they are larger and sharper than the rest, like the teeth of a dog. Thus "the dog" and "the grinders" both refer to the same subject [i.e., teeth].[27]

(b) The Zohar (II, 163b) states that "a sinful person does not grow strong until he kills a man." Faced with this puzzling and implausible statement, Rivlin offered a textual emendation based on his knowledge of zoology.

It appears to me that one should correct the text to read "an animal [*hayuta* instead of *hayava*] does not grow strong until it kills a man". . . . I found in the books of nature that there is a certain animal called the Hyena which is very strong and can live without bread or nourishment for several days. And when it tastes human flesh it can destroy an entire city.[28]

Elsewhere in *Geviei gevia ha-kesef,* Rivlin drew upon his experience as a physician to elucidate the Midrashic comment that "one should not study quickly and in haste. There was once a person who studied in haste, grew ill, and forgot his lesson." He cited the case history of a patient he had seen, who knew the entire Mishna by heart, and would recite it from memory at great speed—a practice which caused him to hyperventilate and grow faint. Rivlin also employed mathematical calculations and geometric diagrams in several passages.[29]

Such scientific tidbits strike the modern reader as intellectually narrow and unimpressive, but they were extremely innovative from the perspective of the East European rabbinic tradition. In eighteenth-century Eastern Europe, there were few precedents for a rabbinic author citing "the books of the Gentiles" and "books of nature" in his *hidushe torah*.

Thanks to Rivlin's prominence and prestige, scientific *hidushim* became quite popular among Shklov's rabbinic scholars. One such *hidush*, by Joshua Zeitlin's son Moshe, was displayed on the verso title page of the Vilna Gaon's glosses to the *'Orakh Hayyim* section of the *Shulhan 'arukh* (popularly referred to as the *bi'ur ha-gra*), published in Shklov in 1803. This large folio volume was a landmark publication of one of the Gaon's most important works; it was edited by R. Elijah's sons, under the supervision of R. Menahem Mendl b. Barukh Bendet, and with the participation of R. Israel b. Shmuel. Printed just beneath the introduction by R. Hayyim of Volozhin was R. Moshe Zeitlin's explication of the Gaon's view on the duration of sunrise. The symbolic prominence of the location given to this scientific *hidush* by the editors was probably not lost upon readers.[30]

Rabbinic animadversions of this kind were psychologically and ideologically important to Shklov's rabbinic elite, because they "proved" that Talmudists could play the game of science just as well as their enlightened brethren and Gentile neighbors. Scientific *hidushim* served to bolster rabbinic social prestige in a community swept by worldly intellectual pursuits, while at the same time reaffirming the primacy of Torah as an object of study and as the foundation of their worldview. The genre was moderately progressive, since it accommodated Torah study to the spirit of the times, and yet, it was essentially conservative, since it subordinated science to the purposes of Torah study. It was the perfect vehicle of creativity for the disciples of the Vilna Gaon in Shklov.

R. Judah Leyb Margoliot: In Search of a Middle Road

A stance similar to Rivlin's was adopted by R. Judah Leyb Margoliot (1747–1811), a traveling Galician rabbi who resided in Shklov in

1785–86, where he composed and published his treatise *Bet midot* (House of Virtues). Margoliot was a known rabbinic author, who had published a volume of responsa, works of ethical and religious instruction, as well as a textbook on the natural sciences prior to his arrival in Shklov. His involvement in the study of science was probably an outgrowth of his visits to Berlin in the 1770s, during which he made the personal acquaintance of Moses Mendelssohn.[31]

In the 1780s, Margoliot became a wandering teacher-preacher, who instructed his audiences in "Talmud, codes, Bible, and 'agadah, as well as the seven sciences and the study of the universe." It was only natural for such an individual to travel to Shklov, despite its distance from Galicia, since the town was known as a burgeoning Jewish cultural center with ties to Berlin. He could have expected to find a receptive audience there, as indeed he did. Margoliot preached to the Shklov community, composed and printed his book *Bet midot* there, and found financial support for his activities.[32]

Bet midot was no run-of-the-mill moralistic tract. As its printer, Zvi Hirsh b. Arye Margoliot (apparently no relation to the author) pointed out in his preface, the book made medieval Jewish rationalist literature accessible to contemporary readers for the first time. He observed that in most cities, one could hardly find a single copy of R. Sayda Ga'on's *'Emunot ve-de'ot*, R. Joseph Albo's *'Ikkarim*, or R. Isaac 'Arama's *'Akedat yitshak*—works upon which Margoliot's treatise was based. And even if one found a copy of these works, they were written in a difficult language and style which rendered them incomprehensible. *Bet midot* was an indispensable guide to this literature, which cited, explained, and paraphrased some of its key passages. In his author's introduction, Margoliot added Aristotle's *Ethics* and *Physics*, and Maimonides' *Guide to the Perplexed* to the list of sources.[33]

Bet midot touched upon several themes found in classical and Jewish philosophical literature. It opened with a discussion of the relative value of intellectual and moral perfection, and sided, perhaps unsurprisingly for a preacher, with the latter. The book's second "chamber" (as its section headings were called) dealt with the virtue of love, and began by clarifying the difference between the Platonic and Aristotelian conceptions of love. The volume was replete with citations of philosophic literature, while references to the Zohar and works of Kabbalah were conspicuously absent.[34]

But the focus of *Bet midot* was ethical, rather than philosophic per se. Margoliot established that love of God was Judaism's central ethical commandment, and most of the book explored how, when, where, and by what means this commandment ought to be fulfilled.[35] Indeed, Margoliot warned *against* the study of philosophy proper, by which he meant the rational investigation of matters of theology and religious faith. Citing Rabenu Tam and R. Asher b. Yehiel, he contended that the dangers of such activity were greater than any purported benefits. Philosophy did not enhance one's love or fear of God, but, on the contrary, weakened them. Margoliot limited his citations of R. Sayda, Maimonides, Albo, and 'Arama to matters of ethics, and assiduously avoided dealing with theology in *Bet midot*.[36]

But within these clearly circumscribed parameters, Margoliot championed the causes of reason and science. He attacked the anti-rationalism and anti-intellectualism of the "fools" who held "that wisdom contradicts faith, and the more a person is wise, the more he will rebel against faith." These individuals failed to distinguish between philosophy and science. Whereas the former was fraught with dangers to one's faith, study of the latter was mandated by rabbinic tradition and law.

For the disciplines of astronomy and mathematics (which is the former's foundation) belong to us, and knowledge of them is incumbent upon us. . . . If R. Elijah Mizrahi [a sixteenth-century Turkish rabbi] and R. Yom Tov Lipman Heller [an early seventeenth-century Polish rabbi] had considered the study of astronomy and mathematics improper, they would not have dealt with these matters and written books about them.
It is revealed and well known that the foundations of these sciences belonged to us. But because we were exiled from our land and became helpless, our wisemen lost their wisdom. It is not proper to drive away the Israelite person from the sciences, which are needed for God's Torah and the welfare of society [*yishuv ha-'olam*].[37]

With the Talmudic phrase *yishuvo shel 'olam*, Margoliot apparently alluded to the practical, everyday benefits which accrued from familiarity with science and technology. He also argued that there was a pressing social need for Jews to be no less versed in such matters than the Gentiles. In language reminiscent of R. Barukh Schick, he argued:

For it does not befit the honor of the Lord's religion and congregation for us to be fools in the eyes of the Gentiles, and to be considered like wild beasts. Does the Lord wish for [the sciences] to be honored in the hearts of our enemies, and for us to be considered fools and idiots? And what will be with the verse "for it is your wisdom and understanding in the eyes of the nations" (Deut. 4:6)?[38]

Margoliot was painfully aware of the Jews' inferiority in this area, and was concerned that their ignorance would be harmful to their social image and standing. This concern was shared by many in his host community of Shklov.

While eager to disseminate worldly knowledge, and ensure that Jews not be considered "fools and idiots," Margoliot was sharply critical of those in Jewish society who adopted Gentile patterns of behavior indiscriminately. He lashed out at the appearance of so-cial circles whose members gathered in the evenings to drink tea and coffee and listen to music, who wore Gentile clothing, and taught their children French and mathematics, rather than Torah. All of this was beyond the pale of proper behavior.[39] Margoliot did not seek a broad-based cultural rapprochement between Jews and Gentiles. Much like R. Barukh Schick, he internalized the Haska-lah's rationalism and science, but rejected its broader tendency toward acculturation.[40]

Hasidic Rejectionism and Enlightened Mitnagdism

Whereas Shklov's rabbinic personalities carefully balanced their acceptance of science and worldly learning against their rejection of broad acculturation, their Hasidic rivals in the Polotsk province enunciated a philosophy of comprehensive rejectionism: Gentiles, their wisdom, and their ways were to be avoided at all costs.

The issue was addressed in a number of letters sent by the leader of Byelorussian Hasidism, R. Menahem Mendl of Vitebsk, from Pal-estine to his followers in Russia. Writing in early 1785, R. Menahem

Mendl lamented that the Russian government had "drawn close to the Jews, to equalize them, God forbid, with Gentiles in several matters." He was alluding to the Imperial decision to consider the Jews as members of the urban estates and to integrate them into the system of municipal governance, both as voters and elected officials. R. Menahem Mendl chastized his followers for participating in the Gentiles' elections (which were conducted in Byelorussia in 1784), and for serving on the magistrates:

The Israelites were redeemed from Egypt by merit of the fact that they did not change their names and language, and did not agree in their hearts to recognize the Egyptian rulers. . . . But you have done otherwise. You have chosen chieftains to head you, and have drawn yourselves close to the Gentiles' practices, sincerely and in your hearts. You considered them proper, and adopted their practices and laws yourselves.[41]

From R. Menahem Mendl's perspective, the Jews were obligated to maintain their political and institutional segregation from the Gentiles.

Several months later, R. Menahem Mendl raised a related issue, warning the Hasidim in Byelorussia to avoid social relations with Gentiles: "Do not walk on one road with them, and may your feet avoid their path, for this is the root of a deadly poison." One must beware of gazing upon Gentiles, or eating with them; contact should be restricted to whatever interaction was necessary in business dealings. R. Menahem Mendl warned of the slippery slope which would result from social contact:

When a Jew first draws close to them, he violates the commandment of "Thou shalt not show mercy unto them" (Deut. 7:2), which the Sages interpret to mean "thou shalt not view them with favor" ('Avoda zara 20a). For once he considers their ways proper, he eats their bread, then drinks their wine, then takes their daughters, and then, God forbid, something else . . .

R. Menahem Mendl also referred to the issue of Gentile wisdom.

The sages' statement on the verse "and his leaf will not whither" (Ps. 1:3) is well known: even the casual conversation of Jewish scholars needs to be studied (Succah 21b), for it is greater than all the secular sciences (hokhmot hitzoniyot). This is known to whoever has eyes that are open to all of God's ways.

The blind ones, however, do not comprehend the sanctity of the Torah, "and consider it to be similar to the teachings of the Gentiles, God forbid."[42]

R. Menahem Mendl reiterated his warnings in a letter to R. Shneur Zalman b. Barukh, written in early 1786, in which he appointed the latter leader of Byelorussian Hasidism. One of his charges to R. Shneur Zalman was to "distance them [the Hasidim] from the practices of the Gentiles and their teachings as much as possible."[43]

On this matter, there was total agreement between R. Menahem Mendl and R. Shneur Zalman. The latter included a prohibition against the study of worldly wisdom in his first published work, the halakhic manual *hilkhot talmud torah:*

It is forbidden to study worldly sciences, as it is said: "you shall speak of them [these words]," and you shall not mix other words with them. Even someone who has already studied the entire Torah should not say, "I have studied the wisdom of Israel, so now I will go study the wisdom of the nations." For it is written, "you shall observe my ordinances and follow them"; you have no right to rid yourself of them. And needless to say, a scholar is obligated to observe [the commandment of] "and you shall meditate upon them day and night" literally. Let him go out and find an hour that is neither day nor night to study [those sciences].[44]

In his theological-ethical treatise *Likute amarim-Tanya*, R. Shneur Zalman added that the impurity of Gentile sciences was greater than the impurity of idle chatter, because preoccupation with the sciences defiled the highest Divine attributes in a person's soul—the attributes of wisdom, discernment, and knowledge *(habad)*.[45]

R. Menahem Mendl's and R. Shneur Zalman's admonitions against having contact with Gentiles, following their practices, and studying their sciences, were not issued in a social vacuum, as purely theoretical pronouncements. They were issued in response to the social and cultural changes in Byelorussian Jewry at the time. Both men were aware of the strong Enlightenment tendency in the Shklov Jewish community, and of the model set by Rivlin, Zeitlin, and others in combining Torah and worldly science. By enjoining their followers to avoid contact with Gentiles and Gentile science,

R. Menahem Mendl and R. Shneur Zalman were warning them not to follow the path of their rabbinist-Mitnagdic rivals to the south. The issue of how to relate to the study of science and worldly disciplines thus became a bone of contention between the leaders of the Hasidic and Mitnagdic camps.

On the Mitnagdic side of the divide, rabbinic figures criticized the Hasidic leaders for their opposition to the study of science, and for their frequent reliance on supernaturalism. The most extensive and penetrating polemic of this kind was offered by R. Barukh Schick, whose father, we should recall (see above, p. 8), had been hounded out of Shklov by violent, aggressive Hasidim.

In his introduction to *Uklides*, Schick hurled a variety of barbs against those "who totally despise all wisdom and science, whatever it may be." The very worst members of this category were "the hidden ones *[ha-tsenu'im]* who wrap themselves in the garb of a 'hasid,' a modest man and a rabbi." Schick's description of them leaves no doubt that he was referring to the Hasidic *tsadikim* (masters). The latter were the epitome of spiritual arrogance, believing that they were, quite literally, the center of the universe, and that all others were obligated to serve them.

In their hearts, they believe that the whole world was created to follow their commands, to carry them on their shoulders, and to sit at their feet. . . . The order of creation was established for their sake. Any person who has been blessed by God with wealth and riches, and does not deliver all his money to them, is guilty of a great sin in their eyes. It is as if he stole money from them. . . . The heavens were created for them, to shine upon them, and the entire world exists in their merit.[46]

This was a caustic Mitnagdic caricature of the doctrine of the *tsadik* as "foundation of the world."

Schick went on to accuse the *tsadikim* of inciting division and conflict in Jewish communities, of showing contempt toward Talmudists, and scheming to depose rabbis. His tirade culminated in a prayer "that the earth open its mouth and devour these sinful people, as it devoured Korach. For their evil is greater than that of Korach."[47]

These were commonplace accusations in the Mitnagdic polemics of the day. But Schick raised them in passing, in the context of a new charge, which had not been mentioned in previous pamphlets and writs of excommunication: the Hasidic leaders were the mortal enemies of science. They were absolute anti-intellectualists and obscurantists, who harbored a visceral hatred of *all* learning and scholarship, whether it was Talmudic or scientific. Their spiritual arrogance made it impossible for them to tolerate wisemen and scholars of any kind.

They arrogantly despise everyone who they hear possesses any positive trait or wisdom. Most of all do they despise anyone who they are told is a great scholar of Torah. For they think to themselves: Who has the audacity to be more wise than them? . . . They say: "There is no one other than me, the earth is mine, I will go forth in battle against all the wisemen."[48]

According to Schick, the Hasidic leaders considered the "wise-man"—here apparently meaning the student of science—to be "a deceiver who neglects the worship of heaven." They were quick to brand him a disbeliever and heretic, "even if his intention was the very opposite, to uphold the law." The Hasidic leaders, as well as other opponents of wisdom in Jewish society, were responsible for chasing numerous Jews away from the study of science, "thereby striking them with blindness, and rendering them an object of scorn and derision in the eyes of the nations."[49]

Schick's critique of Hasidism fused together the traditional Mit-nagdic charge that the Hasidim had contempt for Torah study and Torah scholars, with the later Maskilic charge that they despised science and enlightenment. He asserted, or at least implied, that Talmudists and scientists were natural allies, because both were engaged in advancing wisdom and knowledge, and also faced abuse at the hands of a common enemy—the Hasidim. In this manner, the Mitnagdic and Maskilic critiques of Hasidism were woven into one fabric.

Schick's invocation of the Vilna Gaon, later in the same intro-duction to *Uklides*, was part of this polemical argument. He cited the Gaon's words in praise of studying the sciences not only for their intrinsic value, but also in order to contrast the combination of Torah and science advocated by the towering leader of the Mit-nagdic camp, with the enmity toward both Torah and science exhibited by the leaders of the Hasidic camp. From Schick's perspective as well, the issue of science was one that divided Hasidim and Mitnagdim.[50]

Other rabbinic proponents of science were troubled by a related aspect of Hasidism: the movement's penchant for supernaturalism and miracle claims. R. Judah Leyb Margoliot directly challenged the veracity of Hasidic miracles in *Bet midot*.

> There are those disreputable *ba'ale shem* who wish to be thought of as men of God. They perform marvels before women and the light-headed through devious falsifications and lies. And as they falsify, they invoke the Royal seal [i.e., the name of God]. Especially in our generation, when so many of the hidden mysteries of nature have been uncovered, it is easy for an evil person to trick others into believing that he is a miracle-worker.[51]

Margoliot offered the following examples of fake "miracles": a person could use scientific devices to predict the future (such as knowing whether it will rain by using a barometer); he could use mirrors and telescopes to see concealed objects, and megaphones to project voices and sounds. Margoliot prayed that "God save us from such perversities, and enable us to examine all deeds with true deliberation."[52]

The rejection of Hasidic miracles as hoaxes was not commonplace in Mitnagdic polemics. The topic was absent from most bans, letters of condemnation, and pamphlets, because the Mitnagdim themselves did not question the occurrence of miracles. Their leader, the Vilna Gaon, claimed that he had various supernatural powers, including the ability to create a golem; he said that he had once actually begun creating one, but was ordered from heaven to cease and desist. The Gaon also spoke of having had illuminations from Elijah the prophet and angels. There was no aversion to the supernatural per se in the Mitnagdic camp. R. Elijah's disciple R. Menahem Mendl of Shklov was quite explicit about the matter: "Even in our time, the Lord performs great marvels for the saintly and pious."[53]

When the question of Hasidic miracles was broached by the Mitnagdic polemicist R. Israel Loebel, he argued merely that the ability to perform marvels was not, in itself, proof of one's piety or the truthfulness of one's teachings. Many false prophets, from the sorcerers in Egypt down to Shabbetai Zevi, had performed such acts. If the Hasidic "rabeyim" (as he called them) made miracles, it was no doubt through their use of sorcery and witchcraft. R. Menahem Mendl of Shklov argued, similarly, that the Hasidic leaders knew the "secret of the impure electrum [hashmal de-tumah]; from this you should understand whence their prophecy comes."[54]

Margoliot's condemnation of the bogus miracles wrought by ba'ale shem was not a traditional Mitnagdic critique at all, but an enlightened, Maskilic one. It was an outgrowth of his immersion in the study of natural science, and an expression of his rationalist worldview. In fact, the section on miracles was one of the few passages in his book which was praised by the Berlin Maskil Aaron Halle Wolfsohn, in his otherwise disappointed and critical review of Bet midot in Ha-me'asef.[55]

Hasidic miracles were likewise dismissed as nonsense in the text of the Shklov ordinances against the Hasidic sect, issued by the va'ad medinat rusiya in 1787. In decrying the recent publication of Hasidic books (the first printed Hasidic work, Toledot ya'akov yosef, was printed in 1780), the ordinances took note of their incredulous contents.

All of their books are against the holy Torah and follow a crooked path. Especially the exaggerations and miracle stories [ma'ase nisim] which are told in their books. These are blatant and well-known lies. God forbid that we should believe in such nonsense [divre habai].[56]

The Shklov ordinances were written by none other than R. Benjamin Rivlin, who, as we have seen, was a rabbinic scientist of the first order. Like Schick and Margoliot, his involvement in science led him to develop an enlightened variant of Mitnagdism, which attacked the sect not only from traditional perspectives, but from a modern, "scientific" one as well.

CHAPTER 7

Decline and Dissolution

The growth and flourishing of Shklov as a Jewish cultural center was the result of a confluence of factors: the severing of the Mogilev province from Poland—and its annexation by Russia—in 1772, the town's emergence as one of Russia's commercial windows on the West, the concentration of a group of disciples of the Vilna Gaon in Shklov, and the establishment of Count Semion Zorich's court there in 1778. The town's subsequent decline was likewise the product of several interrelated processes.

Shklov's prominence as a commercial center began to decline after the second and third partitions of Poland, in 1793 and 1795. With the incorporation of Lithuania and the remainder of Byelorussia into the Tsarist Empire, the town was robbed of its strategic position along Russia's Western border, and ceased being a focal point of land-based trade between Russia and its neighbors. For the first time since the establishment of its Jewish community in 1668, Shklov found itself several hundred kilometers removed from an international frontier, a factor which contributed mightily to its gradual decline into economic oblivion.[1]

Zorich's death in 1799 was likewise a significant blow to the town's economic and cultural vitality. Having died without heirs, and with an astronomical level of debt, his court was liquidated by the Imperial treasury, which established a state trusteeship to supervise the sale of his assets. The impressive cultural institutions he established in Shklov were dissolved: the best dancers and musicians in his theater and ballet were engaged by the Imperial State Theater in St. Petersburg; the Shklov Nobility Academy, with its library and laboratory, was incorporated into the St. Petersburg Cadet Corps. Before long, the town was a shadow of its former self.[2]

The impact of these events was felt by the Shklov Jewish community after a time lag of a few years. At first, the class of wealthy Jewish merchants had enough accumulated capital and business contacts to continue running their affairs on their own, without the external stimuli of the border and Zorich's court. A letter from the Jews of Shklov to their far-flung brethren in Buchara, written in December 1802, still boasted about the city:

> Its inhabitants are the wealthiest and most honored men in the land, and trade among the nations. Most of them are merchants from the children of Israel who travel across the earth to import merchandise. And it [Shklov] distributes the treasures of its merchandise to all the surrounding lands.[3]

These boastful words were probably already somewhat exaggerated at the time of their composition. Only a few years later, the Jews of the Mogilev province, including Shklov, were cast into a severe economic crisis. In 1806, acute poverty led a group of thirty-six Jewish families from the region to apply for resettlement to agricultural colonies in New Russia. Less than a year later, the number of applicants for resettlement from the Mogilev province mushroomed to 338 families (or 1,955 souls) and then to 600 families (approximately 3,600 souls). Most of the applicants were rural Jews who were expelled from the countryside, and not inhabitants of cities and towns such as Shklov. But they stressed in their petitions to Tsarist officials that the urban Jewish communities in their province were themselves impoverished, and had proven incapable of absorbing rural migrants.[4]

Shklov's prominence as a political center of Russian Jewry dwindled rapidly after Nota Notkin's death in 1804. As a center of Hebrew printing, it was soon surpassed by Vilna and Grodna. And the liquidation of Zorich's court and its institutions spelled the beginning of the end of Shklov as a center of Jewish cultural openness, modernization, and adaptation. Without the presence of a vibrant European cultural milieu in the midst of the town, Shklov's Jews were no longer challenged to grapple with the questions of science, enlightenment, and acculturation on a daily basis. The town's Jewish commercial class lost its immediate contact with Russian high society, and the rabbinic elite lost the apologetic need to exhibit its worldly, scientific knowledge. Jewish social and cultural life in Shklov became more insular and closed.

From Integration to Apostasy and Beyond: The Odysseys of Perets and Nevakhovich

Meanwhile, the efforts of Shklov's enlightened expatriots in St. Petersburg to improve Russian Jewry's legal and social status ended in disappointment and defeat. The Imperial Statute Concerning the Jews which was issued in December 1804, as a result of the State Committee's deliberations, represented a rejection of Notkin's approach of moderate liberal reform, and an embrace of several of Derzhavin's draconian proposals.

The statute provided for the linguistic and cultural reform of the Jews to be imposed by force: If Jews did not send their children to Russian state elementary schools, they would be required to establish schools of their own which would teach Russian, Polish, or German. Similarly, Jewish financial records and contracts would be recognized by courts of law only if they were written in one of the three above-mentioned European languages. The statute stipulated that by 1812, all rabbis and kahal leaders would be required by law to read and write in either Russian, Polish, or German.[5]

At the same time, the 1804 statute preserved the blanket prohibition on Jewish residence outside the Pale of Settlement, and maintained the double taxation of Jewish merchants. Harshest of all was its stipulation that all Jews were to be expelled from the countryside by 1808, its prohibition on Jews selling or distilling alcoholic beverages, and leasing villages, and its annulment of all debts owed by peasants to such Jews. Taken together, these measures represented an endorsement of Derzhavin's view that for Russians the Jews were an economic and moral threat, whose activities needed to be restricted.[6]

Also incorporated into the 1804 statute was the sharp curtailment of the rabbis' and kahals' authority. Rabbis were prohibited from issuing fines and punishments, and kahals were not allowed to collect taxes for internal purposes, unless special permission was granted by the authorities. The goal was to weaken Jewish autonomous institutions, not to reform them.[7]

For the mass of Russian Jewry, the stipulations about secular schools, the weakening of the rabbinate and kahal, and the expulsion of Jews from the villages were most worrisome of all. Their representatives responded with time-tested devices—massive bribes, foot-dragging, and subterfuge—and were able to neutralize the effects of these provisions. No schools were created, and the kahals continued to exert their powers. The expulsions from the countryside were carried out, but on a much more limited scale than the law had envisioned, thanks to intercessions in St. Petersburg.[8]

For Perets and Nevakhovich, who had harbored high hopes for Jewish integration and emancipation, the 1804 statute was a crushingly disappointing document. The statute failed to facilitate the integration of Jews—even of enlightened, virtuous, productive Jews—into Russian society. It did not enable any category of Jews to join the civil service, to live in Moscow or St. Petersburg, or to enjoy an equal level of taxation with Russian merchants. Indeed, the expulsion from the countryside and other provisions added insult to injury, by legitimizing the popular anti-Jewish prejudices and suspicions which Nevakhovich had decried.

As a result of this legislative outcome, the hopes of Perets and Nevakhovich for Jewish emancipation were shattered, and they reverted to their personal agenda of advancing their careers in St. Petersburg's commercial and literary circles. Thanks to their extraordinary connections and wealth, they were not personally subject to the statute's restrictions on Jewish residence and commercial activity. Nonetheless, the statute lent further impetus to Perets's and Nevakhovich's tendency to de-emphasize their Jewishness and disassociate themselves from Jewish communal affairs.[9]

The exact year in which the two men converted to Lutheranism is uncertain. Historian Iulii Gessen's suggestion of 1813 seems likely, or at least plausible. In 1809, both were listed as subscribers to the renewed Königsberg edition of the Hebrew Haskalah journal *Hame'asef*. In 1810, the minute book of the Shklov burial society still referred to Perets with the honorific title *morenu* ("our teacher") when it recorded the death of his daughter Miriam. In the same year, a Russian author in St. Petersburg wrote to a friend in Moscow about the recent performance of a drama by the "Israelite" playwright, Nevakhovich. But in 1813, rumors were circulating in St. Petersburg's official circles that Perets was on the verge of adopting Christianity.[10]

Perets's conversion was apparently precipitated by personal considerations. Following the death of his wife Feygele at Ustye, he chose to marry his German mistress, Caroline De Somber—a step which required his adoption of Lutheranism. His son, Grigorii, and daughter, Sofia (previously: Tsirl), converted simultaneously with him.[11]

Shortly thereafter, Perets's financial affairs took a sharp turn for the worse. During the 1812 war against Napoleon, he was deeply involved in financing the Russian war effort and arranging the transport of provisions to the troops. He loaned 4 million rubles to the state treasury, but was unable to recoup the debt, and was forced to go into bankruptcy. In 1816, his houses, estates (with two thousand serfs), and other assets were sold in a public auction for 1.5 million rubles, and Perets was left in financial ruin. In a Hebrew letter to his relative Solomon Zeitlin, written in 1822, he complained: "My affairs are in terrible condition, and I can rely on no one, other than on our father in heaven who feeds one and all. I hope that he will not leave me a laughing stock to my enemies." He died in poverty in 1833.[12]

For Perets's son Grigorii, conversion should have opened the way to greater social and professional success. While still a Jew, in 1811, he had been rejected for admission into a St. Petersburg Masonic lodge, on the grounds that Masonic rules prohibited the acceptance of Jews. But his conversion did not open all doors. The Perets family's social standing was based exclusively upon its wealth, and once it disappeared, they were considered to be nothing more than déclassé Jews. Grigorii's career in the Russian civil service languished in low-ranking positions, mostly in the provinces. In 1817, he became involved in the Russian insurrectionist movement known as the Decembrists, by joining a secret cell of Imperial officials who were critical of Tsarist policies and who favored the establishment of a constitutional monarchy in Russia.[13]

Grigorii's residual ties to Judaism and Jewry came to the fore during the course of his conspiratorial activity: The cell adopted, at his suggestion, the Hebrew word for freedom, *herut*, as its secret password, and he instructed new members to read not only the constitutions of various Western countries, but also "certain laws of Moses from the Bible" which proved that God favored a constitutional system of government. According to the cell's initiator and leader, Colonel Fedor Glink, Grigorii spoke to him, inter alia, about "the need for a society on behalf of the liberation of the Jews scattered throughout Russia and Europe, and for their settlement in Crimea or even in the East as a separate nation." Perets "exuded about how to gather in the Jews, transport them with great triumph etc. etc. He also mentioned that his father had once had such a plan, but that it required the partnership of many capitalists." Thus, Grigorii Perets maintained an interest in the Jews' "liberation" several years after his conversion to Lutheranism.[14]

Grigorii's conspiratorial activity came to a close in 1822, when he married Maria Grevenits, the sister of Count Alexander Grevenits (a Russian senator who had married Grigorii's sister Sofia somewhat earlier). He was arrested in the aftermath of the December 1825 uprising (in which he had no direct involvement), was detained in prison for six months, and exiled to Siberia, where he spent the next fourteen years of his life.[15]

Perets's protégé, Yehuda Leyb Nevakhovich, enjoyed a successful career as a Russian author and playwright during the years between his publication of *Vopl* (1803) and his conversion to Christianity (probably in 1813). He issued a booklet of philosophic fiction entitled *Chelovek v prirode ili perepiska dvukh prosveshchenikh druzei* (Man in Nature, or the Correspondence between Two Enlightened Friends) in 1804, and published an essay on Russian history in the most prominent literary journal of the day, *Litsei*, in 1806. The essay, written in reply to a critical article on Russian history published in Germany, was a stridently patriotic defense of Russian national character and institutions. In the same year, 1806, Nevakhovich was admitted into the ranks of the Imperial civil service, perhaps as a token of gratitude for his literary defense of the fatherland.[16]

Nevakhovich's fame reached its climax in 1809, when his drama *The Sullites, or the Spartans of the Eighteenth Century* was performed at the Imperial State Theater to an audience which included Tsar Alexander I. Following the performance, Alexander presented him with a gold snuffbox adorned with jewels, which featured the Tsar's own image engraved on the exterior. At about this time, Nevakhovich developed a close personal friendship with Russia's most important playwright and director of the Imperial State Theater, A. Shakhovskii, and he reportedly helped Shakhovskii compose his biblical tragedy *Deborah*. Shakhovskii's *Deborah* was the only instance in which Nevakhovich worked on a drama with a "Jewish" theme. His own works, *The Sullites* and *Oden, King of the Skifites*—both written while Nevakhovich was himself still an "Israelite"—were devoid of Jewish motives.[17]

Nevakhovich's literary career was disrupted some time after 1810, probably because of the financial ruination of his patron, Perets. Nevakhovich became preoccupied with the more mundane task of earning a living, and from 1817 on, he resided in Warsaw, serving as an official in the Polish Kingdom's Ministry of Finance and engaging in private commerce. His only noteworthy literary enterprise during his later years was a Russian translation of Herder's "Thoughts on the History of Mankind," issued in 1829.

The circumstances of Nevakhovich's conversion to Lutheranism are unclear; like his patron, Perets, he married a German woman, Catherine Michelson. He died in 1831, during a visit to St. Petersburg, and was buried in the capital's German Lutheran cemetery. A poignant quotation from Herder was inscribed on his tombstone: "Here, beneath our gaze, everything is reduced to ashes; time threatens to destroy earthly splendor and earthly joy."[18]

From Russia to Jerusalem: The Disciples of the Vilna Gaon

Shklov's rabbinic elite also underwent a metamorphosis, which took them from their city in a new—and diametrically opposed—direction: to the Land of Israel.

Their migration was pioneered by R. Menahem Mendl b. Barukh Bendet, who set out to the Holy Land in 1808 with a small group of followers. After a brief sojourn in Tiberias, the group settled in Safed. R. Menahem Mendl and his entourage were apparently sent as an advance team for a larger rabbinic convoy which departed the following year, under the leadership of another disciple of the Vilna Gaon, R. Sa'adya b. Natan Nota of Vilna. The convoy included R. Menahem Mendl's son, Natan Nota, R. Benjamin Rivlin's son, Hillel, as well as members of the Zeitlin family, and established the first non-Hasidic Ashkenazic community in the Land of Israel.[19]

In order to sustain their community of some forty families, or 150 souls, R. Menahem Mendl dispatched letters and emissaries to his close associate R. Israel b. Shmuel of Shklov, and to R. Hayyim of Volozhin. They, in turn, proceeded to raise funds locally, in Byelorussia and Lithuania, and pressed for a fraction of the funds collected worldwide for the Land of Israel to be allocated to the new settlement.[20]

Having helped the settlers overcome their initial financial hurdles, R. Israel of Shklov personally headed a second rabbinic convoy to the Holy Land in 1809. By 1813 the community of the *prushim*, or pietists, as they were called, in Safed grew to 461 souls and constructed houses for its yeshiva and synagogue. R. Israel of Shklov was recognized as the community's foremost religious authority, with R. Menahem Mendl and R. Hillel Rivlin subsequently establishing a branch in Jerusalem.[21]

The "'*aliya* of the disciples of the Gaon" was a social movement which generated a great deal of interest and excitement among the rabbinic elite of Lithuania and Byelorussia. R. Israel, who returned to Russia in 1810 to raise funds for the *prushim*, urged his rabbinic colleagues to leave for Palestine, and groups of Talmudists and preachers responded. One contemporary who decided "to join those who conspire with the most heroic designs to leave the land of their birth," was Avraham b. Asher Anshil of Minsk, who described the movement in the following terms:

Each day new groups appear, who wander, walk and journey to the land of their forefathers' inhabitancy. They cast off their gold and silver, and undertake to abandon the land of their birth where they have sojourned, a land which is not theirs. Rather than sojourn there [in Russia], they have chosen to settle, and have embarked upon the journey by sea . . . unto the Holy Land, in order to cleave unto the Lord's inheritance.[22]

The movement included some of the most prominent rabbinic personalities of the time. R. Avraham Danziger, the Vilna Gaon's in-law and author of the halakhic code *Haye 'adam*, is known to have planned to leave for the Land of Israel in 1811. Although his personal designs did not come to fruition, he did compose a halakhic manual for migrants to the Holy Land on the agricultural laws which pertained there, *Sha'are tsedek* (Gates of Righteousness; Vilna, 1812). The elderly R. Benjamin Rivlin, who had single-handedly made Shklov into a center of rabbinic learning in the 1770s, also set out for the Holy Land in 1812, immediately after Russia's defeat of Napoleon. But he fell ill at the outset of his journey, and died in Liepel, on the outskirts of Mogilev. The migratory movement as a whole came to an end in 1813, when a plague broke out in Palestine which devastated the Ashkenazic community.[23]

What motivated the Shklov disciples of the Vilna Gaon to uproot themselves from their established homes, and spearhead a movement of rabbinic *'aliya* to Palestine? Were they driven, as one historian has recently argued, by intense Messianic expectations and by the belief that they could personally precipitate the coming of the Messiah through their actions?[24] An examination of the letters written by the *prushim* shortly after their arrival in Safed suggests otherwise. In their appeal to world Jewry for financial support, published in Shklov in 1810, the *prushim* stated that they had settled in the Land of Israel

"to work it and keep it"; to work it through Divine service, and to keep it through the watch of Torah; to unite the four ells of pristine halakhah with the four ells of the holy and pure land. . . . To restore the Torah to its dwelling place.[25]

The *prushim* aspired to create a utopian religious community, whose members would pursue a life of absolute piety and constant Torah study, without compromises, in the Holy Land. Their goals were pietistic, in a sense mystical, but not Messianic. They sought to attain personal immersion in the word of God—but not to effect the national salvation of Israel, or the metaphysical transformation of the universe.

The underlying motivation for their *'aliya* was stated explicitly by R. Hayyim b. Tuvya Katz of Vilna, a disciple of the Vilna Gaon who settled in Safed along with R. Israel of Shklov, in a private letter to the diaspora.

Our people who come to the Holy Land mostly come to attain perfection, to be among the occupants of the house of study, and to sit and engage in Torah and worship. . . . The Holy Land is more suited for Torah than the diaspora; day and night are equally free for the acquisition of Torah.[26]

The Gaon's disciples inherited his reclusive scholastic tendencies—hence their name *prushim*, which meant recluses. They endeavored to pursue Torah study in an ideal environment, with less distractions and competing obligations than in Lithuania and Byelorussia. The deepening economic crisis which embroiled Shklov and the Mogilev province must, in fact, have forced the "Sages of Shklov" to seek out a more favorable environment for their learned pursuits, just as it had forced other Jews to migrate to New Russia.

The *prushim* themselves drew attention to another motive for their *'aliya*—their desire to observe the "religious commandments contingent upon the land," such as the tithes and Sabbatical year. These commandments were dormant at the time, since neither the Sephardic nor Hasidic communities engaged in agricultural activity. The *prushim* decided to purchase plots of farmland near Safed shortly after their arrival, for the express purpose of growing crops and observing the agricultural commandments. It is interesting to note that the *prushim* never entertained the idea of feeding themselves and earning a livelihood through farm work. The latter was viewed exclusively as a vehicle for observing additional religious prescriptions.[27] R. Avraham Danzig's above-mentioned manual was written to train the migrants in their performance.

There was nothing Messianic about renewing the observance of the "commandments contingent upon the land." The latter had never lost their binding validity and practical applicability—unlike, for instance, the laws of the Temple cult. Their performance had been discontinued because of historical circumstances: the vast majority of Jews no longer lived in Palestine, and the few that did no longer engaged in agriculture. The disciples of the Vilna Gaon were driven by a pietistic impulse to observe the Torah's commandments to the utmost degree possible. Following their master, R. Elijah, who had also once attempted to settle in the Land of Israel, they took this idea to its logical conclusion—or destination.[28]

As a result of the migration of the disciples of the Vilna Gaon from Shklov to the Holy Land, Shklov ceased to be the bastion of rabbinic-Mitnagdic culture it had been for nearly forty years. The yeshiva established by R. Benjamin Rivlin dwindled to a small local institution, which no longer enjoyed national stature or influence. The output of Hebrew printing in the town also declined sharply. Hebrew presses in Shklov issued a total of thirty books between 1813 and 1825, an average of 2.3 books per year, as opposed to 5.7 books per year during the town's heyday, between 1783 and 1799.[29]

The texture of Jewish religious culture in Shklov also changed following the disciples' departure. In the absence of a strong Mitnagdic leadership, Shklov soon became a predominantly Hasidic town, one of the bastions of Habad-Lubavitch. Six of the thirty books printed there between 1813 and 1825 were, in fact, treatises of Habad Hasidism.

Conclusion

During the historical interlude between the first and last partition of Poland, and, arguably, for a decade thereafter, the Byelorussian town of Shklov was the foremost center of Jewish cultural, intellectual, and political activity in the Russian Empire. The "Sages of Shklov" consolidated and strengthened traditional rabbinism in their city and province, and conducted a successful campaign to prevent the spread of the Hasidic movement into their region; the local disciples of the Vilna Gaon transmitted their master's teachings, and were the driving force behind the publication of his works; Shklov's Hebrew printing presses were the most prolific in the Byelorussian-Lithuanian provinces, and were a spur to Jewish literary creativity; and the town's lay leaders, Notkin and Zeitlin, emerged as the de facto representatives and advocates of Russian Jewry before the Imperial Court in St. Petersburg.

Shklov distinguished itself in yet another respect. It was the first Russian Jewish community which confronted—and to a large extent welcomed—the challenges of enlightenment and acculturation. The court of Count Semion Zorich, with its extraordinary cultural institutions and European milieu, exerted a subtle but pervasive influence on the texture of Jewish culture and intellectual life in the city. Members of the Jewish commercial class adopted European social and cultural norms. In the cases of Notkin and Zeitlin, they were able to build upon their European cultural fluency and their patronage relationships with Zorich and other Russian officials to gain entry into Russian high society.

As Western ideas, arts, and sciences flooded the city, Jewish intellectuals were challenged to study and produce works of science, drama, and Hebrew philology, and to formulate new ideas on the reform of Jewish culture and the position of Jews in Russian society.

Because of Shklov's position as a center of trade between Russia and the West, there was extensive personal traffic and contact between its Jewish merchants and intellectuals and the enlightened Jews of Berlin. The Berlin Haskalah provided the Shklovers with a much-needed intellectual vocabulary regarding enlightenment, acculturation, and emancipation, and a model of their implementation in life. Programs for Jewish educational reform abounded. They ranged from narrowly conceived reforms of rabbinic studies (R. Barukh Schick), to plans for the curricular overhaul of the *heder* (N. H. Schulman), to ambitious proposals to create Jewish schools under state auspices (Jacob Hirsch and Nota Notkin). All these plans drew their inspiration from Western Jewish models.

Among the acculturated elite, political concepts and ideas about the position of Jews in Russian society also changed. Notkin argued not only for the alleviation of the Jews' civil status, but for their corporate equalization with nonbonded Russians, and for the admission of a large number of Jews into the Russian civil service. Nevakhovich pleaded for social acceptance and the elimination of anti-Jewish prejudices, which he considered to be remnants of medieval irrational hatred. Basing themselves on the European Enlightenment's ideas of universal equality and religious tolerance, they shifted the objectives of Jewish political discourse from insuring physical security and communal autonomy, to achieving political and social integration into Russian life.

In Shklov, the lay leadership clearly and publicly identified itself with the goal of moderate acculturation. Maskilim such as N. H. Schulman were therefore able to publish their works and propagate their ideas in Shklov without confronting organized opposition or persecution. The town's rabbinic elite accommodated, and, indeed, legitimized within circumscribed boundaries, the pursuit of worldly knowledge and science. This was one of many issues where they followed—and modified—the teachings of their master, the Vilna Gaon, and disagreed sharply with their Hasidic adversaries.

Zorich's death and the collapse of his court, in 1799, and the rejection of Notkin's and Nevakhovich's proposals for the Jews' civil emancipation, in 1804, dealt mortal blows to the processes of enlightenment and acculturation among the Jews of Shklov. From that point on, the protagonists sputtered into different directions. Abraham Perets and Nevakhovich, representatives of the success-fully acculturated commercial and intellectual elite, pursued—and achieved—admission into Russian society at the expense of their affiliation with Jewry; others, such as Zeitlin, retreated from public life and from the pursuit of Jewish cultural and political reform. As for the "Sages of Shklov," they were relieved of the local pressure to accommodate science and worldly learning—and chose a life of intensified Talmudism and pietism in the Land of Israel.

But the memory of the "Shklov Haskalah" reverberated in the works of subsequent Maskilim. Isaac Ber Levinsohn, the "father of the Russian Haskalah," paid tribute to his Shklov forebears in his Yiddish satirical pamphlet *Di hefker velt* (The World of Chaos; Warsaw, 1891). In it, two Ukrainian Jews revealed the corruption and perversion of their kahals and Hasidic rebbes to an astonished visitor from Mogilev. The visitor responded to their tales with shock and indignation. "In our land of Byelorussia, there is no such non-sense; people don't even know what a Hasidic Rebbe or miracle worker is. We have scholars and sages, as in the days of yore." His hosts reacted with exasperated jealousy.[1]

The Galician Maskil Joseph Perl referred to the noble Jews of Shklov in his epistolary novella *Bohen tsadik* (The Test of the Righteous; Prague, 1838), a fantastic exposée of the foibles of all classes and sectors of East European Jewish society. The book's traveling protagonist, Ovadiah b. Petahia, found only one truly righteous figure in all his journeys—a Jewish farmer from the Mogi-lev province who had settled on one of the Jewish agricultural colonies in New Russia. A disciple of the Vilna Gaon, he plowed the fields by day and studied Torah at night. The farmer had settled as a member of the group headed by the Shklov merchant Nahum Finkelstein, who was depicted by Perl as a glorious servant of his people, dedicated to their economic rejuvenation. In the seamy universe of *Bohen tsadik*, the only righteous Jews were from Shklov![2]

The "Shklov Haskalah" left behind it a modest historical legacy. The descendants of some its figures participated in the development of the Haskalah center in Vilna—Joshua Zeitlin's son-in-law, Mordechai Nathanson, was a pillar of Vilna's "reformed" congregation *Tohorat ha-kodesh*, and Naftali Hirtz Schulman's grandson, Kalman Schulman, was a prominent Hebrew author and translator. Through these individuals, Shklov exerted its influence on the formation of the religiously conservative, and intensely literary and scholarly Haskalah subculture that emerged in Vilna a generation later.[3]

But Shklov's significance lies not in its legacy or impact on subsequent events, but in its paradigmatic anticipation of them. For a brief historical interlude, the Jews of this Byelorussian town were offered a preview of the problems which would confront Russian Jewry during the nineteenth century, and, naively and unwittingly, they rehearsed a range of positions and solutions which would be embraced by their descendants.

Notes

Notes to Introduction

1. I. Trunk, "Der va'ad medinas rusiya (raysn)" [The Council of Byelorussia], *YIVO Bletter* 40 (1956): 63–85; N. Vakar, *Belorussia: The Making of a Nation* (Cambridge, Mass., 1956); Maria Barbara Topolska, "Peculiarities of the Economic Structure of Eastern White Russia in the Sixteenth–Eighteenth Centuries," *Studia Historiae Oeconomicae* 6 (1971): 37–49.

2. S. Mtsislavskii (= S. Dubnow), "Evrei v mogilevskoi gubernii" [Jews in the Mogilev Province], *Voskhod* 6 (1886), no. 9: 1–10; I. Trunk, "Geshikhte fun yidn in vitebsk" [History of the Jews in Vitebsk], in G. Aronson (ed.), *Vitebsk amol* (New York, 1956), 1–56. On the Council of Lithuania and other regional organs of Jewish self-government, see Jacob Katz, *Tradition and Crisis* (New York, 1961), 122–34; Y. Heilprin, *Yehudim ve-yahadut be-mizrah 'eropah* [Jews and Judaism in Eastern Europe] (Jerusalem, 1969), 39–60.

3. *Evreiskaia entsiklopediia* (St. Petersburg, 1908–13), "Mogilev," 10: 153–54, "Vitebsk," 5: 639–40; *Pinkas ha-medinah* [Minute book of the Lithuanian Council], ed. S. Dubnow (Berlin, 1925): nos. 503 and 505 (from the year 1656), 628 (from the year 1667). On the Russian invasion and its catastrophic impact on Byelorussian Jewry, see S. Dubnow, "Tson ha-herga: haruge Mohlev 'al nahar Dniepr" [The Slaughtered Sheep: The Victims of Mogilev on the Dniepr], *Ha-pardes* 3 (1896): 94–100; *Istoriia evreiskogo naroda* 11, ed. P. Marek et al. (Moscow, 1914), 72–77.

4. Maria Barbara Topolska, "Szklow i Jego Rola w Gospodarce Bialorusi Wschodniej w XVII i XVIII Wieku" [Shklov and Its Role in the Economy of Eastern Byelorussia in the Seventeenth and Eighteenth Centuries], *Roczniki Dziejow Spolecznych Gospodarczych* 30 (1969): 1–32; Sergei Bershadskii, "Polozhenie o evreakh 1804 goda" [The 1804 Statute on the Jews], *Voskhod* 15 (1895), no. 4: 97–98; *Regesti i Nadpisi* [Registers and Inscriptions], vol. 2 (St. Petersburg, 1910), no. 1326; Murray J. Rosman, *The Lords' Jews: Magnate-Jewish Relations in the Polish-*

Lithuanian Commonwealth in the Eighteenth Century (Cambridge, 1990), 47, see also pp. 62, 108.

5. The census figures were as follows: Shklov—1,367 (*Evreiskaia entsiklopediia* 16: 45); Slutsk—1,577 (14: 392); Pinsk—1,277 (12: 530); Minsk—1,322 (11: 86). Historians concur that the census underreported the Jewish population by approximately 33 percent; see Raphael Mahler, *Yidn in amolikn poyln in likht fun tsifern* [Jews in Old Poland in Numbers], (Warsaw, 1958).

6. S. Mtsislavskii (= S. Dubnow), "Oblastnie kagalnie seimi v voivodstve volynskom i v belorussii (1666–1764)" [Regional Communal Councils in Vohlyn and Byelorussia (1666–1764)], *Voskhod* 14 (1894), no. 4: 24–42, esp. p. 33; Dubnow, *Pinkas ha-medinah*, no. 949; P. Marek, "Beloruskaia synagoga i eia teritoriia" [The Byelorussian Council and Its Territory], *Voskhod* 23 (1903), no. 5: 71–82. Trunk, "Der va'ad medinas rusiya."

7. Trunk, "Der va'ad medinas rusiya," pp. 70–73. During most of the eighteenth century, the provincial rabbinate was occupied by members of the Ginzburg family, one of the great rabbinic clans of East European Jewry, and was passed on from father to son to grandson. See D. Magid, *Toldot mishpehot ginzburg* [History of the Ginzburg Families], (St. Petersburg, 1891), 27, 54–56, 169–70, 196.

8. On Arye Leyb Ginzburg and Yehiel Halperin, see Benzion Eisenstadt, *Rabane Minsk ve-hakhameha* [The Rabbis and Scholars of Minsk], (Vilna, 1898); on Avraham Katzenellenbogen, see Arye Leyb Feinstein, *'Ir tehilah* [Exalted City], (Warsaw, 1886). The career of R. Barukh Schick of Shklov, examined below in chapter 2, is an example of a talented young Talmudist who left "the land of Russia" to study in Minsk and receive rabbinic ordination from Rabbi Katzenellenbogen of Brest-Litovsk.

9. On R. Israel Yaffe, and the subsequent controversy surrounding his alleged Sabbatianism, see S. J. Fuenn, *Kneset yisra'el* [Congregation of Israel], (Warsaw, 1886): 694–95; on R. Elijah Pines, see H. N. Dembitzer, *Kelilat yofi* [City of Beauty] (New York, 1959–60), vol. 1:50b; on R. Jacob b. Judah Schick, see Magid, *Toldot mishpehot ginzburg*, 27–28, 32, and the letters of approbation to his posthumous *Moreh tsedek* [Righteous Instruction] (Shklov, 1783).

10. This is the reasoned estimate of Raphael Mahler, *Divre yeme yisra'el: dorot aharonim* [History of the Jews in Modern Times], vol. 1, book 4 (Merhavia, 1956), 229–31, based on the 1772–73 census conducted by the Russian authorities.

11. Avraham Ya'ari, "Ha-defus ha-'ivri be-Shklov" [Jewish Printing in Shklov], *Kiryat sefer* 22 (1945): 49–72, 135–60; C. Lieberman, "Nosafot le-ha-defus ha-'ivri be-Shklov" [Addenda to Jewish Printing in Shklov], *Kiryat sefer* 25 (1949): 315–320, 26 (1950): 101–111. At the turn of the

nineteenth century, the neighboring town of Kopys also became an important center of Hebrew printing; see C. D. Friedberg, *Toldot ha-defus ha-'ivri bi-polanya* [History of Jewish Printing in Poland] (Antwerp, 1932), 91–93. For a comparison between Shklov and other centers of Hebrew printing in Eastern Europe, see Friedberg.

12. C. H. Rivlin, *Hazon tsiyon: shklov ve-yerushalayim*, [Vision of Zion: Shklov and Jerusalem] (Jerusalem, 1953), 32 (from a poem by R. Joseph Rivlin, scion of Shklov's most prominent rabbinic family); Chaim Meyer Heilman, *Bet rabi* [The Rabbi's House] (Berdichev, 1900), 20a; letter from Shklov to the Bucharian Jews, dated December 1802, appended to *Derishat tsiyon* [Pursuit of Zion] (Frankfurt on the Oder, 1806). The letter's patriotic hyperbole and its claim that Tsar Alexander I "has made us equal with all inhabitants of the land in everything" are indications of its author's emancipationist orientation. The description of the Shklov synagogue is from *Otsar yisra'el* [The Treasury of Israel Encyclopedia], ed. J. D. Eisenstadt (New York, 1917), 10: 208. For a depiction of Shklov in this period based on local folk memory, see Y. Litvin (= S. Hurwitz), "Ven Shklov iz geven erets yisroel" [When Shklov Was the Land of Israel], *Yidishe neshomes* [Jewish Souls], (New York, 1916), 1: chapter 21 (unpaginated).

13. See Michael S. Stanislawski, *Tsar Nicholas I and the Jews: The Transformation of Jewish Society in Russia 1825–1855* (Philadelphia, 1983), 49–52; Mahler, *Divre yeme yisra'el*, vol. 1, book 4, 25–68.

14. Iulii Gessen, *Evrei v rossii* [The Jews in Russia] (St. Petersburg, 1906); I. Tsinberg, "Shklov i ego 'prosvetiteli' kontsa XVIIIogo veka" [Shklov and Its 'Enlighteners' at the End of the Eighteenth Century], *Evreiskaia starina* 12 (1928): 17–44, and in his *Geshikhte fun der literatur bay yidn* [History of Jewish Literature] (New York, 1943), 5: 320–39; 7a: 263–70.

Notes to Chapter 1

1. For an overview of the conflict between Hasidim and Mitnagdim in English, see Bernard Weinryb, *The Jews of Poland* (Philadelphia, 1973), 282–301; and Mordechai Wilensky, "Hasidic-Mitnaggedic Polemics in the Jewish Communities of Eastern Europe: The Hostile Phase," in Gershon D. Hundert (ed.), *Essential Papers on Hasidism* (New York, 1991), 244–71. The classical treatment of the subject is by S. Dubnow, *Toldot Ha-hasidut* [History of Hasidism] (Tel Aviv, 1975, fourth edition). Wilensy's *Hasidim ve-mitnagdim* [Hasidism and Opponents], 2 vols. (Jerusalem, 1970), is an indispensable collection of primary sources.

2. Shneur Zalman b. Barukh of Liady, *'Igrot kodesh kevod kedushat admor ha-zaken* [Sacred Letters of the Old Rabbi], ed. Shalom Duber Levine (Brooklyn, N.Y., 1980), 126; also cited with slight variations by Wilen-

sky, *Hasidim ve-mitnagdim*, 1:40, n. 24. The letter was written in 1805; significantly, R. Avraham did not deny R. Shneur Zalman's charges.

3. Chaim Meyer Heilman, *Bet rabi*, 8; Mikhael Vilensky in *Kiryat sefer* I (1924): 240; R. Joseph Isaac Schneerson, "Avot Ha-Hasidut" [The Fathers of Hasidism], *Ha-tamim* (December 1935): 62–63 and passim. For a critical evaluation of the historical literature produced by the Lubavitch movement, see Ada Rapoport-Albert, "Hagiography with Footnotes: Edifying Tales and the Writing of History in Hasidism," *History and Theory* 27 (1988): 119–59. R. Avraham of Kalisk referred to the *tolk*, and to the charge that he was responsible for the sins of Hasidim in Byelorussia, in a 1801 letter to R. Shneur Zalman, published in David Zvi Hilman (ed.), *'Igrot ba'al ha-tanya u-bene doro* [Letters by the Author of the Tanya and His Contemporaries] (Jerusalem, 1953), 156, and Jacob Barnai (ed.), *'Igrot hasidim me-'erets yisra'el* [Letters of Hasidim from the Land of Israel] (Jerusalem, 1980), 255–56.

4. Yisrael Loebel, *Sefer vikuah* [Book of Disputation] (Warsaw, 1798), 3a; in Wilensky, *Hasidim ve-mitnagdim*, 2: 274: "They consider it permitted to kill, beat, and inform on those who oppose them, as they did to R. Sholem of Lubavitch, and as they did to R. Jacob of Shklov." After serving the community of Shklov for more than twenty years, R. Jacob surfaced in the Lithuanian town of Slutsk, where he died in 1774, suggesting a sudden departure. On R. Jacob, see pp. 23–24 below.

5. This was first pointed out by Immanuel Etkes in his study, "Ha-gra ve-reshit ha-hitnagdut la-hasidut" [The Vilna Gaon and the Beginning of Opposition to Hasidism], in *Temurot ba-historiya ha-yehudit ha-hadasha, kovets ma'amarim shai le-Shmuel Ettinger* [Ettinger Jubilee Volume] (Jerusalem, 1987), 439–58. The Hasidic tradition speaks of two Shklov disputations, one in 1771–72 and another in 1776–77; Heilman, *Bet rabi*, 8, 13.

6. *Zemir 'aritsim ve-harvot tsurim* [The Sounds of Oppressors and Swords of Stone] (Alksenits, 1772), in Wilensky, *Hasidim ve-mitnagdim*, 1: 63. Heilman, *Bet rabi*, 8, reports that the pronouncement was made at a special assembly held several months after the disputation.

7. Wilensky, *Hasidim ve-mitnagdim*, 1: 64.

8. Etkes has noted ("Ha-gra ve-reshit ha-hitnagdut," 444–48) that the Vilna Gaon had a negative view of Hasidism even prior to receiving the writings from Shklov. Nonetheless, from the perspective of our topic it is important to point out that the events in Byelorussia and the disputation in Shklov motivated him to launch a campaign to destroy the movement.

9. Edward C. Thaden, *Russia's Western Borderlands 1710–1870* (Princeton, 1984), 32–55.

10. John D. Klier, *Russia Gathers Her Jews: The Origins of the "Jewish Question" in Russia 1772–1825* (Dekalb, Ill., 1986), 64–65; Iulii Gessen,

Istoriia evreiskogo naroda v rossii [History of the Jewish People in Russia] (Petrograd, 1916), 1: 133–36.

11. Gessen, *Istoriia*, 1: 136, 139; *Evreiskaia entsiklopediia*, "kagal," 8: 88–90.

12. On the status of Jewish self-government in Poland and the debates surrounding the role of the kahal in the 1770s and 1780s, see Raphael Mahler, *Toldot ha-yehudim be-folin* [History of the Jews in Poland] (Merhavia, 1946), 440–456; S. Dubnow, "Evreiskaia pol'sha v epokhu poslednikh razdelov" [Jewish Poland at the Time of the Last Partitions], *Evreiskaia starina* 4 (1911): 441–463; N. M. Gelber, "Die Juden und die Judenreform auf dem vierjährigen Seim," in Ismar Elbogen et al. (eds.), *Festschrift zu Simon Dubnows siebzigsten Geburtstag* (Berlin, 1930), 136–53.

13. "Pinkas kahal kadosh Petrovitz," Yivo Archives, Tcherikover collection, file #917, esp. pp. 69a, 70b, 71a; the text of the statutes was published by Dubnow in Russian translation, "Istoricheskie soobshcheniia: kagalnie ustavi s kontsa 160go do kontsa 180go veka" [Historical Notes: Kahal Constitutions from the Late Sixteenth to the Late Eighteenth Centuries], *Voskhod* 13 (1894), no. 2: 90–105. On the jurisdictional dispute between the two Mstislavls, see "Pinkas kahal kadosh Mtsislav," Yivo Archives, Tcherikover collection, file #918, pp. 98–99.

14. *Polnoe sobranie zakonov rossiiskoi imperii*, vol. 21, no. 15,436; cited by Gessen, *Istoriia*, 1: 136. Gessen suggested that the complaint was submitted by persecuted Hasidim; "K istorii religioznoi borbi sredi ruskikh evreev" [On the History of the Religious Struggle within Russian Jewry], *Voskhod* 22 (1902), no. 1: 131.

15. These reforms have been studied by several historians; Klier, *Russia Gathers Her Jews*, 67–74; Richard Pipes, "Catherine II and the Jews: The Origins of the Pale of Settlement," *Soviet Jewish Affairs* 5 (1975), no. 2: 3–20; Shmuel Ettinger, "Ha-yesodot ve-ha-megamot be-'itsuv mediniuto shel ha-shilton ha-rusi klape ha-yehudim 'im halukot polin" [Principles and Tendencies in the Formation of Russian Policy toward the Jews after the Partition of Poland], *He-'avar* 19 (1972): 20–34. See also the treatment by Isaac Levitats, *The Jewish Community in Russia, 1772–1844* (New York, 1943), 26, 48–49.

16. See the letter of approbation by the rabbinic court of the *medinah* to David Karo, *'Ohel Rahel* [The Tent of Rachel] (Shklov, 1790).

17. On the "Sages of Shklov" see below, chapter 6.

18. On the second Shklov disputation, see the letter by R. Shneur Zalman to his Hasidim in Vilna, in Wilensky, *Hasidim ve-mitnagdim*, 1: 198–99, and Heilman, *Bet rabi*, 13–14. Etkes contends (in "Ha-gra ve-reshit ha-hitnagdut") that only one disputation took place, in 1771–72. I am inclined to follow Wilensky and Heilman on this point, since R. Shneur Zalman refers to one Shklov disputation as a debacle, at which R. Avraham Kalisker was unable to respond convincingly to Mitnagdic

charges, and to the other as a Hasidic victory in which he himself personally participated, and refuted all accusations. The success of the Hasidim at the second disputation led the antagonistic audience to resort to violence.

19. Heilman, *Bet rabi*, 117; see also pp. 13, 35–36, 118–19. Heilman reports that an anti-Hasidic gathering of Russian Jewish communities was convened in Shklov in 1781, simultaneous with the gathering of Polish Jewish communities at the Zelva fair which issued several anti-Hasidic bans.

20. See the 1787 *takanot ha-medinah* against Hasidism which have survived in three different versions, Wilensky, *Hasidim ve-mitnagdim*, 1: 142–59. See also the vehement letter by R. Menahem Mendl b. Barukh Bendet of Shklov, written in 1805, ibid., 1: 315–18, and the caustic remarks of R. Israel b. Shmuel of Shklov, written in 1808–10, in Isaiah Tishby, "Kitrugo shel R. Yisrael Mi-Shklov 'al ha-hasidim" [The Polemic of Rabbi Israel of Shklov against the Hasidim], *Kiryat sefer* 51 (1976): 300–303. For a survey of the major themes in Mitnagdic polemics, see Wilensky's article "Hasidic-Mitnaggedic Polemics" (above n. 1).

21. Wilensky, *Hasidim ve-mitnagdim*, 1: 149–50.

22. Ibid., 348–49.

23. Ibid., 151–52. I have followed the version first published by P. Marek in "Vnutrenaia borba v evreistve v XVIIIom veke" [The Internal Struggle in Jewry in the Eighteenth Century], *Evreiskaia starina* 12 (1928): 126–27, which is fuller and, to my mind, more authentic.

24. Marek, "Vnutrenaia borba," 131, n. 1. The minutes, which were dated the 21st of Elul, 554[. . .] (178 [. . .]), were personally examined by Marek, but never published. I would assume that the year was 5541, based on the month indicated, Elul. According to Hasidic tradition, a *herem* was issued by the Russian Mitnagdim in Shklov at the time of the Polish *herems* at the Zelva fair, in Elul 5541; Heilman, *Bet rabi*, 35. A similar claim regarding official Russian authorization to persecute the Hasidim was made by the *gubernskii kagal* of the Minsk province in 1797: "We have the ability to pursue them and persecute them. For by the grace of God, we have been granted the authority [to do so] by our General Governor." Wilensky, *Hasidim ve-mitnagdim*, 1: 193–94.

25. Wilensky, *Hasidim ve-mitnagdim*, 1: 296–97; *'Igrot kodesh* (above n. 2), 5. R. Shneur Zalman also ordered the Hasidim to act with restraint and not resort to denunciations to the Gentile authorities.

26. See Louis Jacobs, *Hasidic Prayer* (New York, 1973).

27. Wilensky, *Hasidim ve-mitnagdim*, 1: 161–62; *'Igrot kodesh*, 16. See Esther 3:13 and 7:3.

28. Wilensky, *Hasidim ve-mitnagdim*, 1: 166–67; *'Igrot kodesh*, 23–24. Reports of anti-Hasidic persecution in the Mogilev province reached the Hasidic masters in Palestine, R. Menahem Mendl of Vitebsk and R.

Avraham Kalisker; see Barnai, '*Igrot hasidim*, 63–65, 95–96, 104. R. Menahem Mendl and R. Avraham emigrated to Palestine in 1777.

29. Shaul Ginsburg, "Mayse Ushats" [The Incident at Ushats], in *Historishe shriftn* (New York, 1941), 3: 180–81. The threat to the physical well-being of Hasidim in the Mogilev province is a theme in Hasidic traditions about R. Shneur Zalman's son-in-law, R. Avraham Sheynes. R. Avraham grew up in Mitnagdic Shklov, and was the son of one of its leading rabbinic scholars. When he became interested in Hasidism, he ran away from home to R. Shneur Zalman's seat of residence in Liozna. R. Avraham's father wrote to R. Shneur Zalman demanding that his son be sent home, but the son was afraid to go home "lest the people of the place kill me." Only after extracting a vow from Shklov's townsmen before a rabbinic court that they would not cause him any harm, did R. Avraham agree to return. Heilman, *Bet rabi*, 116–17.

30. See the letter by R. Menahem Mendl of Vitebsk, dated 1783–84, in Barnai, '*Igrot hasidim*, 104.

31. Heilman, *Bet rabi*, 35–36. Heilman consistently treats the eastern Byelorussian provinces, which he refers to as "our land" (*medinatenu*), as a discrete region in the history of Hasidism. The one community in the Mogilev province known to have tolerated a Hasidic *minyan* in the period under consideration was Stary Bykhov. Its rabbi, R. Israel Rappoport, was congratulated by R. Shneur Zalman for his efforts to establish peace between the waring camps. Wilensky, *Hasidim ve-mitnagdim*, 1: 298–99; '*Igrot kodesh*, 30–32.

32. Heilman, *Bet rabi*, 12. R. Menahem Mendl may have fled from Minsk, where he was targeted by the Mitnagdim as the "image of jealousy," to the freer atmosphere of the Polotsk province. See Wilensky, *Hasidim ve-mitnagdim*, 1: 65, 102.

33. On R. Shneur Zalman's rise to power, see I. Etkes, "'Aliyato shel rabi Shneur Zalman mi-Liadi le-'emdat manhigut" [The Rise of Rabbi Shneur Zalman of Liady to a Position of Leadership], *Tarbits* 54 (1984–85), 429–39. The issuance of guidelines, some time in the 1780s, restricting the frequency with which Hasidim could visit Liozna is evidence of R. Shneur Zalman's growing popularity as *tsadik*; '*Igrot kodesh*, 53. In the late eighteenth century, Liozna belonged to the Polotsk (later Vitebsk) province; Heilman, *Bet rabi*, 1.

34. Letter by R. Israel of Polotsk, 1778, in Barnai, '*Igrot hasidim*, 73–78.

35. Barnai, '*Igrot Hasidim*, 93; the letter is dated 4 'Adar 5542 [=March 1782].

36. '*Igrot kodesh*, 22, and Wilensky, *Hasidim ve-mitnagdim*, 1: 166 (with slight variations).

37. See, for instance, R. Phinehas b. Judah, *Keter torah* [Crown of Torah] (n.p., 1859), 16b–17a (first edition: Shklov, 1788). A comprehensive analysis of R. Phinehas's thought is provided by Alan L. Nadler's forthcoming book, *A Religion of Limits: The Theology of the Mitnaggedim*.

The list of subscibers to R. Phinehas's commentary on the prayer book *Sha'ar ha-rahamim* [Gate of Mercy] (Shklov, 1788) indicates the existence of non-Hasidic congregations in Vitebsk, Nevel, and Polotsk.

38. The text of the oath is reproduced by Wilensky, *Hasidim ve-mitnagdim*, 1: 323.
39. I. Etkes, "'Aliyato shel rabi Shneur Zalman" (above n. 33).
40. *'Igrot kodesh*, 3–4, 8–9; Barnai, *'Igrot hasidim*, 93.
41. Barnai, *'Igrot hasidim*,174; Hilman, *'Igrot ba'al Ha-tanya u-bene doro*, 35.
42. *'Igrot kodesh*, 44. In another letter, R. Shneur Zalman states explicitly that he is not requesting donations, but is imposing fees "with great threats and decrees"; ibid., 52.
43. Heilman, *Bet rabi*, 132; see the responsa, appended to *Shulhan 'arukh ha-rav* (Vilna, 1904), pt. 4.
44. Cf. I. Etkes, "Rabi Shneur Zalman mi-Liadi ke-manhig shel hasidim" [Rabbi Shneur Zalman of Liady as a Hasidic Leader], *Zion* 50 (1986): 321–54.
45. See the recent treatment by Klier, *Russia Gathers Her Jews*, 75–80, and the literature cited there.
46. *Polnoe sobranie zakonov rossiiskoi imperii*, vol. 23, no. 17, 327; cited by Gessen, "K istorii religioznoi borbi," 132.
47. R. Avigdor's denunciation was first published by Dubnow, "Vmeshatel-stvo ruskogo gosudarstvo v anti-khasidskuyu borbu" [The Interference of the Russian State in the Anti-Hasidic Struggle], *Evreiskaia starina* 3 (1910): 90–109, and is available in Hebrew translation in Wilensky, *Hasidim ve-mitnagdim*, 1: 237–58. The passage in question is on p. 108 of Dubnow's article, and pp. 256–57 in Wilensky.
48. Heilman, *Bet rabi*, 9 (n. 1), 53; similarly p. 40.
49. The title page and other sections of this first edition are reproduced in Yehoshua Mondshein, *Sifre ha-halakha shel ha-admor hazaken* [The Halakhic Works of the Old Rabbi], (Brooklyn, N.Y., 1984), 1–5.
50. Heilman, *Bet rabi*, 119–20.
51. See the list of the heads of habad *minyanim* at the end of the "Liozna ordinances" of March 1796; *'Igrot kodesh*, 78–79.
52. Heilman, *Bet rabi*, 140–43; quote from p. 140.
53. On the final stage of the conflict between 1797 and 1801, see the treatment by Wilensky, *Hasidim ve-mitnagdim*, 1: 210–22, 230–36, based on documents which were unknown to Dubnow. The provincial authorities in Lithuania reiterated the official policy denying the kahal the authority to exercise civil, judicial, and police powers; ibid., p. 212.
54. On the continued harsh Mitnagdism of R. Menahem Mendl and R. Israel of Shklov, see the citations in n. 20 above. On the cemetery controversy, see Shlomo Berman, "Mishpehot kahal kadosh shklov ('al pi pinqas ha-niftarim shel hevrat gemilut hasadim shel 'emet)" [The

Families of the Shklov Jewish Community (Based on the Record Book of the Burial Society)], *Kovets 'al yad*, N.S. I [11] (1936): 166.

55. Article 53 of the *polozheniia o evreakh*; see Shmuel Ettinger, "Takanot 1804" [The Statute of 1804], *He-'avar* 21 (1977): 87–110, esp. p. 109; in Russian—O. Levanda, *Polnii khronologicheskii sbornik zakonov i polozhenii kasayushshchikhsa evream* [Complete Chronological Collection of Laws and Statutes Concerning the Jews], (St. Petersburg, 1874), 60. The texts of R. Shneur Zalman's sermons which he delivered in Shklov in 1804, are contained in *Ma'amare ha-admor ha-zaken* [Essays of the Old Rabbi] (Brooklyn, N.Y., 1957), 1: 1–3, 8–11, 13–15; *Ma'amare ha-admor ha-zaken 5564* (Brooklyn, N.Y., 1980), 43–59.

Notes to Chapter 2

1. *Uklides* [Euclid's Elements] (The Hague, 1780), introduction (unpaginated).
2. For an analysis of the Vilna Gaon's image as a forerunner of the Haskalah, see Immanuel Etkes, "Ha-gra ve-ha-haskalah: tadmit ve-mitziut" [The Vilna Gaon and the Haskalah: Image and Reality], in *Prakim be-toldot ha-hevra ha-yehudit be-yeme ha-benayim ve-ba-'et ha-hadasha mukdashim le-profesor yaakov katz [Katz Jubilee Volume]*, ed. E. Etkes and J. Salmon (Jerusalem, 1980), 192–217. Schick's image as a disciple of the Vilna Gaon has likewise a long history. See, for instance, S. Stanislavskii, "Biograficheskie etiudi" [Biographical Studies], *Voskhod* 10 (1891) no. 12: 143–57, esp. pp. 143, 176.
3. Cf. S. J. Fuenn, *Kiryah ne'emanah* [The Loyal City] (Vilna, 1915), 146; Zinberg, *Geshikhte fun der literatur bay yidn* 5, 320–24; Mahler, *Divre yeme yisra'el*, 1, book 4: 14–16, 53–56.
4. Schick's date of birth: Jacob of Karlin, *Keren 'orah 'al masekhet nazir* [Rays of Light on Tractate Nazir] (Jerusalem, 1959), introduction. R. Jacob and his brother R. Isaac of Karlin were Schick's grandsons. His death is recorded in the *pinkas* of the Slutsk burial society (Jewish National and University Library, 40 927), as rosh hodesh adar 5568 (= 1808). On Schick's father, see the letters of approbation to the latter's posthumous *Moreh tsedek* (Shklov, 1783); on the Ginzburg family and Schick's relation to it, see Magid, *Toldot mishpehot ginzburg*, 27–28, 32, 54–56, 168–71.
5. "Pinkas hevra kadisha shivah keruim," Jewish National and University Library, fols. 4a, 6a, 7a, 10a, 17b, and passim; Avraham Haim Shabad, *Toldot ha-yamim she-'avru 'al hevra kadisha shivah keruim* [History of the Shivah keruim Society] (Vilna, 1909), 7–9. Schick's *semikha* was printed in his edition of *Yesod 'olam* (Berlin, 1777); his former post as *dayyan* figures on the title page to *Uklides*.
6. Schick, *'Amude ha-shamayim-tiferet adam* [Pillars of the Heavens and the Splendor of Man] (Berlin, 1777), 2b.

7. Shabad, *Toldot ha-yamim*, 5, 7–9.
8. *Yesod 'olam*, introduction (unpaginated).
9. See below.
10. *Kitve shabetai donelo* [The Works of Shabbetai Donello], ed. Mutner (Jerusalem, 1949), 36; Joseph Ibn Aknin, *Sefer musar*, ed. Bacher (Berlin, 1911), 75; Meir Aldabi, *Shevile 'emunah* (Tel Aviv, n.d.), 33a.
11. See my article "Rabbi Moshe Isserles and the Study of Science among Polish Rabbis," in Bernard Dov Coooperman (ed.), *Tradition and Crisis Revisited* (Cambridge, 1994).
12. Ibid.; David B. Ruderman, "The Impact of Science on Jewish Culture and Society in Venice," in Gaetano Cozzi (ed.), *Gli Ebrei e Venezia* (Milan, 1987), 417–48.
13. Isaac Eisenstein-Barzilay, "The Background of the Berlin Haskalah," in *Essays on Jewish Life and Thought in Honor of Solo W. Baron* (New York, 1959), 184–185; R. Jonathan of Ruzhany's *Yeshua be-yisra'el* [Salvation in Israel] (Frankfurt, 1720), is a comprehensive commentary to Maimonides' *Hilkhot kidush ha-hodesh*.
14. *Tiferet adam*, 21b–22b, 25b; *'Amude ha-shamayim*, 24b–25a; J. Leibowitz, "Smukhim harvianiim ba-refuah ha-'ivrit" [References to Harvey in Hebrew Medical Literature], *Ha-rofe ha-'ivri* 2 (1957), 36–48; Hillel Levine, "Paradise Not Surrendered: Jewish Reactions to Copernicus and the Growth of Modern Science," in Robert Cohen and Max Watkowsky (eds.), *Epistemology, Methodology, and the Social Sciences* (Dordrecht, 1983), 205–22.
15. *Tiferet adam*, 8a; *'Amude ha-shamayim*, 2b, 5a, 10a–b; on Cardano and Viete, see Charles C. Gillespe (ed.), *Dictionary of Scientific Biography* (New York, 1971–76), 3: 64–67; 14: 18–25.
16. *Tiferet adam*, introduction, 2b. It is difficult to comprehend why Schick singled out Isaac Israeli's *Yesod 'olam* and Joseph Shlomo Delmedigo's *'Elim* for criticism on account of their ignorance of "books in foreign tongues, such as Euclid." Both were replete with references to Euclid and other Greek scientists.
17. N. M. Gelber, "Le-toldot ha-rofim ha-yehudim be-polin ba-me'ah ha-18" [On the History of Jewish Physicians in Poland in the Eighteenth Century], in I. Tirosh (ed.), *Shay le-yeshayahu: sefer yovel le-yeshayahu volfsberg* (Tel Aviv, 1956), 347–71. Gelber lists six Padua graduates from Lithuania and Byelorussia in the eighteenth century.
18. On Gordon, see S. Ginzburg, *Ramhal u-vene doro* [Rabbi Moshe Hayyim Luzzatto and His Contemporaries], (Tel Aviv, 1937), index; I. Tishby, "Darke hafatsatam shel kitve ramhal be-folin ve-lita" [The Dissemination of Luzzatto's Writings in Poland and Lithuania], *Kiryat Sefer* 45 (1977): 139–50. For additional evidence suggesting Gordon's intermediacy between Padua and Shklov, see below.
19. *Tiferet adam*, 4a, 8a.

20. *'Amude ha-shamayim,* 24b, 26a–b, 27a–b, 28b. *Tiferet adam* cites the Bible and Talmud on pp. 6b, 7a, 8a–b, 23a–b, 27b, and passim.
21. I. Tishby, *Mishnat ha-zohar* [Teachings of the Zohar] (Jerusalem, 1971), 1: 140–48, 155–58; A. Altmann, "The Delphic Maxim in Medieval Islam and Judaism," in *Studies in Religious Philosophy and Mysticism* (New York, 1969), 14–19.
22. *Tiferet adam,* 22b, citing Zohar 4: 234a and 235a. See R. Yehuda Ashlag, *Zohar 'Im perush ha-sulam* (Jerusalem, 1957), 17: 148–151, 167; *Tiferet adam,* 28b, citing *Tikune zohar,* 52b; *Tiferet adam,* 13a, citing Zohar 3: 128b; similarly *Tiferet adam,* 18a citing *Tikune zohar,* 128a and others.
23. *Tiferet adam,* 17a, citing Zohar 3: 235a. Y. S. Reggio, an enlightened Italian rabbi, criticized Schick for his utilization of the Zohar for anatomical data, *Otsar nehmad* 1 (1856): 9.
24. *Tiferet adam,* 1a.
25. Ibid., 2a.
26. Ibid.
27. Moshe Hayim Luzzatto, *Adir ba-marom* [Mighty in Heaven], ed. S. Luria (Warsaw, 1880), 2a–b.
28. *Tiferet adam,* 2a; on Gordon see the references in n. 18 above.
29. See Mendl Piekarz, *Bi-yeme tsemihat ha-hasidut* [At the Birth of Hasidism] (Jerusalem, 1978).
30. Shabad, *Toldot ha-yamim,* 16. According to Mahler, *Divre yeme yisra'el,* 1, bk. 4: 53–54, Schick journeyed first to London, studied medicine there, and visited Berlin en route back to Poland. I have found no evidence to support any of these claims. R. Saul Berlin in his letter of approbation to *'Amude ha-shamayim-tiferet adam* states that Schick "came here from the land of Lithuania with a scroll on kiddush ha-hodesh and anatomy."
31. M. A. Shulvass, *Between East and West* (Detroit, 1971).
32. Berl Kagan, *Sefer Ha-Prenumerantn* (New York, 1975), Yiddish introduction, ix–x.
33. See the *haskamot* to *'Amude ha-shamayim-tiferet adam* and *Yesod 'olam,* as well as Schick's introduction to the latter.
34. On the Mendelssohnian circle, see A. Altmann, *Moses Mendelssohn: A Biographical Study* (Philadelphia, 1973), 346–420; Jacob Katz, *Tradition and Crisis* (New York, 1961), 245–74.
35. By contrast, *'Amude ha-shamayim-tireret adam,* published shortly after Schick's arrival, was a simple, low-cost publication. It appears that Schick had not yet made the acquaintance of Berlin's elite at the time of its printing.
36. *Yesod 'olam,* verso, pp. 1, 2.
37. On the Berliners' attitude toward Polish Jews, see N. H. Wessely, *Divre shalom ve-'emet* [Words of Peace and Truth] (Berlin, 1782), 55–56;

148   NOTES TO CHAPTER 2

Aaron Halle Wolfsohn, "Sihah be-'eretz ha-hayim" [A Conversation in
Paradise], *Ha-me'asef* 7 (1797): 55. The anonymous fanatic Mendels-
sohn debates in this imagined dialogue is clearly a Polish Jew; see pp.
56, 58, 123, 131. On Maimon's reception by the Berlin Maskilim, see his
Autobiography, translated by J. Clark Murray (London, 1954), 109–13.
See, more generally, Steven Aschheim, *Brothers and Strangers: The
East European Jew in German and German-Jewish Consciousness,
1800–1923* (Madison, 1982).

38. *Yesod 'olam*, 2a–b.
39. Wessely, *Divre shalom ve-'emet*, 45–46.
40. Maimon, *Autobiography*, 134–37. The original German provides the
    initials of the persons involved. These were Dr. B. and Messrs. F., J.,
    and L.; according to Altmann, the initials refer to Dr. Bloch, Fried-
    lander, Jaroslav, and Levi; *Moses Mendelssohn*, 363.
41. See the partial reprint of Lefin's *Modah le-binah* under the title *Refuot
    ha'am* [Remedies for the People] (Zolkiew, 1794), title page and verso;
    Joseph Klausner, *Historiyah shel ha-sifrut ha-'ivrit ha-hadasha* [History
    of Modern Hebrew Literature] (Jerusalem, 1960), 1: 225–26.
42. Schick spent his later years in Minsk (to 1791), in Ustye, a private
    estate in the Mogilev province of tsarist Russia (to roughly 1797), and
    in Slutsk, where he died in 1808. He published but one book during this
    span of time, a second edition of *Keneh ha-midah* [The Length
    of Measurement] (Shklov, 1791). His most intriguing act was his be-
    coming a member, in 1785, of the Vienna chapter of the Order of the
    Asiatic Brethren, a pseudo-Masonic organization whose members in-
    cluded Austrian aristocrats and Jewish Frankists. Despite this unusual
    association, about which very little is known, there is no basis for
    doubting Schick's religious orthodoxy in the 1780s and 1790s. See G.
    Scholem, "Karyerah shel frankist: Moshe Dobrushka ve-Gilgulav" [The
    Career of a Frankist: Moshe Dobrusha and His Metamorphoses], in
    Mehkarim ve-mekorot le-toldot ha-shabta'ut ve-gilguleha [Studies
    and Sources on the History of Sabbateanism and Its Transformations]
    (Jerusalem, 1974), esp. pp. 160–63. On Schick's Ustye period, see below
    chapter 3.
43. Schick, *Derekh yeshara* [The Straight Path] (The Hague, 1778), intro-
    duction; *Uklides*, postscript appealing for advance subscribers.
44. See above pp. 22.
45. Schick, *Keneh ha-midah* (Prague, 1783), verso.
46. While in Prague, Schick conducted mathematics classes for a group of
    adult students, and enlisted the financial support of several prominent
    citizens of the Jewish community, most notably the members of the
    Jeitteles family. On Prague in this period, see Hillel J. Kieval, "Cau-
    tion's Progress: The Modernization of Jewish Life in Prague, 1780–
    1830," in Jacob Katz (ed.), *Toward Modernity: The European Jewish
    Model* (New Brunswick, N.J., 1987), 71–105.

47. *Uklides*, introduction. These "enemies of wisdom" were a veiled reference to Hasidism; see below, chapter 6.
48. Ibid.
49. Ibid. The position of this sentence is ambiguous; it may be read as a continuation of the words of the Vilna Gaon which precede it, or, alternatively, as Schick's own words. I am convinced that the sentiment is Schick's and is totally uncharacteristic of R. Elijah.
50. *Uklides*, introduction.
51. Arthur Hertzberg, *The French Enlightenment and the Jews* (New York and Philadelphia, 1970), 253–54, 256–57, 279, 294, 309, 311.
52. *Uklides*, introduction. The claim that the rabbis of antiquity had been masters of science, or that the sciences had originated among them and had been lost in the travails of exile, was an old one. What was new in Schick's case was the use of this argument as part of a polemic against the Enlightenment's view of Judaism.
53. Schick, *Keneh ha-midah*, introduction.
54. Wessely, *Divre shalom ve-'emet*, 45–46.
55. On Jewish number mysticism and gematria, see Gershom Scholem, *Kabbalah* (Jerusalem, 1974), 38–39, 54, 337–43.
56. Zohar 3: 47a–48a; see Ashlag, *Zohar 'im perush ha-sulam*, 13: 33–38. One of the accepted interpretations of the passage is that it is incumbent upon one to combine wisdom with foolishness.

Notes to Chapter 3

1. Y. P. Zakalinskaya, *Votchinnie khoziaistva mogilevskoi gubernii v vtoroi polovine XIIIogo veka* [Estate Economies of the Mogilev Province in the Second Half of the Eighteenth Century] (Mogilev, 1958); my thanks to Professor I. R. Christies of University College, London, for making a copy of this rare book available to me. The most recent biographical treatments of Potemkin and Zorich are: A. N. Fateyev, *Potemkin Tavrichevski* (Prague, 1945), and Hans Halm, "Semen Gavrilovic Zoric," *Jahrbücher für der Geschichte Ost-Europas* 8 (1960), no. 1: 1–9. A handy survey of Zorich's estate is available in E. P. Karnovich, *Zamechatelnie bogatstva chastnikh lits v rossii* [Extraordinary Wealth among Private Individuals in Russia] (St. Petersburg, 1874), 314–327.
2. A. S. Pishchevich, autobiography in *Chteniye v imperaterskom obschestve istorii i drevnostei rossiiskikh pri moskovskom universitete*, 1 (1885): 28. Pishchevich visited Shklov in 1787.
3. Aleksandr Barsukov, "Shklovskie avantiuristi" [Shklov Adventurers], in *Razkazi iz ruskoi istorii XVIIIogo veka* [Tales from Russian History in the Eighteenth Century] (St. Petersburg, 1883), 245–49.
4. Christian Hieronymus Julian Schlegel, *Reise aus Polen nach St. Petersburg* (Erfurt-Golga, 1818), 264–65.
5. Schlegel, *Reise*, 255, 266–67.

6. M. I. Meshcherskii and A. N. Korsakov, "Semion gavrilovich zorich," *Russkii arkhiv* 17 (1879), book II, no. 5: 50; Pischevich (above n. 2), p. 31.
7. Schlegel, *Reise*, 272.
8. Meshcherskii and Korsakov, "Zorich," 50, 53; N. B. Drizen, "K istorii krepostnogo teatra: shklovskii balet" [Toward the History of Peasant Theater: The Shklov Ballet], *Stolitsy i usadba* (July 1914): 8–11; G. I. Barishev et al., *Muzikalnii teatr belorussii, dooktriabrskii period* [Musical Theater in Byelorussia: The Pre-October Period] (Minsk, 1990), 194–99, 235–39; and Barishev's *Teatralnaia kultura belorussii 18ogo veka* [The Theatrical Culture of Byelorussia in the Eighteenth Century] (Minsk, 1992), passim.
9. Barishev, *Muzikalnii teatr*, 195, 235.
10. Meshcherskii and Korsakov, "Zorich," 53–56. The Empress's entourage on her visit to Shklov included: Count Grigorii Potemkin, governor-general of New Russia; Count Ivan G. Chernyshev, vice-president of the Admiralty; Count Yakov A. Bruce, governor-general of Moscow; Prince Fedor Bariatinskii; A. D. Lanskoi, then the Empress's favorite; A. A. Bezborodko, the Empress's literary secretary; Prince S. Gagarin and others; ibid., 55, n. 53. Grand Duke Paul, Catherine's eventual successor, visited Shklov with his wife in 1781, ibid., 57.
11. *Russkii biograficheskii slovar'*, 7: 468.
12. Schlegel, *Reise*, 269–72.
13. Ibid., 268–69, 271; Meshcherskii and Korsakov, "Zorich," 90–96; Barsukov, "Shklovskie avantiuristi," esp. pp. 254–56.
14. On Salle-Morant, see Drizen, "Shklovskii balet" (above n. 8), 10; Meshcherskii and Korsakov, "Zorich," 81–82, 95–96; Barsukov, "Shklovskie avantiuristi," 250, 254–56.
15. Meshcherskii and Korsakov, "Zorich," 52. A full list of the employees of Zorich's court in 1783, including its many foreigners, is preserved in the Russsian State Archive of Ancient Acts (RGADA), fond 7, file 2636.
16. Meshcherskii and Korsakov, "Zorich," p. 50; population figures and other information on Shklov's economy and institutions are culled from "Ekonomicheskie primechanie mestechka starii i novii shklov" [Economic Notes on the Towns of Old and New Shklov], RGADA found 1355, file 719, 153–67.
17. "Die einzige Unbequemlichkeit, der man bei seinen Aufenthalt in Sklow unterwerfen, ist dass man bei ein Juden logiren muss, wo man wohl ein oder zwei Zimmer haben kann. Aber sie sind meisstens schlecht und schmuzig." Schlegel, *Reise*, 273.
18. RGADA fond 7, file 2636, mentions several Jews who served as contractors for Zorich's court, including one Joel Berkovitch who was sent to Prussia to purchase playing cards. See also Y. Litvin, "Ven Shklov iz

geven eretz yisroel" [When Shklov Was the Land of Israel], *Yidishe neshomes* [Jewish Souls] (New York, 1916), 1: 2–4. The estimate of tax revenue was made by Jacob Hirsch, in a 1783 memorandum to the Tsarist authorities regarding the creation of Jewish state schools; *Regesti i nadpisi* 3 (St. Petersburg, 1913): 242–43. On Hirsch's memorandum, see below.

19. Drizen, "K istorii krepostnogo teatra" (above n. 8), 10. Yankelevich assumed the family name Dokhovnikova, which may indicate that she converted to Russian-Orthodoxy.

20. R. Judah Leyb Margoliot, *Bet midot* [House of Virtues] (Shklov, 1786), 26b. On Margoliot, see below, chapter 6.

21. Gessen, *Evrei v rossii*, passim, esp. pp. 40–41, 360, 444; S. L. Tsitron, "Reb nosn notkin," *Shtadlonim* [Intercessors] (Warsaw, n.d.), 68–89, esp. pp. 68–70. Gessen and Tsitron provide the fullest portraits of Notkin in the historical literature; unfortunately, Tsitron does not identify his sources.

22. L. V. Engelgardt, *Zapiski* [Notes] (Moscow, 1868), 24, n. 4, cited by Meshcherskii and Korsakov, "Zorich," 54, n. 31.

23. Richard Markgraff, *Zur Geschichte der Juden auf der Messen in Leipzig von 1664–1839* (Bischofswerda, 1894), 69.

24. Y. Litvin, "Nosn nota der shtadlen," *Yiddishe neshomes*, (unpaginated); *Ha-me'asef* 2 (1784–85): 1; *Zemirot yisra'el* (Berlin, 1791), verso. For an analysis of Notkin's proposals to reform Russian Jewry, see below, chapter 5.

25. Pinkhes Kon, "A loyb-lid fun der mohilever kehile lekoved katerina der tsveyter" [A Panegyric by the Mogilev Community to Catherine II], *YIVO historishe shriftn* 1 (1929): 753–760; Chaim Borodianski, "Di loyb-lider lekoved katerina der tsveyter un zeyere mekhabrim" [The Panegyrics to Catherine II and Their Authors], *YIVO historishe shriftn* 2 (1937): 531–37.

26. Y. Litvin, "Ven Shklov iz geven erets yisroel" (above n. 18), 2; Meshcherskii and Korsakov, "Zorich," 58, 87; Zorich's letter to Count Aleksei Borisovich Kurakin, general procurator of Russia, May 1797, recounts Notkin's "service to the fatherland," Gessen, *Evrei v rossii*, 41–42.

27. Gessen, *Evrei v rossii*, 41–42. The partnership between Notkin, Shoshinin, and Ikonov went bankrupt in 1799.

28. M. F. Shugurov, "Istoriia evreev v rossii" [History of the Jews in Russia], *Russkii arkhiv* 32 (1894), no. 2: 166, cited in part by Gessen, *Istoriia evreiskogo naroda v rossii*, 1: 175–76.

29. Gessen, *Istoriia*, 176–77. A legally defined realm of Jewish settlement was created in 1794, after the second partition of Poland, and included the newly acquired Lithuanian and Ukrainian provinces, as well as New Russia; see Klier, *Russia Gathers Her Jews*, 75–76.

30. Gessen, *Evrei v rossii*, 41–42.

31. Ibid., 78.
32. Ibid., 34–36, 81, 361. On Notkin's proposals to the State Committee for the Organization of Jewish Life on reforming the Jews' status, see below, chapter 5.
33. Gessen, *Evrei v rossii*, 42; Tsitron, *Shtadlonim*, 73.
34. Quotation from Litvin, "Nosn nota der shtadlen," 2. On his intercesion on behalf of R. Shneur Zalman, the Smolensk community, and other Jews in distress, see Heilman, *Bet rabi*, 75–76; Gessen, *Evrei v rossii*, 452–53; and idem, "Iz biografii noti khaimovicha notkina" [From the Biography of Nota Haymovitch Notkin], *Buduschnost* 1 (1900), no. 45: 894–95. Several legendary tales about Notkin are related by Tsitron, "Reb nosn notkin," 76–83.
35. Magid, *Toldot mishpehot ginzburg*, 50.
36. J. L. Gordon, "K istorii poseleniia evreev v peterburge" [On the History of Jewish Settlement in St. Petersburg], *Voskhod* 1 (1881), no. 2: 36–37, 42.
37. Biographical portraits of Zeitlin are found in Tsitron, *Shtadlonim*, 28–52, and Zinberg, *Geshikhte fun der literatur bay yidn*, 5: 333–34. See S. L. Fuenn, *Kneset yisra'el* (Warsaw, 1886), 430–31 (on his rabbinical studies), and Gessen, *Evrei v rossii*, 41 (on his brother). On the Zeitlin family see Shlomo Berman, "Mishpehot kahal kadosh shklov," *Kovetz 'al yad*, N.S. 1 (1936): 154–158, 172–73.
38. Tsitron, *Shtadlonim*, 28–29, 36; *Zemirot yisra'el* (Berlin, 1791), subscription list; *Besamim rosh* (Berlin, 1793), verso. On the latter work and the furor it aroused, see Moshe Pelli, *Bi-ma'avake temurah* [In the Struggles over Change] (Tel Aviv, 1988), 149–65.
39. Shai Hurvitz, "Sefer hayai" [The Book of My Life], *Ha-shilo'ah* 40 (1922): 3; see also the portrait by Zeitlin's son-in-law, Mordechai Nathanson, in Fuenn, *Kiryah ne'emanah*, 277–79.
40. Fuenn, *Kneset yisra'el*, 431; idem, *Kiryah ne'emanah*, 277. On the title *nadvornii sovetnik*, see James Hassell, "The Implementation of the Table of Ranks in the Eighteenth Century," *Slavic Review* 29 (1970): 283–95.
41. Fuenn, *Kiryah ne'emanah*, 277. Zeitlin's role model in constructing his court may have been Potemkin, whose "extravagances in the field of clothing, jewelry, the table carriages, horses, palaces and gardens, became legendary"; Isabel de Madariaga, *Russia in the Age of Catherine the Great* (London, 1981), 348.
42. Fuenn, *Kiryah ne'emanah*, 277. Nathanson relates that Schick conducted chemical experiments in Ustye; Hurvitz relates that he wrote a book of mathematics (which he mistakenly identifies as *Uklides*); "Sefer hayai," 5. On Lefin's *Heshbon ha-nefesh*, see Immanuel Etkes, *Rabi yisra'el salanter* (Jerusalem, 1982), 135–46, and the literature cited there.

43. Gordon, "K istorii poseleniia evreev v peterburge," *Voskhod* 1 (1881) no. 2: 31; Gordon relates that Lefin was recommended to Abraham Perets by David Friedlander, "with whom Perets was friends and in frequent contact."

44. Fuenn, *Kiryah ne'emanah*, 277; see A. Ya'ari, "Ha-defus ha-'ivri bi-Shklov" [Jewish Printing in Shklov], *Kiryat sefer* 22 (1945): nos. 116, 147; *Sefer mitzvot katan 'im hagahot hadashot* (Kopys, 1820). Zeitlin's letter for the Volozhin yeshiva was printed in *Ha-peles* 2 (1902), 293. On his close friend and colleague, R. Benjamin Rivlin, who also spent many years in Ustye, see below, chapter 6.

45. Fuenn, *Kiryah ne'emanah*, 277; Hurvitz, "Sefer hayai" (above n. 39), 4; Tsitron, *Shtadlonim*, 31–32. Tsitron, 74, reports that Zeitlin and Notkin, although close friends, differed on how to deal with the Russian authorities. Zeitlin preferred case-by-case intercession in instances of anti-Jewish persecution, whereas Notkin advocated a broader strategy of presenting plans to reform the Jews' social and legal status.

46. S. Beilin, "Perepiska mezhdu bukharskimi evreami i shklovskimi evreami" [The Correspondence between the Jews of Bukhara and Shklov], *Perezhitoe* 2 (1910): 277; Barsukov, "Shklovskie avantiuristi," 35.

47. Emanuel Ringelblum, *Kapitlen geshikhte* [Chapters of History] (Buenos Aires, 1953), 187–90; H. J. Kruger, *Die Judenschaft von Königsberg in Preussen 1700–1812* (Marburg, 1966), 95; on the anonymous pamphlet itself, see Mahler, *Toldot ha-yehudim be-folin*, 442–43.

48. Ringelblum, *Kapitlen geshikhte*, 206–7.

49. *Zer'a kodesh* [Holy Seed] (Berlin, 1797), 16b, 19b, 23b–24a, 25b, 29b–30b (letter by Wessely to Kerner). Kerner was born in the Polish town of Zlotowo, and moved to Shklov as a young man.

50. *Humash netivot ha-shalom*, Genesis (Berlin, 1780); *Ha-me'asef* 2 (1784–85): 1; 3 (1786): 211; Isaac Satanov, *Sefer ha-shorashim* (Berlin, 1787), *Sefer ha-midot* (Berlin, 1790), and *Mishle 'asaf* (Berlin, 1792).

51. B. Weinryb, "Yehude polin ve-lita ve-yahasehem le-breslau" [The Jews of Poland and Lithuania and Their Relations with Breslau], in *Mehkarim be-toldot ha-kalkalah ve-ha-hevra shel yehude polin* [Studies on the Economic and Social History of Polish Jewry] (Jerusalem, 1939), 58–59.

52. *Regesti i nadpisi*, 3: 240–43. A Hebrew translation of Hirsch's memorandum was published in *He-'avar* 19 (1972): 78–80.

53. *Regesti i nadpisi*, 241; *He-'avar*, 79. Hirsch also suggested that tax revenues on the slaughter and sale of kosher meat and other commercial transactions be applied toward the establishment of the schools.

54. Litvin, "Ven Shklov iz geven erets yisroel," 8; Ya'ari, "Ha-defus ha-'ivri bi-Shklov," 60.

Notes to Chapter 4

1. On Lefin, see Mahler, *Divre yeme yisra'el*, 4, book 1: 71–88; and Hillel Levine, "Ben hasidut le-haskalah: 'al pulmus anti-hasidi musve" [Between Hasidism and Haskalah: On a Veiled Anti-Hasidic Polemic], in I. Etkes and J. Salmon (eds.), *Prakim le-toldot ha-hevra ha-yehudit be-yeme ha-benayim ve-ba'et ha-hadasha mukdashim le-profesor yaakov katz* [Katz Jubilee Volume] (Jerusalem, 1980), 122–31, and the literature cited there.

2. The scholarly treatments of Schulman to date are: S. Stanislavskii, "Biograficheskaia zametka" [Biographical Note] *Voskhod* 16 (1896), no. 2: 151–57; I. Zinberg, *Geshikhte fun der literatur bay yidn*, 5: 334–36; and A. R. Malachi, *Masot ve-reshimot* [Essays and Notes], (New York, 1937), 109–14; Katz has been overlooked by modern scholarship.

3. Quotation from Mordechai Plungian's biography of the Manasseh of Ilya, *Ben porat* [Son of Porat] (Vilna, 1858), 67.

4. Study of the *Guide* was a key early phase in the metamorphoses of Mendl Lefin, Solomon Maimon, Manasseh of Ilya, and Isaac Ber Levinsohn into Maskilim. On the Berlin Haskalah's image of Maimonides and the *Guide*, see James H. Lehman, "Maimonides, Mendelssohn, and the Me'asfim," *Leo Baeck Institute Yearbook* 20 (1975): 87–108.

5. Hillel Noah Steinschneider, "Kalman Schulman," *Ha-melitz* (1899), no. 7: 12; Fuenn, *Kiryah ne'emanah*, 160. The incident is related with slight variations by Joshua Heschel Levin, *'Aliyot eliyahu* [The Ascendance of Elijah] (Vilna, 1885), 13a, and Kalman Schulman, *Toldot gedole yisra'el* [History of Great Jews] (Vilna, 1913), 2: 135–36. Schulman exhibited his interest in disseminating knowledge of the *Guide to the Perplexed* in his edition of *Zekher rav* (Shklov, 1804), to which he prefaced a lengthy excerpt from Maimonides' introduction to the *Guide*.

6. Mordechai Plungian, *Ben porat*, 67; *Zekher rav*, introduction (unpaginated), 5; H. N. Steinschneider, "Le-toldot R. Kalman Schulman," *Ha-tsefirah* (1889), no. 172: 703.

7. Pelli, *Be-ma'avake temurah*; Tsemah Tsamriyon, *Ha-me'asef: ktav ha-'et ha-moderni ha-rishon be-'ivrit* [*Ha-me'asef*: The First Modern Hebrew Periodical] (Tel Aviv, 1985), 72–91.

8. "Hakdamat ha-mevi li-vet ha-defus," in R. Manasseh Ben Israel, *Mikveh yisra'el* [The Hope of Israel] (Shklov, 1797).

9. Ibid.

10. The list was printed in Ben Israel's original edition in small typeface at the back of the book. In Schulman's edition, it was presented in large bold print at the very outset of the volume.

11. Aaron Halle Wolfsohn, "Sihah be-'erets ha-hayim" [A Conversation in Paradise], *Ha-me'asef*, 7 (1794–97): 131.

12. See Maimonides, *Guide to the Perplexed*, 1:73, and Isaac Israeli, *Yesod*

'olam [Foundation of the Earth] (Berlin, 1777), 18a, 21b, 36a. Schick, in his notes to *Yesod 'olam*, corrected Israeli's error, and remarked that "the recent wisemen found many dwelling places in the southern half," and that "indeed there are dwelling places opposite our feet." Schick's and Schulman's contemporaries had rather backward notions of geography. The Vilna Gaon contended that the earth was square, based on his understanding of biblical verses. See Levin, *'Aliyot eliyahu*, 62, n. 85.

13. Hayim Avraham Katz, *Simhat levav, hu sefer Hovot ha-levavot 'im biur hadash* [Joy to the Heart: A Commentary on "Duties of the Heart"] (Shklov, 1803), introduction, 4b–5a.

14. The editors of *Ha-me'asef* recommended that Frankfurter-Mendelsohn's book be purchased "especially by the dear Jews of Poland, who don't read the books of the Gentile nations"; *Ha-me'asef* (1810): 96.

15. *Zekher rav*, introduction (unpaginated), 5. Schulman's linear translation drew heavily on a prior translation by Yerahmiel Falk Katz, published in the Brunn 1790 edition of *Zekher rav* (this was first pointed out in *Ha-Magid* 3 [1858], no. 34: 134–35). The linear biblical references and index were Schulman's own innovations.

16. *Zekher rav*, introduction (unpaginated), 4–6.

17. S. Assaf, *Mekorot le-toldot ha-hinukh be-yisra'el* [Sources on the History of Jewish Education] (Jerusalem, 1925), 1: 45–52, 61–63; M. Kleinberger, *Ha-mahshavah ha-pedagogit shel ha-maharal mi-Prag* [The Educational Philosophy of R. Judah Loeb of Prague] (Jerusalem, 1962).

18. *Zekher rav*, introduction (unpaginated), 4.

19. See Katz, *Out of the Ghetto* (Cambridge, Mass., 1973), 66–69; Mordecai Eliav, *Ha-hinukh ha-yehudi be-germanya ·be-yeme ha-haskalah ve-ha-emantsipatsya* [Jewish Education in Germany in the Age of Haskalah and Emancipation] (Jerusalem, 1961).

20. *Zekher rav*, introduction (unpaginated), 5.

21. Solomon Maimon, *Autobiography*, 95, 108, 112, 126, 129; R. Rosenfeld, "Rabi menashe ilyer," *Ha-tekufah* 2 (1918): 226. R. Manasseh of Ilya's lack of fluency in German hampered his quest for general knowledge, and contemporary Galician Maskilim, who were fluent in German, considered his level of knowledge quite backward; S. H. Hurwitz, *Tsiyun le-nefesh rabenu nahman ha-kohen krokhmal* [In Memory of Nahman Krochmal] (Warsaw, 1887), 61.

22. Since the language of the traditional "khumesh taytsh" in the *heder* was itself an archaic form of Yiddish, it was, to begin with, closer to German than contemporary spoken Yiddish. See Shlomo Noble, *Khumesh taytsh* [Bible Translation] (New York, 1943), esp. pp. 13–16. Schulman's translation consciously expunged the Slavic component of Yiddish, and may be considered one of the first examples of Maskilic *daytshmerish*, i.e., employing an intentionally "Germanized" language.

23. *Zekher rav*, introduction (unpaginated), 5; S. J. Fuenn, *Safah la-ne'emanim* [Tongue of the Faithful] (Vilna, 1881), 147. A linear Russian translation of *Zekher rav* was published in Warsaw in 1873 by Naftali Maskil Le-'Eitan, but whether the translation was Schulman's is unclear.

24. *Zekher rav*, final page.

25. Schulman's hymn to the Grand Duchess was *Shir ve-halel* [Song and Praise] (Vilna, 1806); on his later educational ventures, see Steinschneider, "Kalman Schulman" (above n. 5); idem, "Le-todot R. Kalman Schulman" (above n. 6), 703. See also A. Z. Rabinovitz, "Le-toldot ha-hinukh ve-ha-haskalah shel ha-yehudim be-rusiya" [On the History of Jewish Education and Enlightenment in Russia], *Ha-hinukh* 3 (1912–13): 105.

26. Avraham Ya'ari, "Le-toldot ha-drama ha-yisre'elit: drama 'ivrit me-haye yosef ve-ehav" [On the History of Jewish Drama: A Hebrew Drama on Joseph and His Brothers], *Bama* 5–6 (1934): 28–34; Ziporah Kagan, "Mekorot ve-mekori'ut ba-mahaze milhama ba-shalom le-hayim avraham katz" [Sources and Originality in the Play "War against Peace" by Hayim Avraham Katz], *Bama* 43 [96] (1969): 62–77, and 44 [97] (1970): 70–78.

27. Hayim Avraham Katz, *Milhama ba-shalom* [War against Peace] (Shklov, 1797), 2a.

28. Ibid.

29. Introduction to Katz, *Simhat levav*, 5a.

30. Katz, *Milhama ba-shalom*, 2a; the sections were contained in the drama's second part, entitled "open rebuke" *(tohakhat megule)*.

31. This point is examined by Kagan, "Mekorot ve-mekori'ut," 67–69.

32. Katz, *Milhama ba-shalom*, 7a.

33. Ibid., 16a–b, 19a–20a, 23bff. and esp. 25a. Other characters were Mirod, the chief butler, Belkin, the Eunuch, and the anonymous prison warden.

34. Ibid., 13a–b. The story was similar to the legend of Solomon and Asmadai. See Kagan's list of stories and parables in "Mekorot ve-mekori'ut," 73–74.

35. See Kagan, "Mekorot ve-mekori'ut," passim, esp. pp. 68, 74 for further examples. The dialogue between Jacob and the wolf is found in Yosef Dan (ed.), *Sefer ha-yashar* (Jerusalem, 1986): 197–98. On the Yiddish chapbook of the late eighteenth century, see David G. Roskies "The Genres of Yiddish Popular Literature 1790–1860," *Working Papers in Yiddish and East European Jewish Studies* 8 (1975); on Hasidic storytelling in this period, see Yosef Dan, *Ha-sipur ha-hasidi* [The Hasidic Tale] (Jerusalem, 1975), 34–79; Gedalyah Nigal, *Ha-siporet ha-hasidit: toldoteha ve-noshe'ah* [The Hasidic Novella: History and Formulation] (Jerusalem, 1981), 13–23.

36. Katz, *Milhama ba-Shalom*, 2b, and in the body of the drama, pp. 3b, 4b–5a; cf. *Sefer ha-yashar* (ed. Dan), 187–89.

37. Katz, *Milhama ba-Shalom*, 9b; compare with the thoroughly negative, uni-dimensional presentation of Zeliha in *Sefer ha-yashar*, 199–203.

38. The first known text of the *mekhires yosef shpil* was published by Berman of Limburg in Frankfurt in 1707; on this and later versions, see Khone Shmeruk (ed.), *Mahazot mikrai'im be-yidish 1697–1750* [Biblical Dramas in Yiddish, 1697–1750] (Jerusalem, 1983), esp. pp. 26–28, 45–48, and 533–621; Y. Shiper, *Geshikhte fun yidisher teater-kunst un drame fun di eltste tsaytn biz 1750* [History of Jewish Theater and Drama from the Oldest Times until 1750] (Warsaw, 1925), 2:249–50.

39. See Hayim Shirman, "Shmuel romaneli, ha-meshorer ve-ha-noded" [Shmuel Romanelli the Wandering Poet], in *Le-toldot Ha-shira ve-ha-drama ha-'ivrit* (Jerusalem: Mosad Bialik, 1979) 2:277–79, and Gershon Shaked's introduction to *Melukhat sha'ul* (Jerusalem, 1968), esp. pp. 21–28. Shirman, 277, notes that *Ha-kolot yehdalun* "really has no plot, and is actually a series of monologues and dialogues expressing emotions and moods." Shaked, pp. 25–26, notes that "the weaknesses of *[Melukhat sha'ul]* are most evident in its manner of characterization. . . . Most of the characters are abstract, like walking ideas."

40. Katz later contended, in his introduction to *Simhat levav*, 4b–5a, that he published his drama in order to raise funds for his father-in-law, whose financial affairs had severely deteriorated. With an eye toward protecting his father-in-law's pride and honor, he did not wish to disclose his authorship or his motive for publishing the drama at the time.

41. Drizen, "K istorii krepostnogo teatra," 10; Simon Karlinsky, *Russian Drama from Its Beginnings to the Age of Pushkin* (Berkeley, 1985), esp. pp. 63–84, 94–115. Karlinsky notes that didactic prose dramas, using realistic Russian speech, became a prominent genre in the 1760s, in the works of Vladimir Lukin and others.

42. Eliezer Pavir's adapted Yiddish translation, *Gedulas yosef* (first edition: Zolkiew, 1801) went through more than forty editions in the nineteenth century. See Avraham Ya'ari, "R. Eliezer pavir ve-mif'alo ha-sifruti" [Eliezer Pavir and His Literary Activity], *Kiryat sefer* 35 (1960), no. 4: 499–520, and David G. Roskies, "The Medium and Message of the Maskilic Chapbook," *Jewish Social Studies* 41 (1977), no. 2: 275–90.

Notes to Chapter 5

1. *Staats- und Gelehrte Zeitung des Hamburgischen Correspondenten*, 1787, no. 53 (April 3): 2; referred to by R. J. Wunderbar, *Geschichte der Juden in den Provinzen Liv- und Kurland* (Mittau, 1853), 32.

2. Judah Leyb b. Noah (Nevakhovich), *Vopl dshcheri iudeiskoi* (St.

etersburg, 1803), 62–63; in Hebrew: *Kol sha'avat bat yehuda* (Shklov, 1804), 34, [reprinted as a supplement to *He-'avar* 2 (1918)]. The ellipsis points are found in Nevakhovich's original text; he considered the term *zhid* defamatory, and inappropriate for print. On Nevakhovich's work, see below.

3. Cf. John D. Klier, "Zhid: Biography of a Russian Epithet," *Slavonic and East European Review* 60 (1982), no. 1: 1–15. In light of the 1787 petition and Nevakhovich's testimony, Klier's suggestion that the term *zhid* gradually became an anti-Semitic epithet during the first half of the nineteenth century needs to be reconsidered.

4. On the municipal reform see de Madariaga, *Russia in the Age of Catherine the Great*, 329–60; on the statute of 1786, see Klier, *Russia Gathers Her Jews*, 70–74.

5. See Tsitron, *Shtadlonim*, 15–27, 28–30, 34. Based on Derzhavin's report, the Senate ruled in 1801 that most of the Jews' complaints were valid, and that landlords could not treat the inhabitants of their towns like their private serfs. The case, however, was moot; Zorich had died more than a year earlier. See the Senate's ruling in S. A. Bershadskii, "Polozhenie o evreakh 1804 goda" [The 1804 Statute on the Jews], *Voskhod* 15 (1895), no. 4: 97–109.

6. *Shir tefila*, cited by Mahler, *Divre yeme yisra'el*, 1, book 3: 116. The German translation which accompanied the Hebrew text is produced by N. N. Golitsyn, *Istoriia russkogo zakonodatelstva o evreakh* [History of Russian Legislation on the Jews] (St. Petersburg, 1886), 377–79. It reads in part:

> Lass in Seinen tagen Religions-hass und Verfolgung unerhoeret Seyn. Wer Dich, allgerechter Gott, fuerchtet, Deinen ewigen Gesetzen getreu, Dem Landesherren und Dem Vaterlande redlich dienet, Jede Kraft seiner Seele, jedes Vermoegen seines koerpers, dem allgemeinen Wohl Des Staats weiht, dem sey ein gleiches Loos beschieden. Er trage dies last Des Landes [sic] und geniesse froh ihr Glueck; er saettige sich von ihrer Fruchtbarkeit und lebe furchtlose under Dem schatten heiliger unverbruechlicher Gesetze.

Mahler, *Divre yeme yisra'el*, 1, book 4: 231, argues that the poem was written by Wessely, based on its stylistic similarity with other poems. Wessely is known to have composed poems in honor of Empress Catherine II (see above, chapter 3) and Tsar Alexander I. On the latter, see the note in *YIVO Historishe shriftn* 2 (1937): 680.

7. S. Bershadskii, "Polozhenie o evreakh," *Voskhod* 15 (1895), no. 1: 86–92.

8. See S. Ettinger, "Ha-yesodot ve-ha-megamot be-'itsuv mediniuto shel ha-shilton ha-rusi klape ha-yehudim 'im halukot polin" [Principles and Tendencies in the Formation of Russian Policy toward the Jews after the Partition of Poland], *He-'avar* 19 (1972): 20–34, esp. pp. 29–30; Klier, *Russia Gathers Her Jews*, 85–94. The most important and influ-

ential response to this survey was the report submitted by Governor Ivan G. Frizel of Lithuania; see Klier, 88–95.

9. The memorandum was published by Gessen, *Evrei v rossii*, 444–46.

10. Ibid.

11. On Dohm's and Mendelssohn's writings on reforming the Jews' social and economic position in society, see Jacob Katz, *Out of the Ghetto: The Social Background of Jewish Emancipation 1770–1870* (Cambridge, Mass., 1973), 57–64. Joseph II's colonization project is mentioned by Gessen, *Evrei v rossii*, 43. Notkin's colonization proposal was based, in part, upon his own intimate familiarity with New Russia, which he acquired during the years when he served as Potemkin's purveyor.

12. Ettinger, "Ha-yesodot ve-ha-megamot," 30–33; Klier, *Russia Gathers Her Jews*, 95–113. Notkin had submitted a copy of his 1797 memorandum for consideration by Derzhavin, and the latter adopted Notkin's proposal for establishing Jewish colonies in New Russia, transforming it from a plan for voluntary resettlement into one for the forced deportation of "unnecessary" elements.

13. Gessen, *Evrei v rossii*, 83–84.

14. In his memoirs, Derzhavin charged that Notkin offered him a bribe to change the views he expressed in the State Committee for the Organization of Jewish Life; Gavriil Derzhavin, *Sochineniia* [Works], ed. Y. Grota (St. Petersburg, 1876), 6: 763–64.

15. Gessen, *Evrei v rossii*, 84, 452–53.

16. An abridged version of Notkin's memorandum was printed by Derzhavin, *Sochineniia* (St. Petersburg, 1878), 7: 353–55.

17. Ibid., 354.

18. Ibid., 355.

19. Notkin also reiterated his proposal to free Jews from double taxation; ibid., 354.

20. See Isaac Levitats, *The Jewish Community in Russia, 1772–1844* (New York, 1943), 94–97 and the literature cited there.

21. Derzhavin, "zapiski," in *Sochineniia*, 6: 764, also p. 767; Gordon, "K istorii poseleniia evreev v peterburge," 34. The page dedicating the Hebrew version *kol sha'avat bat yehuda* (Shklov, 1804) to Perets is missing from most existing copies of the work, and may have been removed due to his subsequent conversion; Gessen, *Evrei v rossii*, 91, n. 1.

22. Gessen, *Evrei v rossii*, 80–81. Perets was also an active trader at the Breslau fairs; see Bernard Weinryb, "Yehude polin ve-yahasehem le-breslau," in *Mehkarim be-toldot ha-kalkala ve-ha-hevra shel yehude polin* [Studies on the Economic and Social History of Polish Jewry] (Jerusalem, 1939), 53.

23. Hasidic legend presents a thoroughly negative image of Perets. One tale relates that when R. Shneur Zalman was released from his first arrest in 1798, he was taken from the St. Petersburg prison to the nearest

Jewish household, which happened to be Perets's. The latter proceeded to abuse and insult the Hasidic master, and held him under house arrest for several days; Heilman, *Bet rabi*, 65–66. Another late source claims that Perets was the main informer against Hasidim to the Russian authorities; Wilensky, *Hasidim ve-mitnagdim*, 2: 354. This is in sharp contrast to the image of Nota Notkin, who, although no Hasid, was given credit for bringing about R. Shneur Zalman's release; Heilman, *Bet rabi*, 75.

24. Gordon, "K istorii," 31; Y. D. Baum, "Evrei Dekabrist: grigorii abramovich perets" [A Jewish Decembrist: Grigorii Abramovich Perets], *Katorga i ssilka* 25 (1926): 100–102. Perets's daughter Miriam stayed behind in Ustye with her mother, and died in 1810, at a young age; S. Berman, "Mishpehot kahal kadosh shklov," 155.

25. See S. Dubnow, *History of the Jews in Russia and Poland* (Philadelphia, 1916), 1: 340; Gessen, *Evrei v rossii*, 85–87, 114–15.

26. Judah Leyb Nevakhovich, *Kol sha'avat bat yehuda* (Shklov, 1804) [reprinted as a supplement to *He-'avar* 2 (1918)], introduction, 1. On Nevakhovich's role as tutor of Russian, see, Gessen, *Evrei v rossii*, 81; Tsitron, *Shtadlonim*, 39–41.

27. See Wilensky, *Hasidim ve-mitnagdim*, 1: 273, 280–81, 290.

28. Judah Leyb Nevakhovich, *Vopl dshcheri iudeiskoi*, reprinted in the annual scientific-literary supplement to *Budushchnost* 3 (1902): 114–31. See the dedication to Kochubei, 117 (in the Hebrew *Kol sha'avat*, 9). This and all subsequent quotations are from the Russian text; the analogous passages from the Hebrew version are cited in parentheses.

29. *Budushchnost*, 118–19 (*Kol sha'avat*, 11).

30. *Budushchnost*, 125–26 (*Kol sha'avat*, 20–21). In a note, Nevakhovich contended that anti-Jewish student violence was prohibited by Russia's municipal authorities, who were guided by the provisions of Catherine's Charter for Provincial and Municipal Institutions (promulgated in 1775). After a few disorders took place, the perpetrators were imprisoned "and Jews saw for the first time that cruelty was not a Christian obligation."

31. Nevakhovich, "Chustvovanie verno-poddannago . . . ," *Vopl dshcheri iudeiskoi*, (St. Petersburg, 1803), 57–60 (*Kol sha'avat*, 32–33). I would like to express my thanks to Mr. Viktor Kelner of the Public Library, St. Petersburg, for making a copy of the original edition of *Vopl* available to me.

32. *Vopl*, 61–63 (*Kol sha'avat*, 34).

33. *Vopl*, 63–64 (*Kol sha'avat*, 35).

34. *Vopl*, 65–66 (*Kol sha'avat*, 36).

35. *Budushchnost*, 122 (*Kol sha'avat*, 16).

36. *Budushchnost*, 122–23 (*Kol sha'avat*, 16–17). Nevakhovich included a separate apostrophe between "Intolerance, Truth and Peace" in his

pamphlet, in which Intolerance is charged with inflicting endless suffering on the peoples of Europe, and is banished from the land for
eternity. *Vopl*, 50–56 (*Kol sha'avat*, 29–31).
37. *Budushchnost*, 123–24, 126 (*Kol sha'avat*, 17–18, 22).
38. *Budushchnost*, 126 (*Kol sha'avat*, 21–22). An explicit appeal to Christian mercy is made on p. 122 (*Kol sha'avat*, 16): "Oh Christians, who
are famous for your meekness and mercy! Have pity upon us! Turn you
tender hearts to us!"
39. *Budushchnost*, 127–28 (*Kol sha'avat*, 23–24). The last point, comparing
the morals of Jews in different lands, was omitted from the pamphlet's
Hebrew version.
40. Ibid.
41. *Budushchnost*, 131 (*Kol sha'avat*, 28).
42. *Kol sha'avat*, 7–8.
43. Ibid.

Notes to Chapter 6

1. See above, chapters 3 and 4.
2. Introduction to *Sefer megine 'erets* (Shklov, 1803), by R. Elijah's sons,
R. Judah Leyb and R. Abraham, pp. 2b–3a. For references to R. Benjamin Rivlin's yeshiva, see the entry "Shklov" (by Joshua Duber Khav-
kin), in *'Otzar yisra'el*, 10: 208; C. H. Rivlin, *Hazon tziyon: shklov ve-
yerushalayim* [Vision of Zion: Shklov and Jerusalem] (Jerusalem,
1953), 13–14; and S. Berman "Mishpehot kahal kadosh shklov," 147
(which records the death of "our master R. Mendl, who used to sit in
the house of study of our master R. Benjamin").
3. Fuenn, *Kiryah ne'emanah*, 168–69; Berman, "Mishpehot kahal kadosh
shklov," 176–77. The 1787 takkanot and other anti-Hasidic documents
were compiled by Rivlin in a manuscript, which was circulated in his
name. See Wilensky, *Hasidim ve-mitnagdim*, 1: 142.
4. Fuenn, *Kiryah ne'emanah*, 206. R. Avraham's letters of approbation to
books published in Shklov are noted in Ya'ari, "Ha-defus ha-'ivri be-
Shklov," nos. 56, 57. He later moved to the town of Rogola, and was
popularly known as "reb avrohom rogoler." See R. Avraham b. Shlomo
Zalman, *Ma'alot ha-torah* [Virtues of the Torah], ed. Michel Feinstein
and Nissan Waxman (New York, 1946), xiii–xxiii.
5. *Sefer megine 'erets*, 2b–3a; *'Otzar yisra'el*, 10: 208.
6. Arye Leib Frumkin, *Toldot Hakhme yerushalayim* [History of the Sages
of Jerusalem] (Jerusalem, 1929), 3: 158–63; J. J. Dinstag, "Rabenu eliyahu mi-vilna: reshima bibliografit" [Rabbi Elijah of Vilna: A Bibliogra-
phy], *Talpiyot* 4 (1949), no. 1–2: 269–356. Of these works, only the
notes on the *Shulhan 'arukh* were from the Gaon's own manuscript.
The others were based on R. Menahem Mendl's notes, which, in some
cases, were reviewed by the Gaon during his lifetime.

7. Three of R. Menahem Mendl's kabbalistic works were recently reissued, *Mayim 'adirim—menahem tziyon—biurim ve-likutim* [Great Waters—Comfort of Zion—Collected Commentaries] (Jerusalem, 1987).

8. Frumkin, *Toldot Hakhme yerushalayim*, 3: 164–67; Fuenn, *Kiryah ne'emanah*, 169; Khaykl Lunski, "Geoynim un gdoylim fun noentn over" [Sages and Giants of the Near Past], *Dos Vort* 488, 1 Adar (1934), 2; S. Levi, "Rabi yisra'el mi-shklov" [Rabbi Israel of Shklov], *Sinai* 3 (1939), no. 1–2: 30–37.

9. See Rabbi Shlomo Goren, "Ha-gra ve-heyerushalmi," in *Sefer Ha-gra* [Vilna Gaon Volume], ed. Rabbi Yehuda Leib Maimon (Jerusalem, 1954), 4: 45–107.

10. Elijah b. Shlomo Zalman of Vilna, *Ayil meshulash* [Geometry], (Vilna/Grodna, 1833); idem, *Dikduk eliyahu* [Elijah's Grammar] (Vilna/Grodna, 1833). See Dinstag's bibliography, 303–4.

11. Avraham Danziger, *Sefer Tsava'at . . . Yehezkel* (Vilna, 1871), 25.

12. Introduction to R. Elijah's commentary on tractate *Avot, Masekhet avot im perush rashi ve-perush ha-ga'on . . . rabenu eliyahu* (Shklov, 1804).

13. Introduction to Israel b. Shmuel of Shklov, *Pe'at ha-shulhan* (Safed, 1836); cited from the Jerusalem, 1968 edition, 5.

14. Letter to Kalman Schulman, printed as a preface to the latter's *Milhamot ha-yehudim 'im ha-roma'im* [The Jewish Wars with the Romans] (Vilna, 1862), v–vi.

15. Barukh b. Jacob Schick, *Uklides*, introduction, 2.

16. On the Gaon as Talmudist, see Louis Ginzberg, "The Gaon, Rabbi Elijah Wilna," in *Students, Scholars and Saints* (Philadelphia, 1928), 125–145, esp. pp. 135–39, and Hayyim Tchernowitz, *Toldot ha-poskim* [The History of Talmudic Adjudicators] (New York, 1948), 3: 210–33. Orthodox biographies of the Gaon, such as Bezalel Landau, *Ha-Gaon he-hasid mi-vilna* [The Gaon and Saint of Vilna] (Jerusalem, 1978), 217, 225–26, have cast aspersions on the veracity of Schick's quotation, in part because of its implicit criticism of most sages and scholars throughout the ages. This is, in fact, further evidence of its accuracy.

17. H. H. Ben Sasson, "Ishiuto shel ha-gra ve-hashpa'ato ha-historit" [The Personality of the Vilna Gaon and Its Historical Impact], *Zion* 31 (1966): 39–86, 197–216; Jacob J. Dinstag, "Ha-'im hitnaged ha-gra le-mishnato ha-filosofit shel ha-rambam?" [Did the Vilna Gaon Oppose the Philosophic Teachings of Maimonides?], *Talpiyot* 4 (1949), no. 1–2: 253–68.

18. See Immanuel Etkes, "Ha-gra ve-ha-haskalah: tadmit ve-mitziut."

19. Benjamin b. Shlomo Zalman Rivlin, *Geviei gevia ha-kesef* [The Silver Goblet], second edition (Warsaw, 1897), 10 (on Ecclesiastes 9:11); 37 (on Shabbat 10a); 47, and passim. Rivlin cited his master, R. Elijah, numerous times in the volume; see, for instance, pp. 7, 8, 10, 15, 17, 25, 33, 46, and 47.

20. Ibid., 5–6 (on Genesis 18:5–6); 17 (on Isaiah 28:9); 19–20 (on Jer. 22:15); 47, and passim.
21. Ibid., 25–26.
22. Fuenn, *Kiryah ne'emanah*, 272–73.
23. Ibid. Similary, Zeitlin's descendant Shai Hurvitz relates that Rivlin established a chemical laboratory and a botanical preserve at Ustye; "Sefer hayai," 5.
24. Fuenn, *Kiryah ne'emanah*, 272–73; see above, chapter 2, on R. Barukh Schick, and my article, "Rabbi Moshe Isserles and the Study of Science among Polish Rabbis," in Bernard D. Cooperman (ed.), *Tradition and Crisis Revisited* (Cambridge, Mass., 1994).
25. R. Israel b. Shmuel of Shklov, *Pe'at ha-shulhan*, introduction, 5.
26. On R. Elijah's interest in the translation of various works into Hebrew, see the testimonies of R. Avraham Simcha of Mtsislavl (above n. 14), and of R. Barukh Schick (n. 15). For evidence of Rivlin's reading non-Hebrew scientific literature, see the citations from *Geviei* gevia ha-kesef below.
27. Rivlin, *Geviei gevia ha-kesef*, 37.
28. Ibid., 53.
29. Ibid., 51–52, as well as pp. 41–42, 49–50, 50–51.
30. *Sefer magine 'erets*, verso. R. Moshe Zeitlin's mathematical *hidushim* were also published as an appendix to *Sefer tsava* (Shklov, 1803), 11b–12b.
31. On Margoliot, see I. Zinberg, *Toldot sifrut yisra'el* [History of Jewish Literature] (Tel Aviv, 1958), 3: 314–17; (Tel Aviv, 1959), 5: 137–40, and A. R. Malachi, "Rabi yehuda leyb margoliot, ve-hagra mi-vilna" [Rabbi Judah Leyb Margoliot and the Vilna Gaon], *Ha-do'ar*, Tamuz 11, 1959. Margoliot published two editions of his scientific primer *'or 'olam al hokhmat ha-teva* (Frankfurt, 1777, and Novydvor, 1783).
32. See the letters of approbation by R. Avraham Katzenellenbogen of Brest-Litovsk and R. Issachar Ber b. Judah Leyb of Shklov to *Bet midot* (Shklov, 1786).
33. Margoliot, *Bet midot*, 2b–3a. Citations of Aristotle's *Ethics* are on pp. 8a, 9b, 13b, 15b, 16b, and passim.
34. Ibid., 5a–b, 11b. Among the Muslim philosophers cited are Avveroes (p. 5a), Algazzi and Abuhamad (p. 19a). On pp. 23a–b, Margoliot advocated the study of Kabbalah to enhance one's fear of God, but the point was left undeveloped. His own book did not draw upon kabbalistic works.
35. Ibid., 11b–32b.
36. Ibid., 20b–21a. Margoliot conceded that the philosophic books of Jewish sages, such as Maimonides' *Guide*, did not pose a threat to one's faith, but he argued that reading their books would inevitably and unavoidably lead one to peruse the harmful works of non-Jewish philosophers.

37. Ibid., 20b. This distinction between science and philosophy was not new; see R. Moshe Isserles, *She'elot ve-teshuvot ha-rama* [Responsa], ed. A. Siev (Jerusalem, 1971), no. 6, and Kleinberger, *Ha-mahshavah ha-pedagogit she ha-maharal mi-prag*, 148–55.
38. Margoliot, *Bet midot*, 20b.
39. Ibid., 26b; see above chapter 3.
40. Another theme in *Bet midot* which may have been influenced by Maskilic thought is the criticism of blind obedience to custom. Noting that the letters of the Hebrew words *minhag* (custom) and *gehenom* (hell) were identical, he told the story "of a man who visited a town of blind-men and proceeded to scratch out his eyes—lest he deviate from their custom." Ibid., 27a.
41. Barnai, *Igrot hasidim me-'erets yisrael*, 119.
42. Ibid., 130–31. R. Menahem Mendl's deputy, R. Avraham of Kalisk, added his own words of admonition: "One should reject the ways of the Gentiles and their practices, and should consider them like nothingness and emptiness." Ibid., 132.
43. Ibid., 147.
44. Shneur Zalman b. Barukh of Liady, *Shulhan arukh ha-rav* [Code of Jewish Law], "Hilkhot Talmud torah" 3:7 (Brooklyn, N.Y., 1968), 5: 1695–96. R. Shneur Zalman left open the possibility that scholars could study worldly sciences "incidentally," in order to acquire words of Torah and fear of God, but "the rest of the people may not."
45. Shneur Zalman b. Barukh of Liady, *Likute amarim-tanya* [The Tanya] (Brooklyn, N.Y., 1968), 13a–b.
46. Schick, *Uklides*, introduction, 1.
47. Ibid.
48. Ibid.
49. Ibid., p. 2. Schick's characterization bore an uncanny resemblance to that of the Galician Maskil Joseph Perl, writing in 1816: "The study of all sciences is strictly forbidden by this sect. . . . They oppose nothing so strongly as science, culture, and enlightenment. People who possess any light, who study any science, or who wish to contribute toward the cultural level of their brethren are intolerable to them. They call such people heretics (*min, apikoyres*)." Joseph Perl, *Ueber das wessen Der Sekte Hasidim*, ed. A. Rubinstein (Jerusalem, 1977), 147–48.
50. There was, however, also one prominent Mitnagdic rabbinic figure in Russia who vocally opposed the study of science and Gentile wisdom— the preacher R. Pinhas b. Judah of Polotsk. See Allan L. Nadler, "A Religion of Limits: The Theology of Mitnagdism According to Phinehas Ben Judah Maggid of Polotsk," unpublished Ph.D. dissertation, Harvard University, 1988, 266–75.
51. Margoliot, *Bet midot*, 32a–b.
52. Ibid.

53. R. Hayyim of Volozhin, introduction to *Sifra de-tseni'uta 'im biure ha-gra* (Vilna, 1820); R. Menahem Mendl of Shklov's letter to R. Judah Dibutin, in Wilensky, *Hasidim ve-mitnagdim*, 1: 315–16.
54. R. Israel Loebl, *Sefer vikuakh* (Warsaw, 1798), 21a–b, in Wilensky, *Hasidim ve-mitnagdim*, 1: 320–22; R. Menahem Mendl's polemic: ibid., 1: 317.
55. Aaron Halle Wolfsohn, "Bikoret sefarim hadashim," *Ha-me'asef* (1790): 177–86, esp. p. 180. Wolfsohn criticized Margoliot for his "inconsistent" attitudes toward Gentiles, Greek wisdom, and philosophy. He also charged that many of the the the best sections of *Bet midot* were lifted, without attribution, from Naftali Hirtz Wessely's book *Gan na'ul* (Amsterdam, 1765–66).
56. Wilensky, *Hasidim ve-mitnagdim*, 1: 151.

Notes to Chapter 7

1. Litvin, "ven shklov iz geven erets yisroel," *Yidishe neshomes*.
2. On the liquidation of Zorich's estate, see RGADA, fond 1239, ("Palace Archive"), inventory 3, file 37,840.
3. S. Beilin, "Perepiska mezhdu bukharskimi i shklovskimi evreami" [The Correspondence between the Jews of Bukhara and Shklov], *Perezhitoe* 2 (1910): 274–80; the Hebrew text of the letter is reproduced on pp. 276–77.
4. V. Nikitin, *Evrei zemledel'tsi* [Jewish Farmers] (St. Petersburg, 1887), 5–30; S. V. Borovoi, *Evreiskaia zemledel'cheskaia kolonizatsiia v staroi rossii* [Jewish Argicultural Colonization in Old Russia] (Moscow, 1928), 41–53.
5. Points no. 6–10 of the 1804 Statute, published in Levanda, *Polnii khro-nolgicheskii sbornik*, 53–60; for Hebrew translation, see *He-'avar* 22 (1972): 102–10.
6. Points no. 16, 19, 34–38.
7. Points no. 51, 54.
8. See Klier, *Russia Gathers Her Jews*, 144–64; P. Kon, "Vegn efenen yi-dishe shuln in Mohilever un Vitebsker gubernyes in yor 1808" [Concern-ing Opening Jewish Schools in the Mogilev and Vitebsk Provinces in 1808], *Tsaytshrift* 2–3 (1928): 156–63, 753–60.
9. In a petition to the Tsar written in 1826, Perets surveyed his state-contracted commercial activities between 1804 and 1815. They in-cluded: the sale and delivery of salt to the Smolensk, Kursk, Orlov, and Vorozhensk provinces (1804–5 and 1808–12); serving as purveyor to the Russian military's Baltic ports (1805–9); transporting salt from Nizhgorod to the Smolensk province (1808–12); transporting provisions to Russian military forces stationed in Bessarabia (1815); leasing the concessions on foodstuff taxes in St. Petersburg and its district,

Moscow, the Tulsk province, and other areas (1811–15); State Archive of the Russian Federation (GARF), fond 109, file 3188, pp. 9–12.

10. Gessen, *Evrei v rossii*, 136–39; also Baum, "Evrei Dekabrist," 103; *Hame'asef*, Tammuz 5569; Berman, "Mishpehot kahal-kadosh shklov," 155; A. Rogachevski, "Vernopoddanii evrei: novie dannie o leibe nevakhoviche" [Loyal Jewish Subject: New Information on Leyb Nevakhovich], *Vestnik evreiskogo universiteta v moskve* 1 (1992): 133. The rumors on Perets' immanent conversion are referred to in a letter from Count Dubrovin to A. Arakcheev; Golitsyn, *Istoriia russkogo zakonodatelstva*, 988.

11. Gordon, "K istorii poseleniia evreev v peterburge," 31–32; V. and L. Perets, *Dekabrist grigorii abramovitch Perets* [The Decembrist Grigorii Abramovich Perets], (Leningrad, 1926), 9, 13–14.

12. Gordon, "K istorii," 32; P. Berliner, "Bankir Perets" [The Banker Perets], *Novii voskhod* (1913), no. 1: 45–48. Perets's letter indicates that he did not lose all ties with the Zeitlin family after his conversion. Indeed, R. Joshua Zeitlin is reported to have remembered Perets in his will, and to have stipulated that, in the event that the Empire forced all Jews to sell their lands, "it is my desire that my estate Ustye be purchased by my son-in-law Perets"; Hurvitz, "Sefer hayai," 6.

13. Baum, "Evrei Dekabrist," 102–3; Perets and Perets, *Dekabrist*, 25.

14. Baum, "Evrei Dekabrist," 106–7, 121. Cf. Notkin's plan for the settlement of Jews in Crimea, above chapter 5. Residual ties to Judaism also persisted with Sofia who, after her conversion and marriage, continued to light Sabbath candles on Friday nights; Gordon "K istorii," 32.

15. Baum, "Evrei Dekabrist," 111, 128, Perets and Perets, *Dekabrist*, 14, 36–43. After his release, Grigorii suffered from illness, loneliness, and social stigmatization, and finally died in 1855.

16. Gessen, *Evrei v rossii*, 95–96; Rogachevski, "Vernopoddanii evrei," 131–32.

17. Gessen, *Evrei v rossii*, 137; Rogachevski, "Vernopoddanii evrei."

18. Gessen, *Evrei v rossii*, 137–38. Nevakhovich's sons were both Russian literati; the older one, Alexander, was a playwright, and the younger, Mikhail, a cartoonist and publisher.

19. Frumkin, *Toldot Hakhme yerushalayim*, 3: 138–40, 158–64, 170, 223–24. See also Yosef Yoel Rivlin, "Ha-gra ve-talmidav ve-yishuv erets yisra'el" [The Vilna Gaon and His Disciples and the Settlement of the Land of Israel], in *Sefer Ha-gra* [Vilna Gaon Volume], ed. Yehuda Leib Maimon (Jerusalem, 1954), 4: 111–62, esp. pp. 120–25. The writings of Y. Y. Rivlin on the early history of the Ashkenazic *yishuv* in Palestine, and C. H. Rivlin's *Hazon tsiyon: shklov ve-yerushalayim* [Vision of Zion: Shklov and Jerusalem] (Jerusalem, 1953) are based, in large part, upon oral traditions passed on in the Rivlin family and the cryptic historical poems of their ancestor, R. Yoseph Rivlin, written in Jerusa-

lem in 1858. These writings contain valuable information, as well as dubious legends, and need to be used with extreme caution.

20. Frumkin, *Toldot*, 3: 139–40.
21. Ibid., 140, 164–67; Y. Y. Rivlin, "Ha-gra ve-talmidav," 125–26. See also the articles by S. Levi, "Rabi yisrael mi-shklov," and Avraham Ya'ari, "Shelihuto shel r. yisra'el mi-shklov" [The Mission of R. Israel of Shklov], *Sinai* 3 (1939), no. 1–2: 30–37, 52–65. Y. Y. Rivlin, "Mishpahat rivlin be-'erets yisra'el" [The Rivlin Family in the Land of Israel], in *Yad yosef yitzhak rivlin: sefer zikaron* (Ramat Gan, 1964), 48–49, relates that the Jerusalem settlement was established in 1811; the generally accepted date is 1816.
22. Quote from Avraham b. Asher Anshil of Minsk, *'Amud ha-yemini* (Minsk, 1811), cited by A. Morgenstern, *Meshihiut ve-'erets yisra'el* [Messianism and the Land of Israel], (Jerusalem, 1985), 68–69.
23. Morgenstern, *Meshihiut*, 69–72; Mordechai Nathansohn's memoirs on Rivlin, in Fuenn, *Kiryah ne'emanah*, 279.
24. This is Morgenstern's hypothesis in *Meshihiut*.
25. Ya'ari, "Shelihuto shel r. yisra'el mi-shklov," 57; also in his book, *'Igrot erets yisra'el* [Letters from the Land of Israel], 2nd ed. (Ramat Gan, 1971), 330.
26. Ya'ari, "Shelihuto," 62, 63 (in *'Igrot erets yisra'el*, 339, 340). On R. Hayim Katz see Frumkin, *Toldot*, 3: 140, 168–69.
27. Ya'ari, "Shelihuto," 60, 64 (in *'Igrot erets yisra'el*, 336, 341). The letters do not mention the purchase of farmland in the context of the community's economic struggle, but rather as a separate item. Jews in the diaspora could fulfill the "commandments contingent upon the land" by sending donations for the purchase of farmland, and becoming legal partners in its ownership.
28. Cf. Morgenstern, *Meshihiut*, 116–17.
29. See Ya'ari, "Ha-defus ha'ivri bi-Shklov"; Y. Y. Rivlin, "Ha-gra ve-talmidav," 117, n. 16.

Notes to Conclusion

1. Isaac Ber Levinsohn, *Di hefker velt* [The World of Chaos], ed. B. Nathanson (Warsaw, 1902), 31–32.
2. Joseph Perl, *Bohen tsadik* [The Test of the Righteous] (Prague, 1838), 97–106. Historical documents refer to Finkelstein as being from Cherikov, not from Shklov; see Borovoi, *Evreiskaia zemledel'cheskaia kolonizatsiia*, 41–44.
3. On Nathanson, Kalman Schulman, and the Haskalah in Vilna, see Israel Klausner, *Vilna—yershalayim de-lita: dorot rishonim, 1495–1881* [Vilna—the Jerusalem of Lithuania: Early Generations, 1495–1881] (Tel Aviv, 1986), passim.

Bibliography

Archival Materials

Moscow. Russian State Archive of Ancient Acts (RGADA).
  Secret Chancellory and Secret Expeditions (Fond 7).
  Economic Notes (Fond 1355).
  Palace Archive (Fond 1239).
Moscow. State Archive of the Russian Federation (GARF).
  Archive of Third Department (Fond 109).
New York. YIVO Institute for Jewish Research
  Tcherikover Collection.
Jerusalem.
  Jewish National and University Library Manuscript Division. Pinkasim.

Published Materials

Altmann, Alexander. *Studies in Religious Philosophy and Mysticism*. New York, 1969.
————. *Moses Mendelssohn: A Biographical Study*. Philadelphia, 1973.
Aschheim, Steven. *Brothers and Strangers: The East European Jew in German and German-Jewish Consciousness, 1800–1923*. Madison, Wis., 1982.
Assaf, Simha. *Mekorot le-toldot ha-hinukh be-yisra'el* [Sources on the History of Jewish Education]. 4 vols., Tel Aviv, 1925–1942.
Avraham b. Shlomo Zalman. *Ma'alot ha-torah* [Virtues of the Torah]. Ed. Michel Feinstein and Nissan Waxman. New York, 1946.
Barishev, G. I. *Teatralnaia kultura belorussii 180go veka* [The Theatrical Culture of Byelorussia in the Eighteenth Century]. Minsk, 1992.
Barishev, G. I. et al. *Muzikalnii teatr belorussii: dooktriabrskii period* [Musical Theater in Byelorussia: The Pre-October Period]. Minsk, 1990.
Barnai, Jacob (ed.). *'Igrot hasidim me-'erets yisrael* [Letters of Hasidim from the Land of Israel]. Jerusalem, 1980.
Barsukov, Aleksandr. *Razkazi iz ruskoi istorii XVIIIogo veka* [Tales from Russian History in the Eighteenth Century]. St. Peterburg, 1883.

Baum, Y. D. "Evrei Dekabrist: grigorii abramovich perets" [A Jewish Decembrist: Grigorii Abramovich Perets]. *Katorga i ssilka* 25 (1926): 97–128.

Beilin, S. "Perepiska mezhdu bukharskimi evreami i shklovskimi evreami" [The Correspondence between the Jews of Bukhara and Shklov]. *Perezhitoe* 2 (1910): 274–80.

Ben Sasson, H. H. "Ishiuto shel ha-gra ve-hashpa'ato ha-historit" [The Personality of the Vilna Gaon and Its Historical Impact]. *Zion* 31 (1966): 39–86, 197–216.

Berlin, Saul. *Besamim rosh* [Incense of Rabbi Asher]. Berlin, 1793.

Berliner, P. "Bankir Perets" [The Banker Perets]. *Novii voskhod* (1913), no. 1: 45–48.

Berman, Shlomo. "Mishpehot kahal kadosh shklov ('al pi pinqas ha-niftarim shel hevrat gemilut hasadim shel 'emet)" [The Families of the Shklov Jewish Community (Based on the Record Book of the Burial Society)]. *Kovets 'al yad*, N.S. 1 [11] (1936): 133–87.

Bershadskii, Sergei. "Polozhenie o evreakh 1804 goda" [The 1804 Statute on the Jews]. *Voskhod* 15 (1895), no. 1: 82–104; no. 4: 86–109; no. 6: 33–63.

Borodianski, Chaim. "Di loyb-lider lekoved katerina der tsveyter un zeyere mekhabrim" [The Panegyrics to Catherine II and Their Authors]. *YIVO historishe shriftn* 2 (1937): 531–37.

Borovoi, S. V. *Evreiskaia zemledel'cheskaia kolonizatsiia v staroi rossii* [Jewish Argicultural Colonization in Old Russia]. Moscow, 1928.

Dan, Yosef. *Ha-sipur ha-hasidi* [The Hasidic Tale]. Jerusalem, 1975.

Dembitzer, H. N. *Kelilat yofi* [City of Beauty]. 2 vols., New York, 1959–1960.

Derzhavin, Gavriil. *Sochineniia* [Works]. Ed. Y. Grota, 9 vols., St. Petersburg, 1864–1883.

Dinstag, Jacob J. "Ha-'im hitnaged ha-gra le-mishnato ha-filosofit shel ha-rambam?" [Did the Vilna Gaon Oppose the Philosophic Teachings of Maimonides?]. *Talpiyot* 4 (1949), no. 1–2: 253–68.

———. "Rabenu eliyahu mi-vilna: reshima bibliografit" [Rabbi Elijah of Vilna: A Bibliography]. *Talpiyot* 4 (1949), no. 1–2: 269–356.

Drizen, N. B. "K istorii krepostnogo teatra: shklovskii balet" [Toward the History of Peasant Theater: The Shklov Ballet], *Stolitsy i usad'ba*, July 1914, 8–11.

Dubnow, S. "Evrei v mogilevskoi gubernii" [Jews in the Mogilev Province]. *Voskhod* 6 (1886), no. 9: 1–10.

———. "Istoricheskie soobscheniia: kagalnie ustavi s kontsa 16ogo do kontsa 18ogo veka" [Historical Notes: Kahal Constitutions from the Late Sixteenth to the Late Eighteenth Centuries]. *Voskhod* 13 (1894), no. 2: 90–105.

———. "Oblastnie kagalnie seimi v voivodstve volynskom i v belorussii (1666–1764)" [Regional Communal Councils in Vohlyn and Byelorussia (1666–1764)]. *Voskhod* 14 (1894), no. 4: 24–42.

———. "Tson ha-herga: haruge Mohlev 'al nahar Dniepr" [The Slaughtered Sheep: The Victims of Mogilev on the Dniepr]. *Ha-pardes* 3 (1896): 94–100.

———. "Vmeshatelstvo ruskogo gosudarstvo v anti-khasidskuyu borbu" [The Interference of the Russian State in the Anti-Hasidic Struggle]. *Evreiskaia starina* 3 (1910): 90–109.

———. "Evreiskaia pol'sha v epokhu poslednikh razdelov" [Jewish Poland at the Time of the Last Partitions]. *Evreiskaia starina* 4 (1911): 441–63.

———. *History of the Jews in Russia and Poland.* Translated by I. Friedlander, 3 vols., Philadelphia, 1916–1926.

———. *Toldot Ha-hasidut* [History of Hasidism]. Fourth edition, Tel Aviv, 1975.

——— (ed.). *Pinkas ha-medinah* [Minute Book of the Lithuanian Council]. Berlin, 1925.

Eisenstadt, Benzion. *Rabane Minsk ve-hakhameha* [The Rabbis and Scholars of Minsk]. Vilna, 1898.

Eisenstadt, J. D. (ed.). *Otsar yisrael* [The Treasury of Israel Encyclopedia]. Ten vols., 2nd edition, Jerusalem, 1951.

Eisenstein-Barzilay, Isaac. "The Background of the Berlin Haskalah." In Joseph Blau (ed.), *Essays on Jewish Life and Thought in Honor of Solo W. Baron.* New York, 1959, 200–239.

Eliav, Mordechai. *Ha-hinukh ha-yehudi be-germanya be-yeme ha-haskalah ve-ha-emantsipatsya* [Jewish Education in Germany in the Age of Haskalah and Emancipation]. Jerusalem, 1961.

Elijah b. Shlomo Zalman of Vilna. *Masekhet avot im perush rashi ve-perush ha-ga'on . . . rabenu eliyahu* [Commentary on Tractate Avot]. Shklov, 1804.

———. *Ayil meshulash* [Geometry]. Vilna/Grodna, 1833.

———. *Dikduk eliyahu* [Elijah's Grammar]. Vilna/Grodna, 1833.

———. *Sifra de-tseni'uta 'im biure ha-gra* [Commentary of Sifra de-tseni'uta]. Vilna, 1820.

Engelgardt, L. V. *Zapiski* [Notes]. Moscow, 1868.

Etkes, Immanuel. "Ha-gra ve-ha-haskalah: tadmit ve-mitsiut" [The Vilna Gaon and the Haskalah: Image and Reality]. In I. Etkes and J. Salmon (eds.), *Prakim be-toldot ha-hevra ha-yehudit be-yeme ha-benayim ve-ba-'et ha-hadasha mukdashim le-profesor yaakov katz* [Katz Jubilee Volume]. Jerusalem, 1980, 192–217.

———. "'Aliyato shel rabi Shneur Zalman mi-Liadi le-'emdat manhigut" [The Rise of Rabbi Shneur Zalman of Liady to a Position of Leadership]. *Tarbits* 54 (1984–1985): 429–39.

———. "Rabi Shneur Zalman mi-Liadi ke-manhig shel hasidim" [Rabbi Shneur Zalman as a Hasidic Leader]. *Zion* 50 (1986): 321–54.

———. "Ha-gra ve-reshit ha-hitnagdut la-hasidut" [The Vilna Gaon and the Beginning of Opposition to Hasidism]. In Shmuel Almog et al. (eds.),

Temurot ba-historiya ha-yehudit ha-hadasha, kovets ma'amarim shai le-Shmuel Ettinger [Ettinger Jubilee Volume]. Jerusalem, 1987, 439–58.

Ettinger, Shmuel. "Ha-yesodot ve-ha-megamot be-'itsuv mediniuto shel ha-shilton ha-rusi klape ha-yehudim 'im halukot polin" [Principles and Tendencies in the Formation of Russian Policy toward the Jews after the Partition of Poland]. *He-'avar* 19 (1972): 20–34.

———. "Takanot 1804" [The Statute of 1804]. *He-'avar* 21 (1977): 87–110.

Evreiskaia entsiklopediia. 16 vols., St. Petersburg, 1908–1913.

Fateyev, A. N. *Potemkin Tavrichevski*. Prague, 1945.

Feinstein, Arye Leyb. *'Ir tehilah* [Exalted City]. Warsaw, 1886.

Fishman, David. "Rabbi Moshe Isserles and the Study of Science among Polish Rabbis." In Bernard Dov Coooperman (ed.), *Tradition and Crisis Revisited*. Cambridge, 1994.

Friedberg, C. D. *Toldot ha-defus ha-'ivri be-polanya* [History of Jewish Printing in Poland]. Antwerp, 1932.

Frumkin, Arye Leib. *Toldot Hakhme yerushalayim* [History of the Sages of Jerusalem]. 3 vols., Jerusalem, 1926–1929.

Fuenn, S. J. *Safah la-ne'emanim* [Tongue of the Faithful]. Vilna, 1881.

———. *Kneset yisra'el* [Congregation of Israel]. Warsaw, 1886.

———. *Kiryah ne'emanah* [The Loyal City]. Second edition, Vilna, 1915.

Gelber, N. M. "Die Juden und die Judenreform auf dem vierjährigen Seim." In Ismar Elbogen et al. (eds.), *Festschrift zu Simon Dubnows siebzigsten Geburtstag*. Berlin, 1930, 136–53.

———. "Le-toldot ha-rofim ha-yehudim be-polin ba-me'ah ha-18" [On the History of Jewish Physicians in Poland in the Eighteenth Century]. In I. Tirosh (ed.), *Shay le-yeshayahu: sefer yovel le-yeshayahu volfsberg*. Tel Aviv, 1956, 347–71.

Gessen, Iulii. "Iz biografii noti khaimovicha notkina" [From the Biography of Nota Haymovitch Notkin]. *Buduschnost* 1 (1900), no. 45: 894–95.

———. "K istorii religioznoi borbi sredi ruskikh evreev" [On the History of the Religious Struggle within Russian Jewry]. *Voskhod* 22 (1902), no. 1: 116–35.

———. *Evrei v rossii* [The Jews in Russia]. St. Petersburg, 1906.

———. *Istoriia evreiskogo naroda v rossii* [History of the Jewish People in Russia]. 2 vols., Petrograd, 1916–1917.

Gillespe, Charles C. (ed.). *Dictionary of Scientific Biography*. 16 vols., New York, 1971–1976.

Ginzberg, Louis. *Students, Scholars and Saints*. Philadelphia, 1928.

Ginzburg, S. *Ramhal u-vene doro* [Rabbi Moshe Hayyim Luzzatto and His Contemporaries]. Tel Aviv, 1937.

Ginzburg, Shaul. *Historishe verk* [Historical Works]. 3 vols., New York, 1939–1941.

Golitsyn, N. N. *Istoriia russkogo zakonodatelstva o evreakh* [History of Russian Legislation on the Jews]. St. Petersburg, 1886.

Gordon, J. L. "K istorii poseleniia evreev v peterburge" [On the History of Jewish Settlement in St. Petersburg]. *Voskhod* 1 (1881), no. 1: 111–23; no. 2: 29–47.

Halm, Hans. "Semen Gavrilovic Zoric." *Jahrbücher für der Geschichte Ost-Europas* 8 (1960), no. 1: 1–9.

Hassell, James. "The Implementation of the Table of Ranks in the Eighteenth Century." *Slavic Review* 29 (1970): 283–95.

Heilman, Chaim Meyer. *Bet rabi* [The Rabbi's House]. Berdichev, 1900.

Heilprin, Yisrael. *Yehudim ve-yahadut be-mizrah 'eropah* [Jews and Judaism in Eastern Europe]. Jerusalem, 1969.

Hertzberg, Arthur. *The French Enlightenment and the Jews*. New York and Philadelphia, 1970.

Hilman, David Zvi (ed.). *'Igrot ba'al ha-tanya u-bene doro* [Letters by the Author of the Tanya and His Contemporaries]. Jerusalem, 1953.

Hundert, Gershon D. (ed.). *Essential Papers on Hasidism*. New York, 1991.

Hurvitz, Shai. "Sefer hayai" [The Book of My Life]. *Ha-shiloah* 40, no. 1 (1922): 1–14.

Israel b. Shmuel of Shklov. *Pe'at ha-shulhan*. Jerusalem, 1968.

Israeli, Isaac. *Yesod 'olam* [Foundation of the Earth]. Berlin, 1777.

Isserles, Moshe. *She'elot ve-teshuvot ha-rama* [Responsa]. Ed. A. Siev, Jerusalem, 1971.

Jacob of Karlin. *Keren 'orah 'al masekhet nazir* [Rays of Light on Tractate Nazir]. Jerusalem, 1959.

Jacobs, Louis. *Hasidic Prayer*. New York, 1973.

Jonathan of Ruzhany. *Yeshua be-yisra'el* [Salvation in Israel]. Frankfurt, 1720.

Kagan, Berl. *Sefer Ha-Prenumerantn* [The Book of Prenumerants]. New York, 1975.

Kagan, Ziporah. "Mekorot ve-mekori'ut ba-mahaze 'milhama ba-shalom' le-hayim avraham katz" [Sources and Originality in the Play "War against Peace" by Hayim Avraham Katz]. *Bama* 43 [96] (1969): 62–77; and 44 [97] (1970): 70–78.

Karlinsky, Simon. *Russian Drama from Its Beginnings to the Age of Pushkin*. Berkeley, 1985.

Karnovich, E. P. *Zamechatelnie bogatstva chastnikh lits v rossii* [Extraordinary Wealth among Private Individuals in Russia]. St. Petersburg, 1874.

Karo, Joseph. *Sefer megine 'erets* [Code of Jewish Law]. Shklov, 1803.

Katz, Hayim Avraham. *Milhama ba-shalom* [War against Peace]. Shklov, 1797.

———. *Simhat levav, hu sefer Hovot ha-levavot 'im biur hadash* [Joy to the Heart: A Commentary on "Duties of the Heart"]. Shklov, 1803.

Katz, Jacob. *Tradition and Crisis*. New York, 1961.

———. *Out of the Ghetto: The Social Background of Jewish Emancipation 1770–1870*. Cambridge, Mass., 1973.

Kerner, Moshe. *Zer'a kodesh* [Holy Seed]. Berlin, 1797.

Kieval, Hillel J. "Caution's Progress: The Modernization of Jewish Life in Prague, 1780–1830." In Jacob Katz (ed.), *Toward Modernity: The European Jewish Model*. New Brunswick, N.J., 1987, 71–105.

Klausner, Israel. *Vilna—yershalayim de-lita: dorot rishonim, 1495–1881* [Vilna—the Jerusalem of Lithuania: Early Generations, 1495–1881]. Tel Aviv, 1986.

Klausner, Joseph. *Historiyah shel ha-sifrut ha-'ivrit ha-hadasha* [History of Modern Hebrew Literature]. 6 vols., Jerusalem, 1960.

Kleinberger, M. *Ha-mahshavah ha-pedagogit shel ha-maharal mi-prag* [The Educational Philosophy of R. Judah Loeb of Prague]. Jerusalem, 1962.

Klier, John D. "Zhid: Biography of a Russian Epithet." *Slavonic and East European Review* 60 (1982), no. 1: 1–15.

———. *Russia Gathers Her Jews: The Origins of the "Jewish Question" in Russia 1772–1825*. Dekalb, Ill., 1986.

Kon, Pinkhes. "Vegn efenen yidishe shuln in Mohilever un Vitebsker gubernyes in yor 1808" [Concerning Opening Jewish Schools in the Mogilev and Vitebsk Provinces in 1808]. *Tsaytshrift* 2–3 (1928): 156–63, 753–60.

———. "A loyb-lid fun der mohilever kehile lekoved katerina der tsveyter" [A Panegyric by the Mogilev Community to Catherine II]. *YIVO historishe shriftn* 1 (1929): 753–60.

Landau, Bezalel. *Ha-Gaon he-hasid mi-vilna* [The Gaon and Saint of Vilna]. Jerusalem, 1978.

Lederhendler, Eli. *The Road to Modern Jewish Politics*. Oxford, 1991.

Lefin, Menahem Mendl. *Refuot ha'am* [Remedies for the People]. Zolkiew, 1794.

Lehman, James H. "Maimonides, Mendelssohn, and the Me'asfim." *Leo Baeck Institute Yearbook* 20 (1975): 87–108.

Leibowitz, J. "Smukhim harvianiim ba-refuah ha-'ivrit" [References to Harvey in Hebrew Medical Literature]. *Ha-rofe ha-'ivri* 2 (1957): 36–48.

Levanda, O. *Polnii khronologicheskii sbornik zakonov i polozhenii kasayushshikhsa evream* [Complete Chronological Collection of Laws and Statutes Concerning the Jews]. St. Petersburg, 1874.

Levi, S. "Rabi yisrael mi-shklov" [Rabbi Israel of Shklov]. *Sinai* 3 (1939), no. 1–2: 30–37.

Levin, Joshua Heschel. *'Aliyot eliyahu* [The Ascendance of Elijah]. Vilna, 1885.

Levine, Hillel. "Ben hasidut le-haskalah: 'al pulmus anti-hasidi musve" [Between Hasidism and Haskalah: On a Veiled Anti-Hasidic Polemic]. In I. Etkes and J. Salmon (eds.), *Prakim be-toldot ha-hevra ha-yehudit be-yeme ha-benayim ve-ba-et ha-hadasha mukdashim le-profesor yaakov katz* [Jacob Katz Jubilee Volume]. Jerusalem, 1980, 122–31.

———. "Paradise Not Surrendered: Jewish Reactions to Copernicus and the Growth of Modern Science." In Robert Cohen and Max Watkowsky (eds.), *Epistemology, Methodology, and the Social Sciences*. Dordrecht, 1983, 205–22.

Levinsohn, Isaac Ber. *Di hefker velt* [The World of Chaos]. Ed. B. Nathanson, Warsaw, 1902.

Levitats, Isaac. *The Jewish Community in Russia, 1772–1844*. New York, 1943.

Lieberman, C. "Nosafot le-ha-defus ha-'ivri be-Shklov" [Addenda to "Jewish Printing in Shklov"]. *Kiryat sefer 25* (1949): 315–20; 26 (1950): 101–11.

Litvin, Y. (pseud. for S. Hurwitz). *Yidishe neshomes* [Jewish Souls]. 5 vols., New York, 1916–1917.

Lunski, Khaykl. "Ge'oynim un gdoylim fun noentn over" [Sages and Giants of the Near Past]. *Dos Vort* 488, 1 Adar, (1934).

Luzzatto, Moshe Hayim. *Adir ba-marom* [Mighty in Heaven]. Ed. S. Luria, Warsaw, 1880.

Madariaga, Isabel de. *Russia in the Age of Catherine the Great*. London, 1981.

Magid, David. *Toldot mishpehot ginzburg* [History of the Ginzburg Families]. St. Petersburg, 1891.

Mahler, Raphael. *Toldot ha-yehudim be-folin* [History of the Jews in Poland]. Merhavia, 1946.

———. *Divre yeme yisra'el: dorot aharonim* [History of the Jews in Modern Times]. 4 vols., Merhavia, 1956–1962.

———. *Yidn in amolikn poyln in likht fun tsifern* [Jews in Old Poland in Numbers]. Warsaw, 1958.

Maimon Solomon, *Autobiography*. Translated by J. Clark Murray, London, 1954.

Maimon, Yehuda Leib (ed.). *Sefer Ha-gra* [Vilna Gaon Volume]. Jerusalem, 1954.

Malachi, A. R. *Masot ve-reshimot* [Essays and Notes]. New York, 1937.

———. "Rabi yehuda leyb margoliot, ve-hagra mi-vilna" [Rabbi Judah Leyb Margoliot and the Vilna Gaon]. *Ha-do'ar*, Tamuz 11, 1959.

Manasseh b. Israel. *Mikveh yisra'el* [The Hope of Israel]. Shklov, 1797.

Marek, P. "Beloruskaia synagoga i eia teritoriia" [The Byelorussian Council and Its Territory]. *Voskhod* 23 (1903), no. 5: 71–82.

———. "Vnutrenaia borba v evreistve v XVIIIom veke" [The Internal Struggle in Jewry in the Eighteenth Century]. *Evreiskaia starina* 12 (1928): 102–89.

——— (ed.). *Istoriia evreiskogo naroda* [History of the Jewish People]. Vol. 11, Moscow, 1914.

Margoliot, Judah Leyb. *Bet midot* [House of Virtues]. Shklov, 1786.

Markgraff, Richard. *Zur Geschichte der Juden auf der Messen in Leipzig von 1664–1839*. Bischofswerda, 1894.

Menahem Mendl b. Barukh Bendet. *Mayim 'adirim—menahem tziyon—biurim ve-likutim* [Great Waters—Comfort of Zion—Collected Commentaries]. Jerusalem, 1987.

Meshcherskii, M. I., and Korsakov, A. N. "Semion gavrilovich zorich." *Russkii arkhiv* 17 (1879), book 2, no. 5, 37–99.

Mondshein, Yehoshua. *Sifre ha-halakha shel ha-admor ha-zaken* [The Halakhic Works of the Old Rabbi]. Brooklyn, N.Y., 1984.

Morgenstern, A. *Meshihiut ve-'erets yisra'el* [Messianism and the Land of Israel]. Jerusalem, 1985.

Mussafia, Benjamin. *Zekher rav*. Shklov, 1804.

Nadler, Allan L. "A Religion of Limits: The Theology of Mitnagdism According to Phinehas Ben Judah Maggid of Polotsk," unpublished Ph.D. dissertation, Harvard University, 1988. (Forthcoming as *A Religion of Limits: The Theology of the Mitnaggedim*.)

Nevakhovich, Judah Leyb. *Vopl dshcheri iudeiskoi* [Russian: "The Lament of the Daughter of Judah"]. St. Petersburg, 1803. [Reprinted, in part, in the annual supplement to *Budushchnost* 3 (1902): 114–31.]

———. *Kol sha'avat bat yehuda* [Hebrew: "The Lament of the Daughter of Judah"]. Shklov, 1804. [Reprinted as a supplement to *He-'avar* 2 (1918).]

Nigal, Gedalyah. *Ha-siporet ha-hasidit: toldoteha ve-noshe'ah* [The Hasidic Novella: History and Formulation]. Jerusalem, 1981.

Nikitin, V. *Evrei zemledel'tsi* [Jewish Farmers]. St. Petersburg, 1887.

Noble, Shlomo. *Khumesh taytsh* [Bible Translation]. New York, 1943.

Pelli, Moshe. *Bi-ma'avake temurah* [In the Struggles over Change]. Tel Aviv, 1988.

Perets, V. and Perets, L. *Dekabrist grigorii abramovitch Perets* [The Decembrist Grigorii Abramovich Perets]. Leningrad, 1926.

Perl, Joseph. *Bohen tsadik* [The Test of the Righteous]. Prague, 1838.

———. *Ueber das wessen Der Sekte Hasidim*. Ed. A. Rubinstein, Jerusalem, 1977.

Phinehas b. Judah. *Sha'ar ha-rahamim* [Gate of Mercy]. Shklov, 1788.

———. *Keter torah* [Crown of Torah]. N.p., 1859.

Piekarz, Mendl. *Bi-yeme tsemihat ha-hasidut* [At the Birth of Hasidism]. Jerusalem, 1978.

Pipes, Richard. "Catherine II and the Jews: The Origins of the Pale of Settlement." *Soviet Jewish Affairs* 5 (1975), no. 2: 3–20.

Plungian, Mordechai. *Ben porat* [Son of Porat]. Vilna, 1858.

Rabinovitz, A. Z. "Le-toldot ha-hinukh ve-ha-haskalah shel ha-yehudim be-rusiya" [On the History of Jewish Education and Enlightenment in Russia]. *Ha-hinukh* 3 (1912–1913): 100–115.

Rapoport-Albert, Ada. "Hagiography with Footnotes: Edifying Tales and the Writing of History in Hasidism." *History and Theory* 27 (1988): 119–59.

Regesti i Nadpisi [Registers and Inscriptions]. 3 vols. St. Petersburg, 1899–1913.

Ringelblum, Emanuel. *Kapitlen geshikhte* [Chapters of History]. Buenos Aires, 1953.

Rivlin, Benjamin b. Shlomo Zalman. *Geviei gevia ha-kesef* [The Silver Goblet]. Second edition, Warsaw, 1897.

Rivlin, C. H. *Hazon tsiyon: shklov ve-yerushalayim* [Vision of Zion: Shklov and Jerusalem]. Jerusalem, 1953.

Rivlin, Y. Y. "Mishpahat rivlin be-'erets yisra'el" [The Rivlin Family in the Land of Israel]. In *Yad yosef yitzhak rivlin: sefer zikaron*. Ramat Gan, 1964.

Rogachevski, A. "Vernopoddanii evrei: novie dannie o leibe nevakhoviche" [Loyal Jewish Subject: New Information on Leyb Nevakhovich]. *Vestnik evreiskogo universiteta v moskve* 1 (1992): 129–32.

Roskies, David G. "The Genres of Yiddish Popular Literature 1790–1860." *Working Papers in Yiddish and East European Jewish Studies* 8 (1975).

———. "The Medium and Message of the Maskilic Chapbook." *Jewish Social Studies* 41 (1977), no. 2: 275–90.

———. *The Lost Art of Yiddish Story-Telling*. Cambridge, Mass., 1995.

Rosman, Murray J. *The Lords' Jews: Magnate-Jewish Relations in the Polish-Lithuanian Commonwealth in the Eighteenth Century*. Cambridge, Mass., 1990.

Ruderman, David B. "The Impact of Science on Jewish Culture and Society in Venice." In Gaetano Cozzi (ed.), *Gli Ebrei e Venezia*. Milan, 1987, 417–48.

Russkii biograficheskii slovar' [Russian Biographical Dictionary]. 25 vols., St. Petersburg, 1896–1918.

Schick, Barukh b. Jacob. *'Amude ha-shamayim-tiferet adam* [Pillars of the Heavens and the Splendor of Man]. Berlin, 1777.

———. *Derekh yeshara* [The Straight Path]. The Hague, 1778.

———. *Uklides* [Euclid's Elements]. The Hague, 1780.

———. *Keneh ha-midah* [The Length of Measurement]. Prague, 1783; Shklov, 1791.

———. *Moreh tsedek* [Righteous Instruction]. Shklov, 1783.

Schlegel, Christian Hieronymus Julian. *Reise aus Polen nach St. Petersburg*. Erfurt-Golga, 1818.

Schneerson, Joseph Isaac. "Avot Ha-Hasidut" [The Fathers of Hasidism]. *Ha-tamim*, no. 2 (December 1935): 43–55.

Scholem, Gershom. *Kabbalah*. Jerusalem, 1974.

———. *Mehkarim ve-mekorot le-toldot ha-shabta'ut ve-gilguleha* [Studies and Sources on the History of Sabbateanism and Its Transformations]. Jerusalem, 1974.

Schulman, Kalman. *Milhamot ha-yehudim 'im ha-roma'im* [The Jewish Wars with the Romans]. Vilna, 1862.

———. *Toldot gedole yisra'el* [History of Great Jews]. 2 vols., Vilna, 1913.

Shabad, Avraham Chaim. *Toldot ha-yamim she-'avru 'al hevra kadisha shivah keruim* [History of the Shivah keruim Society]. Vilna, 1909.

Shiper, Y. *Geshikhte fun yidisher teater-kunst un drame fun di eltste tsaytn biz 1750* [History of Jewish Theater and Drama from the Oldest Times until 1750]. 2 vols., Warsaw, 1925.

Shirman, Hayim. *Le-toldot Ha-shira ve-ha-drama ha-'ivrit* [On the History of Hebrew Poetry and Drama]. 2 vols., Jerusalem, 1979.

Shmeruk, Khone (ed.). *Mahazot mikrai'im be-yidish 1697–1750* [Biblical Dramas in Yiddish, 1697–1750]. Jerusalem, 1983.

Shneur Zalman b. Barukh of Liady. *Ma'amare ha-admor ha-zaken* [Essays of the Old Rabbi]. Vol. 1, Brooklyn, N.Y., 1957.

———. *Likute amarim-tanya* [The Tanya]. Brooklyn, N.Y., 1968.

———. *Shulhan 'arukh ha-rav* [Code of Jewish Law]. Brooklyn, N.Y., 1968.

———. *'Igrot kodesh kevod kedushat admor ha-zaken* [Sacred Letters of the Old Rabbi]. Ed. Shalom Duber Levine, Brooklyn, N.Y., 1980.

———. *Ma'amare ha-admor ha-zaken 5564* [Essays of the Old Rabbi 1804]. Brooklyn, N.Y., 1980.

Shugurov, M. F. "Istoriia evreev v rossii" [History of the Jews in Russia]. *Russkii arkhiv* 32 (1894), no. 2: 55–93, 129–81.

Shulvass, M. A. *Between East and West*. Detroit, 1971.

Stanislavskii, S. "Biograficheskie etudi" [Biographical Studies]. *Voskhod* 10 (1891), no. 12: 143–57.

———. "Biograficheskaia zametka" [Biographical Note]. *Voskhod* 16 (1896), no. 2: 151–57.

Stanislawski, Michael S. *Tsar Nicholas I and the Jews: The Transfomation of Jewish Society in Russia 1825–1855*. Philadelphia, Jewish Publication Society of America, 1983.

Steinschneider, Hillel Noah. "Le-toldot R. Kalman Schulman." *Ha-tsefirah* (1889), no. 172: 703.

———. "Kalman Schulman." *Ha-melitz* (1899), no. 7: 12.

Tchernowitz, Hayyim. *Toldot ha-poskim* [The History of Talmudic Adjudicators]. 3 vols., New York, 1948.

Thaden, Edward C. *Russia's Western Borderlands 1710–1870*. Princeton, 1984.

Tishby, Isaiah. *Mishnat ha-zohar* [Teachings of the Zohar]. 2 vols., Jerusalem, 1971–1976.

———. "Kitrugo shel R. Yisrael Mi-Shklov 'al ha-hasidim" [The Polemic of Rabbi Israel of Shklov against the Hasidim]. *Kiryat sefer* 51 (1976): 300–303.

———. "Darke hafatsatam shel kitve ramhal be-folin ve-lita" [The Dissemination of Luzzatto's Writings in Poland and Lithuania]. *Kiryat sefer* 45 (1977): 101–50.

Topolska, Maria Barbara. "Szklow i Jego Rola w Gospodarce Bialorusi Wschodniej w XVII i XVIII Wieku" [Shklov and Its Role in the Economy of Eastern Byelorussia in the Seventeenth and Eighteenth Centuries]. *Roczniki Dziejow Spolecznych Gospodarczych* 30 (1969): 1–32.

———. "Peculiarities of the Economic Structure of Eastern White Russia in the Sixteenth–Eighteenth Centuries." *Studia Historiae Oeconomicae* 6 (1971): 37–49.

Trunk, I. "Der va'ad medinas rusiya (raysn)" [The Council of Byelorussia]. *YIVO Bletter* 40 (1956): 63–85.

———. "Geshikhte fun yidn in vitebsk" [History of the Jews in Vitebsk]. In G. Aronson (ed.), *Vitebsk amol*. New York, 1956, 1–56.

Tsamriyon, Tsemah. *Ha-me'asef: ktav ha-'et ha-moderni ha-rishon be-'ivrit* [*Ha-me'asef:* The First Modern Hebrew Periodical]. Tel Aviv, 1985.

Tsitron, S. L. *Shtadlonim* [Intercessors]. Warsaw, n.d.

Vakar, N. *Belorussia: The Making of a Nation*. Cambridge, Mass., 1956.

Weinryb, Bernard. *Mehkarim be-toldot ha-kalkalah ve-ha-hevra shel ye-hude polin* [Studies on the Economic and Social History of Polish Jewry]. Jerusalem, 1939.

———. *The Jews of Poland*. Philadelphia, 1973.

Wessely, Naftali Hirtz. *Divre shalom ve-'emet* [Words of Peace and Truth]. Berlin, 1782.

Wilensky, Mordechai. *Hasidim ve-mitnagdim* [Hasidim and Opponents]. 2 vols., Jerusalem, 1970.

———. "Hasidic-Mitnaggedic Polemics in the Jewish Communities of Eastern Europe: The Hostile Phase." In Gershon D. Hundert (ed.), *Essential Papers on Hasidism*. New York, 1991.

Wolfsohn, Aaron Halle. "Bikoret sefarim hadashim." *Ha-me'asef* 4 (1790): 177–86.

———. "Sihah be-'eretz ha-hayim" [A Conversation in Paradise]. *Ha-me'asef* 7 (1794–1797): 219–98.

Wunderbar, R. J. *Geschichte der Juden in den Provinzen Liv-und Kurland*. Mittau, 1853.

Ya'ari, Avraham. "Le-toldot ha-drama ha-yisre'elit: drama 'ivrit me-haye yosef ve-ehav" [On the History of Jewish Drama: A Hebrew Drama on Joseph and His Brothers]. *Bama* 5–6 (1934): 28–34.

———. "Shelihuto shel r. yisra'el mi-shklov" [The Mission of R. Israel of Shklov]. *Sinai* 3 (1939), no. 1–2: 52–65.

———. "Ha-defus ha-'ivri bi-Shklov" [Jewish Printing in Shklov]. *Kiryat sefer* 22 (1945): 49–72, 135–60.

———. "R. Eliezer pavir ve-mif'alo ha-sifruti" [Eliezer Pavir and His Literary Activity]. *Kiryat sefer* 35 (1960), no. 4: 499–520.

———. *'Igrot erets yisra'el* [Letters from the Land of Israel]. Second edition, Ramat Gan, 1971.

Zakalinskaya, Y. P. *Votchinnie khoziaistva mogilevskoi gubernii v vtoroi polovine XIIIogo veka* [Estate Economies of the Mogilev Province in the Second Half of the Eighteenth Century]. Mogilev, 1958.

Zinberg, I. "Shklov i ego 'prosvetiteli' kontsa XVIIIogo veka" [Shklov and Its "Enlighteners" at the End of the Eighteenth Century]. *Evreiskaia starina* 12 (1928): 17–44.

———. *Geshikhte fun der literatur bay yidn* [History of Jewish Literature]. 8 vols., New York, 1943; vol. 9, Waltham and New York, 1965.

Zipperstein, Steven J. "Haskalah, Cultural Change, and Nineteenth Century Russian Jewry: A Reassessment." *Journal of Jewish Studies* 34 (1983), no. 2: 191–207.

Index

.